Polarized Politics

Polarized Politics

Congress and the President in a Partisan Era

EDITED BY

JON R. BOND

Texas A&M University

AND

RICHARD FLEISHER

Fordham University

CQ PRESS

A Division of Congressional Quarterly Inc.

Washington, D.C.

CQ Press
A Division of Congressional Quarterly Inc.
1414 22nd St. N.W.
Washington, D.C. 20037
202-822-1475
800-638-1710
www.cqpress.com

Designed and typeset by Nighthawk Design, Grand Rapids, Michigan
Cover design by Ed Atkeson

Printed in the United States of America

04 03 02 01   5 4 3 2

Library of Congress Cataloging-in-Publication Data

Polarized politics: congress and the president in a partisan era / edited by Jon
R. Bond and Richard Fleisher
    p.   cm.
Includes bibliographic references and index.
ISBN 1-56802-494-0 (casebound : alk. paper) — 1-56802-493-2 (paperback)
1. Presidents—United States. 2. United States. Congress. I. Bond, Jon R. II
Fleisher, Richard.

JK585 .P65 2000
324'.0973—dc21   99-059253

To friendship and collaboration

CONTENTS

FIGURES AND TABLES

Figures

Tables

PREFACE

T he origins of this volume date back to the fall of 1997, when the two of us had a phone conversation about our research on presidential-congressional relations and noted that a marked increase in party conflict in American politics had occurred during the 1990s. We were also aware that much of our previous work, as well as that of other scholars, was based on observations of presidential-congressional interactions during a period of low partisanship. We wondered whether our basic understanding of rivalry between the branches would need to be modified in light of heightened party conflict. We discussed a number of research options for exploring the effect of party polarization on presidential-congressional interactions and decided to seek some help. We thought the best strategy was to hold a conference on the subject, followed, we hoped, by the publication of an edited work. The conference provided a forum for the insights of several scholars whose work has influenced us over the past two decades.

The Program in American Politics at Texas A&M University provided the necessary resources. This program is jointly sponsored by the Department of Political Science in the College of Liberal Arts and the Center for Presidential Studies in the George Bush School of Government and Public Service. One of the goals of the program is to bring scholars to College Station to talk about a wide range of subjects in American politics. Bond proposed holding a conference exploring the theme of congressional-presidential relations in a partisan era to Ken Meier, director of the program. We are grateful that he saw the merits of this proposal and agreed to fund it. And we are grateful to Charles A. Johnson, head of the Department of Political Science, and to George C. Edwards III, director of the Center for Presidential Studies, for providing the funding for Ken to give away.

Next, the two of us sat down to consider potential conference participants. We listed a number of scholars whose previous work had made significant contributions to our understanding of Congress, the presidency, and partisanship. Faced with the constraints of a finite budget and the busy schedules of the scholars we chose, we agreed on a conference program of five papers reporting original research on various aspects of the conference theme. After the conference, held February 5–6, 1999, we identified some issues that the papers had not addressed and commissioned two more essays. We wrote introductory and concluding chapters and headnotes to each substantive chapter to round out the volume.

We believe this book raises (and answers) important questions about the meaning of political party and party polarization in the workings of the national government. The chapters analyze polarized politics as it manifests itself in words and actions. Covering a variety of subjects, such as elections, agenda setting, committee decision making, and developments on the floor, the chapters demonstrate the intricacies of the relationship between the president and Congress. We hope that students of American politics will find the book a useful addition to the literature and that instructors will find it a valuable pedagogical tool to introduce students to the study of the president and Congress in a highly partisan period.

In bringing this project to fruition, we accumulated a large number of debts along the way. George Edwards, Charlie Johnson, and Ken Meier deserve a great many thanks for making it possible for us to bring a group of such accomplished, collegial scholars to Texas A&M for an enjoyable and informative two days. The yeoman work of Kristin Campbell and Michelle Chin is much appreciated. Their superior organizational skills and assiduous attention to detail compensated for our lack of these qualities and ensured that the conference ran smoothly. Jim Cottrill, Patrick Ellcessor, Brad Epps, Glen Krutz, and Carl Richard also contributed timely and valuable assistance that we greatly appreciate. Lisa Blum and Colleen Hoffman juggled different accounts and made sure the bills were paid in compliance with a host of complex rules that Jon was not willing to learn. We also thank those who attended the conference, asked stimulating questions, and offered useful observations for the presenters to consider.

We owe many thanks to Brenda Carter, director of college publishing at CQ Press. Her enthusiasm and encouragement as well as advice at many points along the way helped us bring this project to fruition. It was also a pleasure to work with Gwenda Larsen, Carolyn Goldinger, and the CQ Press staff. In addition, Rich would like to thank Deans Michael Gillan, Robert Grimes, S.J., Robert Himmelberg, and Jeffrey von Arx, S.J., of Fordham University for providing him with release time to work on the final stages of editing the book.

We also have to thank members of both parties for creating this most interesting period of political history. Without their initiation of partisan warfare, we would not have conceived the idea for this volume.

Finally, the chapter authors deserve special thanks. We are grateful that these scholars found time in their busy schedules to contribute some of their current research to this volume. The essays were delivered on time, and we were delighted by the quality of scholarship and insight. But also important to us was the opportunity to join with these scholars in an active collaboration. The Bond-Fleisher friendship and collaboration on research began more than twenty years ago when we were graduate students at the University of Illinois. Our friendship has grown stronger over the years, and we believe the products of our research are better because of the collaboration—the research experience has certainly been more enjoyable.

In a delightful essay published about the time politics in Washington started to become less collegial, Aaron Wildavsky (1986) pointed out that all research is collaborative. Collaboration may be indirect, as when we build upon and amend the work of predecessors. Evidence of indirect collaboration can be seen in this volume's footnotes and references; in a sense, we have been collaborating with the cited authors for years. Or collaboration may be direct, as in a joint project in which researchers divide the work and interact with one another to produce a finished manuscript, as in this book. A volume such as this is the ultimate example of the latter, and we are pleased to have had the opportunity to expand our circle of active collaborators. It is to friendship and collaboration that we dedicate this book.

Jon R. Bond
Richard Fleisher

CONTRIBUTORS

John H. Aldrich (Ph.D. University of Rochester) is the Pfizer-Pratt University Professor of Political Science at Duke University. He specializes in American politics and behavior, formal theory, history, and methodology. He is the author of *Why Parties* and *Before the Convention* and a series of books on elections, the most recent of which is *Change and Continuity in the 1996 and 1998 Elections*. He has served as president of the Southern Political Science Association. He has received grants from the National Science Foundation and the National Endowment for the Humanities, and has served as coeditor of the *American Journal of Political Science* and as a Fellow at the Center for Advanced Study in the Behavioral Sciences.

Andrew W. Barrett is an assistant lecturer and Ph.D. candidate in political science at Texas A&M University. His primary areas of study include presidential rhetoric and presidential-congressional relations. He has published articles on the presidency in the *American Journal of Political Science* and *Presidential Studies Quarterly*.

Jon R. Bond (Ph.D. University of Illinois at Urbana—Champaign) is professor of political science at Texas A&M University. He has published articles on presidential-congressional relations, congressional elections, and public policy in the *American Political Science Review, Journal of Politics, American Journal of Political Science, Political Research Quarterly, Legislative Studies Quarterly, American Politics Quarterly,* and *Polity.* He is coauthor with Richard Fleisher of *The President in the Legislative Arena.* He was an American Political Science Association Congressional Fellow and has served as coeditor of the *Journal of Politics* and on the executive councils of the Midwest Political Science Association and Pi Sigma Alpha. He is a member of the Publications Committee of the American Political Science Association.

George C. Edwards III (Ph.D. University of Wisconsin, Madison) is Distinguished Professor of Political Science at Texas A&M University and director of the Center for Presidential Studies in the Bush School. He also holds the Jordan Professorship in Liberal Arts and is editor of *Presidential Studies Quarterly*. His books include *At the Margins: Presidential Leadership of Congress, Presidential Approval, Presidential Leadership, National Security and the U.S. Constitution, Implementing Public Policy*, and *Researching the Presidency*. He has published articles in the *American Political Science Review, American Journal of Political Science, Journal of Politics, Presidential Studies Quarterly, American Politics Quarterly*, and *Congress and the Presidency*.

Erika Falk is a doctoral student at the Annenberg School for Communication at the University of Pennsylvania. She supervised the Annenberg grant team that conducted research on civility in Congress for use at the bipartisan congressional retreats held in 1997 and 1999 in Hershey, Pennsylvania. She has published articles in the *Journal of Women and Language, Howard Journal of Communications*, and *PS: Political Science and Politics*.

Richard Fleisher (Ph.D. University of Illinois at Urbana—Champaign) is professor of political science at Fordham University. He has published articles on presidential-congressional relations, congressional elections, constituency influence in roll call voting, and electoral realignments in *American Political Science Review, Journal of Politics, American Journal of Political Science, Political Research Quarterly, Legislative Studies Quarterly, American Politics Quarterly*, and *Political Science Quarterly*. He is coauthor of *The President in the Legislative Arena*. He is currently serving as chair of his department and continuing his research on congressional decision making.

Tim Groeling is a Ph.D. candidate in political science at the University of California, San Diego. He has published in the *Journal of Politics*.

Gary C. Jacobson (Ph.D. Yale University) is professor of political science at the University of California, San Diego. He specializes in the study of U.S. elections, parties, interest groups, and Congress. He is the author of *Money in Congressional Elections*, which won the Gladys E. Kammerer Award and the Leon Epstein Award; *The Politics of Congressional Elections*; and *The Electoral Origins of Divided Government* and coauthor of *The Logic of American Politics* and *Strategy and Choice in Congressional Elections*. He served on the Board of Overseers of the National Elections Studies, the Council of the American Political Science Association, the APSA Committee on Research Support, and as treasurer of APSA. He is a fellow of the American Academy of Arts and Sciences.

Kathleen Hall Jamieson (Ph.D. University of Wisconsin) is dean of the Annenberg School for Communication and director of the Annenberg Public Policy Center at the University of Pennsylvania. She is the author or coauthor of ten books on politics and media, including *Beyond the Double Bind: Women and Leadership; Packaging the Presidency,* which won the Winans–Wichelns Book Award; and *Eloquence in an Electronic Age,* which won the Speech Communication Association's Golden Anniversary Book Award. *Everything You Think You Know about Politics and Why You're Wrong* will be published in April 2000.

Samuel Kernell (Ph.D. University of California, Berkeley) is professor of political science at the University of California, San Diego. His research interests focus on the presidency. His books include *Going Public: New Strategies of Presidential Leadership; Strategy and Choice in Congressional Elections,* with Gary Jacobson; *The Logic of American Politics,* with Gary Jacobson; and *Principles and Practice of American Politics: Classic and Contemporary Readings,* coedited with Steven S. Smith.

David W. Rohde (Ph.D. University of Rochester) is University Distinguished Professor of Political Science at Michigan State University. He is the author of books and articles on various aspects of American national politics. He is a former American Political Science Association Congressional Fellow and former editor of the *American Journal of Political Science.* Among his recent works are *Parties and Leaders in the Postreform House* and *Change and Continuity in the 1996 and 1998 Elections* (coauthor).

Barbara Sinclair (Ph.D. University of Rochester) is Marvin Hoffenberg Professor of American Politics at the University of California, Los Angeles. Her publications on the U.S. Congress include articles in the *American Political Science Review, American Journal of Political Science, Journal of Politics,* and *Legislative Studies Quarterly.* Her books include *Congressional Realignment; Majority Leadership in the U.S. House; The Transformation of the U.S. Senate,* winner of the Richard F. Fenno Prize and the D. B. Hardeman Prize; *Legislators, Leaders and Lawmaking: The U.S. House of Representatives in the Postreform Era;* and *Unorthodox Lawmaking: New Legislative Processes in the U.S. Congress.*

CHAPTER 1

Congress and the President in a Partisan Era

Richard Fleisher and Jon R. Bond

In the fall of 1995 a Democratic president and the leaders of the Republican-controlled Congress were jockeying for strategic advantage in what was to become an epic showdown over the 1996 budget. President Bill Clinton was wounded from the stinging defeats suffered in the 1994 midterm elections in which his party lost control of both houses of Congress for the first time in forty years, and the Republicans thought they could force him to accept a budget much closer to their preferences than to his own. Looking for an opportunity to seize the initiative and regain some luster, the president dug in his heels and vetoed the Republican budget. The result was a partial shutdown of the government. During this clash, both sides worked hard—in words and deeds—to turn public opinion in their favor for strategic advantage in the next election. In politics, as in life, sometimes you're the bug; sometimes you're the windshield. This time the Republicans played the role of the unfortunate bug. The resulting compromise budget was interpreted as a victory for the president. Clinton was reelected, and the Democrats picked up nine seats in the House.

In 1997 the same set of actors were on a collision course over the budget. Once again the Republican leadership in Congress believed that Clinton, a lame-duck president further weakened by the stigma of being only the second president in history to be impeached by the House and tried in the Senate, would be forced to accept Republican spending priorities. But the president again resisted. Memories of the earlier shutdown loomed large as negotiations between the president and Republican leaders grew increasingly acrimonious. Although the next election was more than two years away, neither side seemed willing to risk the public's disfavor by shutting down the government again. In the resulting compromise, each side claimed victory.

1

Battles between Congress and the president are not new in American politics. Because the power to make national policy in the United States is shared between Congress and the president, conflict is expected—even intended. Certainly, American history provides numerous examples of politicians in each of the national institutions using their powers to gain political advantage. In setting up a system of government based on the principles of divided power and checks and balances, the Framers were seeking to protect liberty. To reduce the chances that the government would enact laws that infringe on fundamental rights, they created a system that makes it difficult to pass *any* law. Making policy in such a system requires compromise. Coalitions built in support of successful policies are often large and bipartisan (Krehbiel 1998).

Historically, however, the U.S. Congress has been characterized by weak partisanship. As Richard Neustadt (1960, 33) observes, "What the Constitution separates our parties do not combine." Consequently, much of what we know about presidential-congressional relations is based on observations of interactions in a weak partisan environment (Bond and Fleisher 1990; Edwards 1989). Beginning in the 1980s, politics in Congress and the White House became much more partisan. We know less about presidential-congressional relations in a partisan environment.

The budget battles described above seem to differ from the type of conflict anticipated in American politics. Although the American system is known for undisciplined parties characterized by decentralized decision making, the major players in these conflicts were the leaders of the political parties; rank-and-file partisans remained remarkably cohesive in their support for the party position. Furthermore, the compromises reached seemed less satisfying. In earlier days the end of policy battles meant that both sides had accepted the compromise because the game had been played the way the Framers had intended. This time there were few congratulations offered to tough-but-respected opponents for a hard-fought struggle played by the rules. No! Today, every new struggle seems to be viewed as another sortie in a partisan war, with each party seeking to use its control of a seat of government power to demonize the other for partisan advantage. These battles reflect a more general change: the emergence of polarized politics.

The Rise of Polarized Politics

Several scholars argue that politics in Congress and the presidency became more partisan in the 1980s (Aldrich 1995; Fleisher and Bond 1996a,

1996b; Rohde 1991; Sinclair 1995). Evidence supporting this claim typically consists of data showing an increase in the percentage of roll call votes on which a majority of Democrats voted against a majority of Republicans. Figure 1–1 shows trends in party votes—votes in which a majority of one party votes against a majority of the other—in the House and Senate from 1953 to 1998, averaged by Congress to smooth the curves. From low points in the late 1960s, the proportion of party votes in both chambers began to increase gradually through the 1970s. During the Reagan presidency, party voting accelerated dramatically. After the 1982 midterm election, party voting in the House escalated to more than 50 percent of the votes and has remained that high in most years since. In recent years, the House divided along party lines on nearly two-thirds of roll calls. The trend in the Senate appears to lag the House by several years. Party voting in the Senate continued a gradual upward drift until 1986, when Democrats

Figure 1–1 Party Votes in Congress, 1953–1998

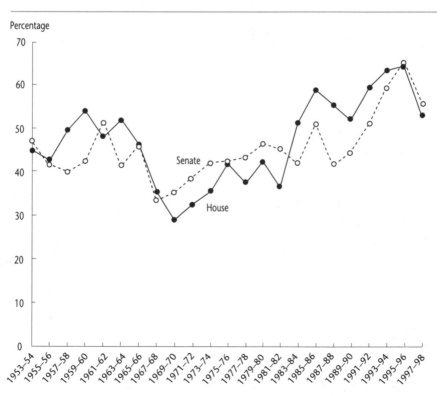

Source: Norman J. Ornstein, Thomas E. Mann, and Michael J. Malbin, *Vital Statistics on Congress, 1997–1998* (Washington, D.C. : CQ Press, 1998).

regained control. After a brief decline in partisanship from 1987 to 1989, we see a sharp increase in the proportion of party votes. Since 1990 the Senate has divided along party lines on a majority of votes and even surpassed the House in partisanship in the 104th (1995–1996) and 105th (1997–1998) Congresses. Figure 1–2 shows a similar increasing tendency for members to vote with their fellow partisans on these party votes.

David Rohde (1991) was among the first to notice the striking increase in partisanship in the 1980s. He argues that the impetus for this increase was electoral. During the 1950s and 1960s, many new liberal Democrats were elected to Congress. Frustrated by a *de facto* governing coalition of conservative southern Democrats and Republicans, these junior Democrats pushed through a series of reforms in the 1970s designed to reinvigorate the Democratic caucus. Although these reforms had some early consequences (for example, the replacement of several committee chairs in 1975), the surge in party voting did not occur until another electoral force—full implementation of the 1965 Voting Rights Act—altered the

Figure 1–2 Party Unity Scores by Congress, 1954–1998

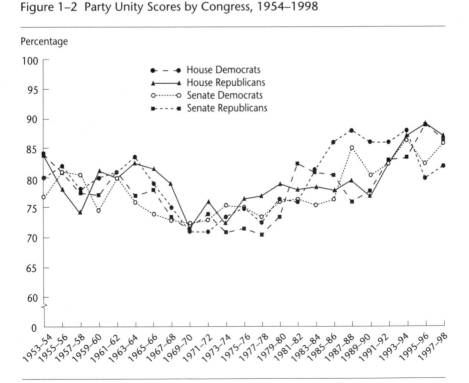

Source: Norman J. Ornstein, Thomas E. Mann, and Michael J. Malbin, *Vital Statistics on Congress, 1997–1998* (Washington, D.C. : CQ Press, 1998).

nature of southern Democratic constituencies. As more African American voters entered the electorate in the South in the 1970s and 1980s, the electoral interests and policy preferences of southern and northern Democrats converged. As differences within the parties declined, differences between them increased. Democratic party leaders in Congress were more willing to use the powers available to them. The result was greater partisanship.

Republicans also became more partisan in the 1980s. The election of Ronald Reagan and the Republican takeover of the Senate in 1980 were viewed by many as a mandate to enact a conservative agenda. Although Democrats maintained control of the House, President Reagan did not have to compromise much to score quick victories on budget and tax cuts. A traditional conservative coalition of Republicans and southern Democrats gave him a working majority to pass high-priority items. These early victories were remarkable not because Democratic support was unusually high—it was only average; rather, they were remarkable because Republican support was nearly unanimous (Fleisher and Bond 1983, 754–56).

The success of an uncompromising posture, however, was short-lived. After the 1982 midterm election, the Democrats solidified their hold on the House, and the conservative coalition no longer constituted a majority (Bond and Fleisher 1990, 87). Democratic leaders began to use their powers and the rules of the House to stymie the Republican agenda and structure policy choices for partisan advantage (Sinclair 1992). Feeling the frustration of decades of minority status, the Republicans turned to a new breed of strident leaders who were less inclined to compromise on the conservative agenda. These changes in the Republican Party accelerated the movement toward greater partisanship in Congress. After becoming the majority party in 1994, the House Republicans used their power to push a policy agenda known as the Contract with America. The contract met with more resistance in the Senate, where the minority party leadership, taking a lesson from the strategy the Republicans employed when they were the minority, used the Senate's rules to stymie significant portions of it. Other parts of the Republican plan were blocked by presidential veto (Bader 1996; Gimpel 1996). Since the mid-1980s opposing party leaders have acted as if they would sooner fight than compromise, but at other times they have worked out compromises on significant legislation (Gilmour 1990).

The rise in partisan conflict has occurred during a period when the electoral process has tended to divide control of the national institutions between the parties. Figure 1–3 shows the percentage of elections that produced divided party control of the presidency and at least one chamber of Congress since the 1800s. The most recent period is marked by an overwhelming

Figure 1–3 Elections Producing Divided Government

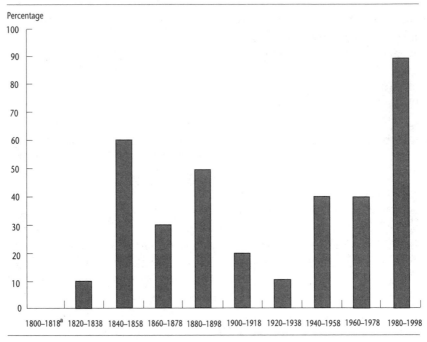

a. None of the ten elections from 1800 to 1818 resulted in divided government.

occurrence of divided government: nine of the ten elections from 1980 to 1998 resulted in divided party control of the presidency and Congress. Although divided government was common in some earlier periods in American history, the last two decades of the twentieth century are remarkable for the unprecedented frequency of divided party control of our national governing institutions.

Does It Matter?

Recent scholarship on American politics has engaged in a number of debates about "gridlock," divided government, and the role of political parties in the gridlock/divided government nexus. One often-heard point is that American government is characterized by gridlock: weak parties in a government of fragmented power with checks and balances make it difficult for the government to pass laws in response to popular preferences. But voters are unable to hold policy makers accountable through the electoral process. Why? The same weak parties and fragmented power also make it difficult to assign blame for government's lack of responsiveness. The result—either from confusion or design (Fiorina 1996)—is an increasing tendency for voters to place different parties in control of Congress and the presidency. But divided government only exacerbates the problem. Gridlock grows worse as government repeatedly fails to produce policies to address the nation's problems. Assigning blame for the government's failure is difficult because voters cannot determine which chamber—or which party—is more responsible for it.

The other side of this argument suggests that divided government does not matter. There are two versions. David Mayhew's version (1991) suggests that government produces about the same amount of major new legislation under divided and unified government. The other version (Brady and Volden 1998; Krehbiel 1998) argues that gridlock occurs under unified as well as divided government.

Woven through this debate about the effects of divided government are arguments about American political parties. Some early commentary extolled the virtues of a responsible party model characterized by strong parties presenting coherent bundles of policies to voters (APSA Committee on Political Parties 1950). Voters could then choose between clear party choices; the winning party would use control of the institutions of government to enact the policies that voters chose; and voters could hold the governing party accountable if it failed to produce (Schattschneider 1942). This commentary was more normative than descriptive of the way American politics actually worked (or works). It was, however, in part a normative response to problems of governing believed to result from weak parties. Empirical research clearly demonstrates that American political parties are not as strong as the disciplined parties in parliamentary systems and that the strength of U.S. parties has varied over time. As noted above, following one of the low points of party strength near the middle of the twentieth century, party splits in Congress became much more common at the century's end.

The effect of partisanship on gridlock has also been the subject of some debate. One view is that if policy making is difficult under any circumstances, government is brought to its knees by the combined effects of divided party control and intense partisanship (Cutler 1988; Ginsberg and Shefter 1990; Sundquist 1988). Jockeying for political advantage in the next election, each party uses its control of a different part of government to block the other's policy initiatives. Major legislation needed to solve the nation's problems is stalled like traffic during rush hour. Voters have difficulty holding unresponsive policy makers accountable as each side blames the other for the gridlock made worse by intense partisanship.

More recent scholarship questions the role that parties play in the ability of government to govern. Although the arguments are careful and nuanced, some researchers conclude that parties—even if they are cohesive—do not matter. What matters is the distribution of individual preferences within the legislature, especially the preferences of individuals at certain "pivot points" in the process (Krehbiel 1998). In the House, where rules permit the majority to prevail, the preference of the median member is the pivot. But legislation must also pass the Senate, where the rules protect the interests of the minority by permitting opponents to filibuster, and then it must survive a potential presidential veto. Stopping a filibuster requires sixty votes; overriding a presidential veto takes two-thirds in both chambers. These features of the system mean that the preferences of members at the sixty-vote pivot in the Senate and the two-thirds pivot in both House and Senate often determine whether new policies will pass. As David Brady and Craig Volden (1998, 135) argue, "It is not parties that cause gridlock; rather it is preferences of the members of the House and Senate in combination with supermajoritarian institutions like Rule XXII that cause gridlock."[1] Keith Krehbiel (1998) goes a step further, arguing that what may appear as partisanship is really individualistic behavior within an institutional setting that provides members with resources to vote with, ignore, or even thwart the actions of party leaders.

Set against intensely partisan conflicts in the 1990s—most notably, government shutdowns, the impeachment and trial of a president, and increasingly acrimonious debate—the scholarship raises several important questions. Do parties matter? If so, how and why do they matter? Why has partisan conflict increased? How has the rise of partisanship affected presidential-congressional interactions? Does it matter whether partisan control of Congress and the presidency is unified or divided? Has partisanship affected democratic accountability?

The chapters in this book present original research that addresses these questions. The essays collectively demonstrate that party control does indeed matter, and the authors offer arguments and evidence indicating how and why it matters. The evidence also shows that whether party control of Congress and the presidency is divided or unified matters, not only in passing legislation, but in other ways as well. At the same time, these essays suggest that the argument that American government is characterized by gridlock and an incapacity to govern is too strong.

---

1. Rule XXII is the Senate rule requiring sixty votes to invoke cloture and end debate.

CHAPTER 2

Party Polarization in National Politics: The Electoral Connection

Gary C. Jacobson

We begin with a chapter focusing on elections, Gary Jacobson's "Party Polarization in National Politics: The Electoral Connection." Members of Congress get their jobs through election, and, if they want to keep these jobs, they must satisfy the preferences of voters. This electoral connection has a strong impact on members' partisan behavior. The activities of congressional party leaders also affect the level of partisanship. First, however, voters must send representatives to Congress who share a wide range of policy preferences. If voters' decisions are only weakly influenced by party, or if party identifiers in different parts of the country have vastly different policy preferences, the winning candidates generally reflect these views. A wide range of policy preferences within each party in Congress results in a substantial overlap across parties, which makes it difficult for party leaders to develop a coherent party program and secure consistent support from their partisans. When partisan preferences in the electorate become stronger and more coherent, congressional behavior becomes more partisan.

This chapter and several others in this volume demonstrate that partisanship in Congress grew considerably during the 1980s and 1990s. Jacobson shows us that members' increasing party loyalty is not out of step with the policy preferences of the constituents they represent: members of Congress and individual citizens have become more polarized along party lines. Yet citizens may not be satisfied with what Congress does. To be sure, polarization in Congress reflects a more partisan electorate, but polarization in Congress is exaggerated relative to polarization of the public. This exaggeration results from the power of party leaders to control the legislative agenda through rules. (In Chapter 3 John Aldrich and David Rohde present their theory of "conditional party government," which explains how and why this happens.) In addition, some elements in the public continue to hold more moderate policy views than the winning candidates. Jacobson believes that the prospects for the future are likely to include more intraparty coherence

9

and intense interparty conflict, especially under divided government. From the electoral perspective, divided party control is likely to continue because there are a sufficient number of voters who are in the middle, while parties in Congress are more polarized than the electorate.

I n December 1998 the House of Representatives voted to impeach President Bill Clinton. The vote was radically partisan: all but four Republicans voted for at least one of the four articles of impeachment, and only five Democrats voted for any of them. Grant every member's claim of a conscience vote, and it becomes all the more remarkable that 98 percent of Republican consciences dictated a vote to impeach the president, while 98 percent of Democratic consciences dictated the opposite. The Senate's verdict after the impeachment trial was only slightly less partisan. Every Democrat voted for acquittal, and 91 percent of the Republicans voted for conviction on at least one article.

Research on congressional roll call voting, notably by several authors represented in this volume, makes it clear that party line voting on the impeachment issue was not an aberration, but the culmination of a trend nearly two decades old. The proportion of partisan roll call votes and party loyalty on these votes have been increasing in both houses of Congress since the 1970s (Aldrich 1995; Rohde 1991; Sinclair 2000), reflecting growing ideological polarization of the congressional parties (Fleisher and Bond 1996a, 2000; Poole and Rosenthal 1997). To appreciate how dramatically the parties have diverged since the 1970s, look at Figure 2–1, which displays the distribution of House members' scores on a common measure of political ideology in selected Congresses spanning the past three decades. These scores, known as DW-NOMINATE scores, are calculated from all non-unanimous roll call votes cast from the 80th Congress through the 105th Congress. Each member's pattern of roll call votes locates him or her on a liberal-conservative dimension ranging from -1.0 (most liberal) to 1.0 (most conservative), allowing us to compare the distribution of positions along the dimension taken by Democrats and Republicans in different Congresses.[1]

---

1. For an explanation of the methodology for computing these scores and justification for their interpretation as measures of liberal-conservative ideology, see Poole and Rosenthal (1997), chapters 3 and 11, and McCarty, Poole, and Rosenthal (1997). DW-NOMINATE scores are updated versions of their D-NOMINATE measure; I am obliged to Keith Poole for providing them for this chapter and to Gregory Bovitz for helping me process them. Because of the way the dynamic element

In the 93d Congress, the ideological locations of House Democrats and Republicans overlapped across the middle half of the scale, and the gap between the two parties' modal locations was comparatively small. In the 97th Congress, the overlap was a bit less extensive but still sizable. By the 101st Congress, the parties had become noticeably more polarized. The 105th Congress, which voted on Clinton's impeachment, was the most sharply polarized of all, with not a single Republican falling below zero on the scale, and only four Democrats scoring above zero.[2]

Trends in partisan polarization in the House over a somewhat longer period are summarized in Figure 2–2, which displays the difference in median and mean DW-NOMINATE scores of House Republicans and Democrats in the Congress immediately following each presidential election from 1952 through 1996. Note particularly how dramatically the gap between the parties' average ideological locations grew in the 1990s; in the 105th Congress, the parties' medians and means were more than 0.7 points apart on this 2-point scale. According to Keith Poole and Howard Rosenthal, the first DW-NOMINATE dimension captures, in addition to liberal-conservative ideology, the primary cleavage that distinguishes the two parties, and hence the scores also serve as measures of party loyalty (1997, 46).[3] From this perspective, party unity on the House impeachment vote was simply a manifestation of a broader pattern of partisan polarization highlighted by the nearly complete disappearance of conservative Democrats and liberal Republicans (although a few moderates remain in both parties). The numbers above the columns in the last panel of Figure 2–1 show how many members bolted their party on impeachment. Note that all but two of the nine who defected on impeachment belong to the small set of members who still have DW-NOMINATE scores adjacent to or overlapping those of members of the opposing party.

The Republicans persisted in their attempts to impeach and remove Clinton even though every one of the myriad national polls taken from the eruption of the Monica Lewinsky scandal in January 1998 through the end of the trial in February 1999 found the public opposed to impeachment

---

(*continued*) affects the scores, a few members (0.1 percent) for a few Congresses have scores less than −1.0 or more than 1.0. I have placed them in the closest category within the −1.0 to 1.0 range.

2. The pattern for the 105th Congress (1997–1999) is not merely a consequence of the Republican takeover of the House in 1994; polarization was nearly as sharp in the 103d Congress (1993–1995).

3. Scores on the horizontal axes of Figures 2–1 through 2–5 indicate the range between the number specified and the next higher score.

Figure 2–1 Ideological Positions on Roll Call Votes

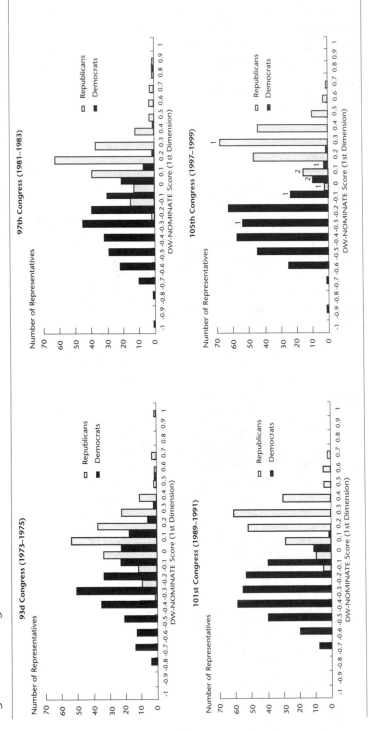

Source: Compiled by the author from Poole and Rosenthal DW-NOMINATE Scores (http://voteview.gsia.cmu.edu.dwnl.htm).

Note: The entries are frequency distributions of Republican and Democratic members of Congress on a liberal-conservative dimension based on non-unanimous roll call votes in which 1 represents the most conservative position and -1 represents the most liberal. Each bar indicates the number of representatives falling into the specified range. For example, in the 105th Congress, sixty-two Republicans had scores between .03 and .04 on the scale.

Figure 2–2 Difference in Median and Mean DW-NOMINATE Scores of Republicans and Democrats, 83d Through 105th Congresses

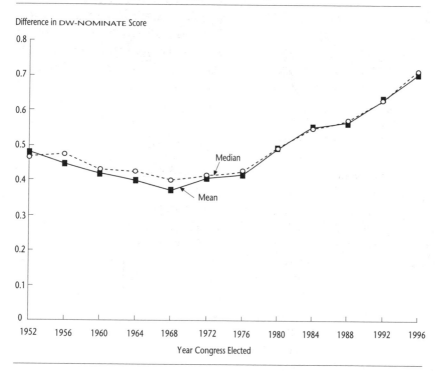

Difference in DW-NOMINATE Score

Year Congress Elected

Note: The entries are the difference between the mean and the median positions on the DW-NOMINATE scale of House Republicans and Democrats in the specified Congress. The larger the difference, the farther apart the two parties are ideologically.

and conviction, typically by margins of about two to one.[4] Yet the public, like Congress, was from start to finish sharply polarized on the issue. In poll after poll, a solid majority of self-identified Republicans favored Clinton's impeachment and removal, while more than 80 percent of self-identified Democrats remained opposed. In the end, 68 percent of Republicans wanted the Senate to convict and remove Clinton, while only 30 percent favored acquittal; among Democrats, 89 percent favored

4. Polling coverage of Clinton and his travails was extraordinarily heavy. The summary conclusions about public opinion reported in this chapter are based on polls conducted by or on behalf of Gallup, CNN, CBS News, the *New York Times, Time,* the Pew Research Center, ABC News, the *Washington Post,* NBC News, the *Wall Street Journal,* and the *Los Angeles Times* and reported at *http://www.pollingreport.com, http://www.gallup.com,* and *http://www.people-press.org* during 1998 and 1999.

acquittal, while only 10 percent preferred conviction.[5] Members of Congress may have voted their consciences, but their consciences were wonderfully in tune with the preferences of their core supporters. Congressional Republicans acted against the manifest preferences of a majority of Americans on a highly salient issue, and they may yet pay for it in the 2000 election by losing the House and—much less likely—the Senate.[6] But they voted the way the majority of Republican voters wanted them to.

Partisan voting on impeachment thus reflected, albeit in an exaggerated and skewed fashion, sharply divided electoral constituencies. It also reflected the power of majority party leaders in the contemporary House to enforce discipline, notably on the adoption of a rule governing the impeachment bill that did not permit consideration of a censure resolution. Moderate Republicans were left with no alternative short of impeachment. These two forces—the emergence of distinct and increasingly homogenous electoral coalitions in both parties and, in consequence, the greater willingness of members to submit to party discipline—are the chief explanations that have been offered for the broader rise in party unity and ideological divergence since the 1970s (Fleisher and Bond 2000; Rohde 1991). Respect for the power of the electoral connection usually concedes causal priority to electoral change. Yet voters can respond only to the options presented by the parties' candidates. If legislative parties become more dissimilar and unified as their respective electoral coalitions become more dissimilar and homogenous, it is also true that the choices offered by more polarized, unified parties encourage polarized electoral responses.

My goal in this chapter is to review the electoral changes that both underlie and reflect the more unified and divergent congressional parties of the 1990s. The story contains few surprises, but fresh observations from the most recent elections point uniformly to a near-term future that is, if anything, substantially more conducive to partisan coherence and division, intensifying conflicts not only within the legislature, but especially—under divided government—between the president and Congress.

Most of the analysis is presented graphically, for this is the most efficient way to summarize and appreciate the various interrelated trends. I

---

5. Gallup/CNN/USA *Today* Poll, February 12–13, 1999, reported at *http://www.pollingreport.com/scandals.htm*, February 15, 1999.

6. A little arithmetic suggests that, if the distribution of partisan preferences on impeachment were similar across districts (and assuming independents duplicate the district's breakdown, as they duplicate the breakdown in national polls), Republicans would have to outnumber Democrats 71:29 for a district majority to favor impeachment.

begin with some observations on changes in partisanship and voting behavior since the 1970s. Next, I show how the electoral coalitions of House
Democrats and Republicans have consequently diverged. The circle is completed by an examination of how patterns of roll call voting have become
increasingly predictable from electoral decisions, fulfilling one major condition for responsible party government. An ironic effect of these changes
may have been to make divided government even more popular, for the
parties in government have polarized much more sharply than have party
identifiers in the electorate.

The Growth of Partisan Coherence in the Electorate

The consensus explanation for the rise in party cohesion in Congress since
the 1970s is party realignment in the South. The short version is that the
civil rights revolution, particularly the Voting Rights Act of 1965, brought
southern blacks into the electorate as Democrats, while moving conservative whites to abandon their ancestral allegiance to the Democratic Party
in favor of the ideologically more compatible Republicans. The movement
of jobs and people to the South also contributed to larger numbers of Republican voters, who gradually replaced conservative Democrats with conservative Republicans in southern House and Senate seats. The constituencies that elected the remaining Democrats became more like
Democratic constituencies elsewhere, so the roll call voting of southern
Democrats became more like the roll call voting of Democrats from other
regions. The southern realignment left both congressional parties with
more politically homogeneous electoral coalitions, reducing internal disagreements and making stronger party leadership tolerable.

This analysis is certainly correct as far as it goes. The realignment of
southern political loyalties and electoral habits has been thoroughly documented (Black and Black 1987; Frymer 1995; Hood, Kidd, and Morris
1999; Nadeau and Stanley 1993; Stanley 1988; Wattenberg 1991). Figure 2–3 summarizes the principal trends. As the proportion of Republicans among major party identifiers has risen, so has the share of southern
House and Senate seats won by Republican candidates.[7] Starting from al-

---

7. Independents who said they leaned toward either party are treated as partisans.
Republican Party ID is the Republican share of major party identifiers. The South
is defined as the eleven states of the former Confederacy. Some of the data presented in this and subsequent tables are from Miller and the NES (1998) and
Sapiro, Rosenstone, and the NES (1999).

Figure 2–3 The Rise of the Republican South, 1952–1998

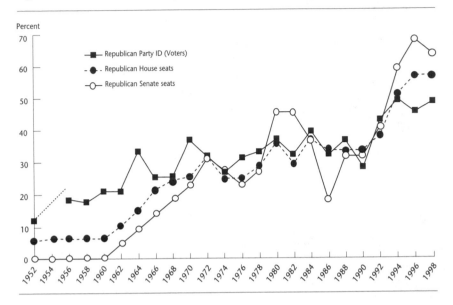

Source: National Election Studies.

most nothing in the 1950s, Republicans now enjoy parity with the Democrats among voters and hold solid majorities of southern House and Senate seats.

Realignment in the South contributed to the increasing ideological homogeneity of the parties, but it is by no means the whole story. Other forces have also necessarily been at work, for links between ideology and party identification have grown stronger outside the South as well. Since 1972 the National Election Studies (NES) have asked respondents to place themselves on a 7-point ideological scale ranging from extremely liberal to extremely conservative.[8] On average, nearly 80 percent of respondents who say they voted in House elections are able to locate their position on the scale. As Figure 2–4 shows, tau-b correlations between the voters' positions on the liberal-conservative scale and the NES's 7-point party identification scale have grown noticeably stronger since 1972 outside the South as well as within. Like other measurements of correlation, the tau-b statistic takes values from −1 (a perfect negative relationship) through 0 (no relationship) to 1 (a perfect positive relationship). In the

8. The categories are extremely liberal, liberal, slightly liberal, moderate or middle of the road, slightly conservative, conservative, and extremely conservative.

Figure 2–4 Correlation Between Party Identification and Ideology of House
Voters, 1972–1998

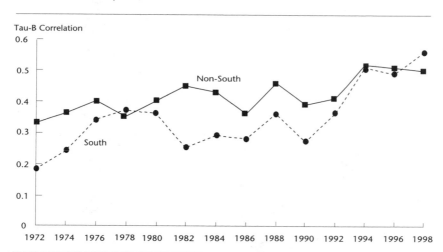

analysis presented here and in Figure 2–5, the higher the tau-b correlation, the stronger the positive relationship between party identification and the other variable of interest.[9] The increase was steeper for southern voters, and by 1994 they had become indistinguishable on this score from voters elsewhere.

A similar pattern of growing partisan coherence within the electorate is evident in correlations between voters' party identification and positions on several of the NES's issue scales displayed in Figure 2–5.[10] On every issue—ranging from the government's economic role, to race, to women's role in society, to abortion policy—the overall trend is upward, with tau-b correlations reaching their highest levels on four of the five scales in 1998. Notice that although economic issue positions are normally most strongly related to partisanship—reflecting the venerable New Deal cleavage—the steepest increases have occurred on social issues. For

---

9. I use the tau-b statistic to measure the relationship because the analysis is of ordinal variables. Alternative measures of association, including the product-moment correlation, reveal precisely the same trends. All of these analyses are confined to respondents who reported voting for one of the major party candidates in the House election. For details on the tau-b statistic, see Blalock (1960, 232–234).

10. Issue positions are measured with 7-point scales, except for the abortion issue, which is a 4-point scale. See the Appendix for details on the questions generating the scales.

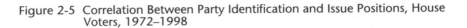

Figure 2-5 Correlation Between Party Identification and Issue Positions, House
Voters, 1972–1998

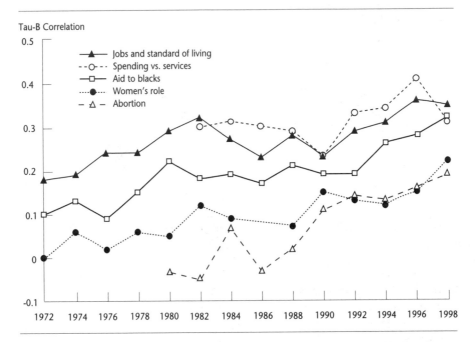

Tau-B Correlation

Legend:
- Jobs and standard of living
- Spending vs. services
- Aid to blacks
- Women's role
- Abortion

example, in 1980 opinions on abortion were unrelated to party identification; now we observe a substantial correlation. In 1980 only 30 percent of voters who opposed abortion under all circumstances identified themselves as Republicans; by 1998, 71 percent did so.[11]

More generally, in 1972 the voter's positions on the various scales—ideology, jobs, aid to blacks, and women's role—predicted party identification (Republican, independent, or Democrat) with only 62 percent accuracy; in 1998 the same four variables predicted party identification with 74 percent accuracy.[12] Clearly, citizens now sort themselves into the appropriate party (given their ideological leanings and positions on issues) a good deal more consistently than they did in the 1970s, with the largest increases in consistency occurring in the 1990s. Not surprisingly, partisan

---

11. For additional evidence regarding the partisan effects of the abortion issue, see Adams (1997).

12. Based on logit equations, with the 3-point party identification scale as the dependent variable and leaners treated as partisans, the baseline (null) predictive accuracy for 1972 was 49 percent, for 1998, 50 percent.

evaluations of presidential candidates, presidents, and the parties themselves have become more divergent as well (Fleisher and Bond 1996a).

The Revival of Electoral Consistency

Both the southern realignment and growing ideological coherence of
electoral coalitions have contributed to greater consistency in voting behavior. Among individual voters, party loyalty has risen and ticket splitting
has diminished since the 1970s. Figures 2–6 and 2–7 display the pertinent
data. Party loyalty in congressional elections declined from the 1950s
through the 1970s but has subsequently rebounded, recovering about
two-thirds of the decline. Party loyalty in presidential elections is trickier
to measure, because some years have featured prominent independent or
third party candidacies (specifically 1968, 1980, 1992, and 1996), while
the rest have not. But even with Ross Perot drawing votes from both parties in 1996, 84 percent of partisans voted for their party's presidential
candidate, a higher proportion than in any election from 1952 through
1980. If we consider as defectors only those who voted for the other *major* party's candidate, the rate of defection in both 1992 and 1996 was only

Figure 2–6 Party Loyalty in Congressional Elections, 1952–1998

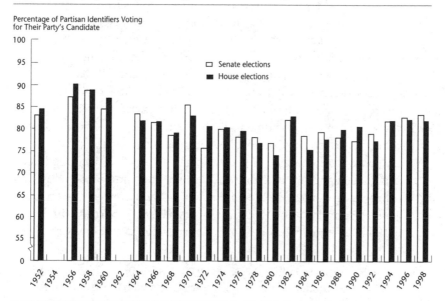

Percentage of Partisan Identifiers Voting
for Their Party's Candidate

☐ Senate elections
■ House elections

Figure 2–7 Ticket Splitting, 1952–1998

Percent Voting a Split Ticket

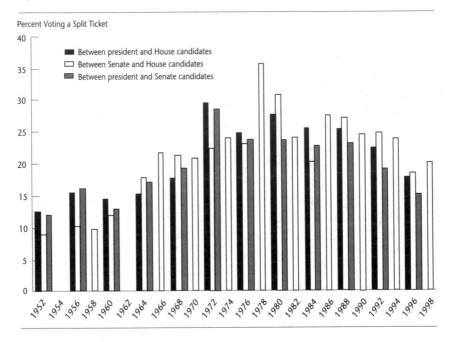

10 percent, the lowest of any election in the NES time series (1988 had the next lowest rate).

The trend in ticket splitting—voting for candidates of different parties on the same ballot—appears, not accidentally, as the inverse of the trend in party loyalty. Ticket splitting was relatively infrequent in the 1950s, grew more common through the 1970s, and since has declined to the levels last seen in the early 1960s. The declines since the 1970s in partisan defections and ticket splitting are probably even greater than these NES data indicate, because both phenomena have been artificially inflated since 1978 by changes in the wording and administration of the vote question that produce an overreport of votes for House incumbents.[13]

An important consequence of greater party loyalty and decreased ticket splitting is that aggregate electoral results have become more consistent across offices. For example, the simple correlation between a party's district-level House and presidential vote shares has risen sharply from its low point in 1972, as Figure 2–8 indicates. Both the decrease between 1952

---

13. A reasonable estimate is that the post–1978 surveys understate party loyalty by about three percentage points; see Box-Steffensmeier, Jacobson, and Grant (1999); Jacobson and Rivers (1993).

Figure 2–8 Correlations Between District-Level House and Presidential Voting, 1952–1996

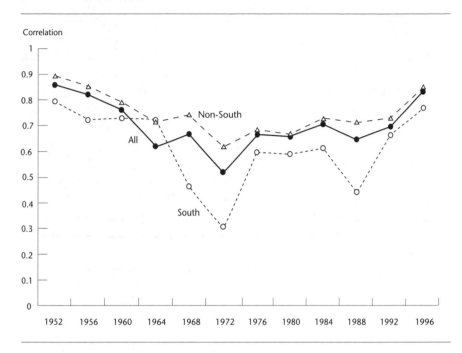

and 1972 and the increase since 1972 are steepest for southern districts, but the same U-shaped trend occurs in districts outside the South as well. By 1996 the association between House and presidential voting had re-bounded to a level last seen in the 1950s (.77 in the South, .85 elsewhere, and .83 overall). Similarly, a district's presidential vote predicted which party's candidate would win the House seat with greater accuracy in the 1990s than at any time since the 1950s. The trend toward electoral dis-integration across offices I documented a decade ago has clearly gone into reverse since then (Jacobson 1990).

Diverging Electoral Constituencies

The growth in partisan coherence, consistency, and loyalty among voters has made the two parties' respective electoral constituencies—that is, the voters who supported the party's winning candidates—politically more homogeneous and more dissimilar. It has also given the president and con-gressional majorities more divergent electoral constituencies when the branches are divided between the parties.

To begin with an elementary but telling example, according to NES surveys, 48 percent of the respondents who voted for members of the Democratic House majority in 1972 also voted for Richard Nixon; 36 percent of the voters supporting the Democratic House winners voted for Ronald Reagan in 1984; but only 27 percent of the voters supporting members of the Republican House majority voted for Clinton in 1996. The comparatively small proportion of shared electoral constituents was surely one source of Clinton's difficulties with the Republican congressional majority in a divided government (Fleisher and Bond 2000).

More generally, the respective parties' electoral constituencies have diverged ideologically since the 1970s, with the parties' most active supporters moving the farthest apart. I measure differences in the ideological makeup of electoral constituencies by subtracting the mean ideological self-placement of NES respondents who voted for one set of winning candidates from the mean for respondents who voted for another set of winning candidates. Ideological divisions among activist constituents are gauged by repeating the analysis for respondents who reported engaging in at least two political acts in addition to voting during the campaign.[14] Figure 2–9 displays the changes in the ideological distinctiveness of the electoral constituencies of House Republicans and Democrats and of southern and nonsouthern Democrats since 1972.[15]

In the 1970s the ideological differences between the two parties' electoral constituencies were modest and no wider than the gap between southern and nonsouthern Democrats' electoral constituencies.[16] By the 1990s the difference between the parties' electoral constituencies had more than doubled, to about 1.2 points on the 7-point scale, and the Democrats' regional divergence had entirely disappeared. Realignment in the South again explains only part of this change, for the gap between Republican and Democratic constituencies also grew (from 0.7 to 1.1 points) outside the South. Note also that the mean ideological difference between

---

14. The acts include trying to persuade others to vote for a candidate, going to political meetings or rallies, working for a party or candidate, wearing a campaign button or putting a bumper sticker on a car, and donating money to a party or candidate's campaign; about one in five voters is an activist by this measure.

15. The 1998 survey contained too few southern voters for winning Democrats to permit meaningful analysis.

16. Indeed, for four of the six election years prior to 1984, the difference in mean ideological self-placement of southern Democratic and Republican constituencies was statistically insignificant at $p<.05$.

Figure 2–9 Difference in Mean Ideological Self-Placement of House Activist
and Electoral Constituencies, 1972–1998

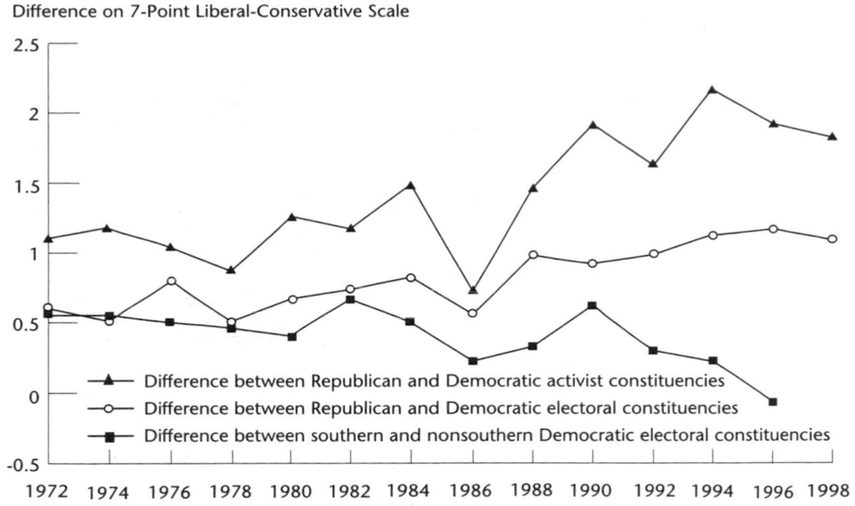

Difference on 7-Point Liberal-Conservative Scale

—▲— Difference between Republican and Democratic activist constituencies
—○— Difference between Republican and Democratic electoral constituencies
—■— Difference between southern and nonsouthern Democratic electoral constituencies

the parties' most active electoral constituents widened even more, nearly doubling to about two points on the scale.

Figure 2–10 presents the equivalent data for Senate electoral constituencies, except that entries are calculated from the three surveys up to and including the year indicated on the chart, so that data from voters electing the entire Senate membership are used to calculate in each observation. The same pattern of ideological polarization between the parties' respective electoral and activist constituencies appears, although somewhat muted, reflecting the greater heterogeneity of the Senate's larger electorates.

The ideological gap between the president's electoral constituency and the congressional majority's electoral constituency under conditions of divided government also has doubled. In 1972 Nixon voters were on average only 0.7 points more conservative than voters for the House Democrats elected that year. In 1996 the House Republicans' electoral constituency was 1.4 points more conservative than Bill Clinton's electoral constituency.[17] The gap between the most active segment of each electoral

17. The equivalent gaps for the elections of 1980, 1984, and 1988 were .97, .88, and 1.04, respectively.

Figure 2–10 Difference in Mean Ideological Self-Placement of Senate
Activist and Electoral Constituencies, 1976–1998

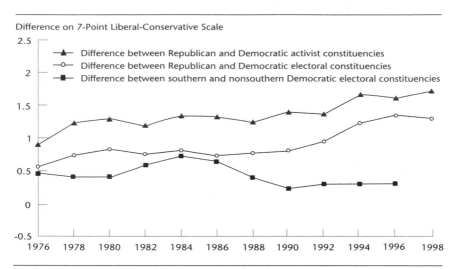

Difference on 7-Point Liberal-Conservative Scale

— ▲ — Difference between Republican and Democratic activist constituencies
— ○ — Difference between Republican and Democratic electoral constituencies
— ■ — Difference between southern and nonsouthern Democratic electoral constituencies

constituency widened even more, from 1.3 points in 1972 to 2.2 points in 1996. An equivalent analysis of self-placement on issue positions tells the same story; on every issue dimension examined in Figure 2–5, the congressional parties' respective electoral coalitions are farther apart in the 1990s than they were at the beginning of the time series.

A discussion of changes in electoral coalitions would not be complete without confirming how profoundly the southern realignment has affected the demographic composition of the remaining Democratic coalition. Although it is not news, it is still worth highlighting just how dependent successful southern Democratic candidates are on African American voters. Figure 2–11 presents the pertinent data. For representatives, the entry is simply the proportion of all votes for the winning Democrat that were cast by black voters in each election year. For senators, it is the African American proportion of all votes for winning southern Democrats in the trio of elections culminating in the year listed. Therefore, the Senate entries indicate the proportion of African Americans in the electoral constituencies of all southern senators in the Congress following the specified election. Blacks were once a negligible part of the electoral constituencies of southern Democrats in Congress. Now they supply more than one-third of their votes. Add to this the fact that southern whites who continue to identify themselves as Democrats now share the socioeconomic profile of white Democrats elsewhere (Nadeau

Figure 2–11 Share of Votes for Southern Democratic Representatives and Senators Provided by African American Voters, 1956–1996

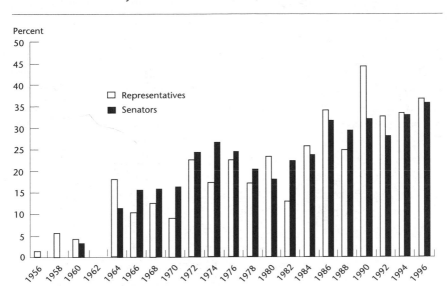

and Stanley 1993), and the nearly complete disappearance of conservative southern Democrats in Congress is no mystery at all.[18]

Chicken or Egg?

Evidence from examination of the electorate, then, is fully consistent with the standard argument that partisan polarization in Congress reflects electoral changes that have left the parties with more homogeneous and more dissimilar electoral coalitions. When the focus of analysis is Congress, electoral change seems to be the independent variable: changes in roll call voting reflect changes in electoral coalitions. When the focus is on elections, however, it becomes apparent that causality works at least as strongly in the opposite direction: voters sort themselves out politically by responding to the alternatives represented by the two parties.

18. Data for 1998 are not included because the number of southern respondents who voted for winning House and Senate Democrats (23 and 12, respectively) is too small for meaningful analysis. Such as they are, the 1998 results are not inconsistent with previous years—six of the twenty-three House voters and three of the twelve Senate voters were African Americans.

Realignment in the South *followed* the national Democratic Party's decision to champion civil rights for African Americans and the Republican Party's choice of Sen. Barry Goldwater, who voted against the Civil Rights Act of 1964, as its standard-bearer that year. Partisan divisions on the abortion issue surfaced first in Congress, then in the electorate (Adams 1997). Electorates diverged ideologically after the parties had diverged ideologically; the divisions in Congress and among activists during and after the Reagan years left the two parties with more distinctive images, making it easier for voters to recognize their appropriate ideological home. Conservatives moved into the Republican ranks, while liberals remained Democrats (Abramowitz and Saunders 1998; Carmines and Layman 1997). Notice that most of the trends among voters identified in the figures show their largest movement in the 1990s, *after* the firming up of congressional party lines in the 1980s.

This is not to say, however, that members of Congress simply follow their own ideological fancies, leaving voters no choice but to line up accordingly. As vote-seeking politicians, they naturally anticipate voters' potential responses and so are constrained by them. The Republican "southern strategy" emerged because Republican presidential candidates sensed an opportunity to win converts among conservative white southerners. Ambitious Republicans adopted conservative positions on social issues to attract voters alienated by the Democrats' tolerance of nontraditional life styles but indifferent at best to Republican economic policies. Democrats emphasized "choice" on abortion because they recognized its appeal to well-educated, affluent voters who might otherwise think of themselves as Republicans. In the budget wars of the past two decades, Democrats have vigorously defended middle class entitlements such as Social Security and Medicare, while Republicans have championed tax cuts because each position has a large popular constituency. In adopting positions, then, politicians are guided by the opportunities and constraints presented by configurations of public opinion on political issues. Party polarization in Congress depended on the expectation that voters would reward, or at least not punish, voting with one's party's majority.

In reality, therefore, the relationship between mass and elite partisan consistency is inherently interactive. Between the 1970s and the 1990s, changes in electoral and congressional politics reinforced one another, encouraging greater partisan consistency and cohesion in both. One important result is that the linkage between citizens' decisions on election day and the actions of the winners once they assume office has become much tighter. Indeed, election results predict congressional roll call voting on issues that fall along the primary liberal-conservative dimension accurately enough to meet one of the fundamental conditions for responsible party government. This is evident when we regress DW-NOMINATE scores on two variables, party and the district-level presidential vote, and observe how much of the variance they explain. The presidential vote stands here as a serviceable if somewhat imprecise measure of district ideology: the higher the Republican share of the vote in any given election, the more conservative the district. The results are summarized in Figure 2–12, which tracks the proportion of variance in first-dimension DW-NOMINATE scores explained by party and presidential vote, individually and in combination, in the Congresses immediately following each presidential election since 1952.

As we would expect from the information in Figures 2–1 and 2–2, the capacity of party to account for roll call voting on the liberal-conservative dimension declined from the 1950s to the 1970s but since then has risen steeply. The predictive accuracy of the district-level presidential vote remained lower than that of party through most of the period, reaching a low point in 1976 (a consequence of Jimmy Carter's initial appeal to conservative southerners), but then rising to its highest levels in the time series during the 1990s. The *relative* contribution of district ideology to explaining House members' positions on the liberal-conservative dimension tends to be greatest in the 1960s and 1970s, when party's contribution is lowest. Between 1976 and 1996, both variables become increasingly

Figure 2–12   Variance in Roll Call Ideology Explained by District Presidential
Vote and Party, 1952–1996

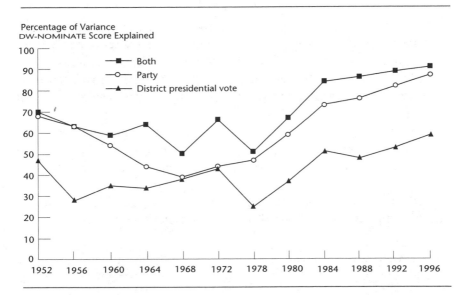

accurate predictors of congressional voting, to the point where by the 105th Congress, party and presidential vote account for a remarkable 91.5 percent of the variance in representatives' DW-NOMINATE scores.

The voting patterns of House members, then, are increasingly predictable from elementary electoral variables: the party of the winner and the district's ideology as reflected in its presidential leanings (with these two variables themselves correlated in 1996 at the highest level since the 1950s). With this development, voters have a much clearer idea of how their collective choices in national elections will translate into congressional action on national issues. Because party labels are so much more predictive of congressional behavior, voters have good reason to use them more consistently to guide voting decisions.

The same circumstances that make the party label such an informative cue also deepen the dilemma faced by moderate voters, however. And, despite the growing divergence between the parties' respective electoral coalitions, most Americans still cluster in the middle of the ideological spectrum. In surveys from the 1990s, about 60 percent of House voters place themselves in one of the middle three positions on the 7-point liberal-conservative scale, down only modestly from about 68 percent in the 1970s. Polarization in Congress has outstripped polarization in the electorate, so the proportion of citizens placing themselves between the two parties has not diminished.[19] Therefore, although the 1998 NES survey found party line voting to be near its highest level in thirty years, it also found that

- only 45 percent of voters preferred the continuation of the two-party system to elections without party labels (29 percent) or new parties to challenge the Republicans and Democrats (26 percent);
- 84 percent thought that the phrase "too involved in partisan politics" described Congress quite well (40 percent) or extremely well (44 percent);
- 56 percent preferred control of the presidency and Congress to be split between the parties, 24 percent preferred one party to control both institutions, and the rest did not care.

With elite polarization outstripping mass polarization, the advent of a central component of responsible party government—unified parties with

---

19. The share of voters placing themselves between the points where they place the parties on the 7-point liberal-conservative scale has not changed appreciably since the 1970s, remaining at about 30 percent.

distinct policy positions—may have had the paradoxical effect of strengthening support for divided government. The more divergent the parties' modal ideological positions, the more reason the remaining centrist voters have to welcome the moderating effect of divided government (Fiorina 1996). But under divided government, the more divergent the parties, the more rancorous the conflict between the president and Congress, and rancorous political conflict is welcomed by almost no one.

The Clinton impeachment put the bitterest of partisan conflicts on full display, and the public did not find it a pretty sight. After the Senate acquitted Clinton, members of Congress, particularly on the Republican side, began looking for ways to soften the image of rabid partisanship that the impeachment had imparted. The trends examined here suggest that any success they achieve is destined to be temporary. Party divisions in Congress have increasingly sturdy electoral roots, particularly among activists, as well as strong institutional reinforcement from the congressional parties. Both parties' holds on their respective branches is tenuous, guaranteeing intense electoral competition across the board in 2000. The party that achieves the upper hand has an excellent chance of winning control of the whole federal government; if the Republicans can win the presidency, they are almost certain to capture undivided national power for the first time in nearly half a century. With so much at stake, no partisan political advantage is likely to be left unexploited. The only constraint on undiluted partisanship is the fear of losing ground by *looking* too partisan; if impeachment politics is any indication, it is not much of a constraint. All signs point to a new partisan era in national politics that is likely to continue for the foreseeable future.

Appendix

The following questions were used to create the 7-point issue position scales analyzed and reported in Figure 2–5. The variable number is listed as it appears in the code book for the 1952–1996 Cumulative Data File (Miller et al. 1998).

V809. "Some people feel that the government in Washington should see to it that every person has a job and a good standard of living. Others think that the government should just let each person get ahead on his own. Where would you place yourself on this scale, or haven't you thought much about it?" The end points of the scale are (1) "Government see to job and good standard of living" and (7) "Government let each person get ahead on his own."

V830. "Some people feel that the government in Washington should make every possible effort to improve the social and economic position of blacks. Others feel that the government should not make any special effort to help blacks because they should help themselves. Where would you place yourself on this scale, or haven't you thought much about it?" The end points of the scale are (1) "Government should help blacks" and (7) "Blacks should help themselves." Wording varies slightly from survey to survey.

V834. "Recently there has been a lot of talk about women's rights. Some people feel that women should have an equal role with men in running business, industry, and government. Others feel that women's place is in the home. Where would you place yourself on this scale or haven't you thought much about this?" The end points of the scale are (1) "Women and men should have an equal role" and (7) "Women's place is in the home."

V838. "There has been some discussion about abortion during recent years. Which one of the opinions on this page best agrees with your view? You can just tell me the number of the opinion you choose."

1. By law abortion should never be permitted.
2. The law should permit abortion only in case of rape, incest, or when the woman's life is in danger.
3. The law should permit abortion for reasons other than rape, incest, or danger to a woman's life, but only after the need for the abortion has been clearly established.
4. By law, a woman should always be able to obtain an abortion as a matter of personal choice.

V839. "Some people think the government should provide fewer services, even in areas such as health and education, in order to reduce spending. Other people feel that it is important for the government to provide many more services even if it means an increase in spending. Where would you place yourself on this scale, or haven't you thought much about this?" The end points of the scale are (1) "Government should provide many fewer services: reduce spending a lot" and (7) "Government should provide many more services: increase spending a lot."

CHAPTER 3

The Consequences of Party Organization in the House: The Role of the Majority and Minority Parties in Conditional Party Government

John H. Aldrich and David W. Rohde

Political scientists have long recognized that political parties in the United States are weak compared to their counterparts in most parliamentary democracies. Yet, as Gary Jacobson's analysis in the previous chapter demonstrates, the strength of parties varies over time, and Jacobson has identified some of the reasons for the rise in partisanship over the last decade or so. Political scientists also debate the consequences of variation in partisanship on behavior and policy making in Congress. On one side are scholars such as Keith Krehbiel (1998) who argue that parties and partisan activity are not essential to a sound theoretical understanding of Congress. A theory is by definition an abstraction. In building theoretical abstractions, political scientists make simplifying assumptions about a political process or institution in order to focus attention on the essential aspects to explain and predict some behavior. For example, a theory can ignore certain details about the "real" Congress so long as the simplification contains the essential components that make Congress work.

Krehbiel's theory focuses on the distribution of preferences in Congress and the importance of preferences of individuals at "pivot points," which are defined by rules that require 60 percent of senators to stop a filibuster and two-thirds of both houses to override a presidential veto. This theory ignores parties: because American parties are too weak to ensure cohesion of their members, the majority does not have a great advantage over the minority. Instead, according to Krehbiel (1998, 171), "competing party organizations bidding for pivotal votes may roughly counterbalance one another, so final outcomes are not much different from what a simpler but completely specified nonpartisan theory predicts." So even though parties are a big part of Congress, *theoretically*

31

they can be ignored because they are not essential to explaining and predicting what Congress does.

On the other side of the debate are John H. Aldrich and David W. Rohde. In their chapter, Aldrich and Rohde address those scholars who question the importance of parties in the legislative process. Their goal is to show both theoretically and empirically how and why parties matter. The chapter is grounded in the theory of "conditional party government," which the authors have developed both individually and collaboratively. The theory of conditional party government is based on the assumption that legislators have multiple goals: policy and reelection. When members of Congress hold preferences that are similar to those of fellow partisans and different from the preferences of members of the opposition, these members are likely to prefer strong party leaders in the legislature. Homogeneous preferences within parties and disagreement between parties provide a necessary "condition" for strong party leadership. If the condition of homogeneous preferences is met, then rank-and-file members (who now agree on policy) give party leaders the tools and resources to achieve the party's policy goals, and they expect leaders to use them. Moreover, party control of the legislature matters because the power and resources of majority and minority parties are asymmetric—that is, they are not equal. Majority party leaders have more leverage over the process than minority party leaders. Use of the powers (for example, agenda control, rules of debate, and timing of votes) by the majority party skews policy away from the median member of the chamber and toward the median of the majority party. This process helps us understand why party polarization in Congress is more exaggerated than the party polarization of ordinary citizens documented by Jacobson in Chapter 2. In addition to presenting important theoretical and empirical information about Congress, this chapter demonstrates how scholars develop and test scientific theories by criticizing and revising each other's work.

═══════

For some time, we have sought to develop and test a theory of the role of parties in Congress (especially in the House) that we call "conditional party government."[1] In this chapter we continue to develop that theory by presenting some amplifications of the argument and by offering some systematic evidence about one aspect of it. In particular, we compare our views and research results with those presented in

1. The earlier work includes Rohde (1991); Aldrich (1995); and Aldrich and Rohde (1996; 1997; 1997–1998; 1998; 2000b).

the work of Keith Krehbiel (1991, 1993, 1998). The issue in contention is whether the influence of the majority and minority parties on members' behavior and on legislative outcomes is symmetric or whether the majority party has a disproportionate impact.

In the first section, we review the theoretical basis of conditional party government. Next we contrast our view of the balance between the majority and minority parties with Krehbiel's view. Finally, we seek to clarify some of the expectations of our theory.

The Theory of Conditional Party Government

The theory of conditional party government begins with the policy preferences that members bring with them to the House and that they choose to make known by their votes and other policy-making actions. These preferences may be shaped by the legislators' personal views, as well as the desire to be reelected. Parties as electoral institutions are therefore likely to exert a strong influence on legislators' beliefs and actions. We also assume that the parties may affect members' behavior through their partisan legislative institutions. Further, the relative effectiveness of the party as a legislative institution depends on electoral results, in particular, by affecting the degree to which the "condition" in conditional party government is satisfied. By that we mean the degree to which the preferences of party members are homogeneous, especially within the majority party, and different between the parties. Because the degree of satisfaction of this condition is partially due to electoral forces, the electoral and internal legislative party are closely related.

In our conception, the main factors shaping the relationship between the electoral and the institutional arenas are the patterns of political preferences within different parts of members' constituencies (geographic, reelection, and primary in Richard Fenno's [1973] terms), and especially those of party activists. Central to this conception is the view (also building on Fenno) that actors have multiple motives, and that both the electoral and policy goals of participants are important. Party activists care about policy, and they want their candidates to share and pursue those policy interests. When the preferences of activists and ordinary voters within the primary and reelection constituencies of a given party vary substantially across districts in different parts of the country, the preferences of representatives within that party's House contingent probably will be fairly heterogeneous. This diversity of policy preferences was the case, for example, for Democrats in the late 1960s, when northern and southern

Democrats were in conflict over issues such as civil rights and the Vietnam War, and the southerners often sided with the Republicans against their northern co-partisans (Rohde 1991).

If, on the other hand, the preferences within the primary and reelection constituencies of a party's representatives become more similar across districts, we would expect the policy preferences of those representatives (or their successors) also to become more similar. This convergence of preferences was, in our view, what happened during the 1970s and 1980s. In southern districts, for example, more black voters were added to the rolls, which liberalized the Democratic primary constituencies and led to the creation of Republican constituencies made up of white southern Democrats who left the party and northern Republicans who had migrated. As a result, southern Democratic candidates became more similar to northern Democratic candidates, and some of them were successful. Other southern districts, however, elected GOP members who were like their northern colleagues, but more conservative.

Three sets of consequences depend on the increasing degree to which this condition—homogeneous parties and policy differences between the parties—is satisfied. First, the more the condition is met, the more likely are party members to give their legislative party institutions and party leadership stronger powers and greater resources. Second, the greater the satisfaction of the condition, the greater the party's expectation that the party will use those powers and resources more often. Third, provided that the majority party has (because it is the party that organizes the House) more powers and resources to employ than the minority party, then legislation should reveal that fact. In particular, the greater the degree of satisfaction of the condition in conditional party government, the farther policy outcomes should be skewed from the center of the whole Congress toward the center of opinion in the majority party.

What Is at Issue?

As indicated earlier, the most persistent critic of party theories has been Keith Krehbiel. Basing his position both on theory and data, he has argued that partisan effects are neither implied by a well-specified theory nor consistent with available evidence. In discussing Krehbiel's positions, we will sometimes refer to aspects of his viewpoint as "pure majoritarian theory" rather than as "informational theory" as he does. We do this not to be argumentative, but rather to focus attention on where we agree and disagree. First, we do not disagree with the idea that the members try to structure the institution so as to get committees to provide expertise and information. That is, we do not reject informational motives for the members. Rather, the disagreement here is whether this is their only theoretically relevant motivation in organizing the legislature (Rohde 1994).[2] Our contention is that other motives, linked to partisan policy and electoral interests, are relevant because they induce different behavior and result in different outcomes than those expected by Krehbiel's theoretical argument. Second, we do disagree about whether the influence on outcomes in this process is symmetric between the majority and minority parties. Krehbiel assumes that it is and that therefore the center of the relevant policy dimension—that is, the median member who has preferences at the midpoint of preference rankings—will control outcomes and consequently determine choices of organizational structure. We make other assumptions, which we believe imply that, under certain theoretically specified circumstances, outcomes will be skewed away from the chamber median preference and toward the majority party's median preference.

In discussing his view of the symmetric balance between parties, Krehbiel (1998, 171) states:

> The point is not that majority-party organizations and their deployment of resources are inconsequential. Rather it is to suggest that competing party organizations bidding for pivotal votes may roughly counterbalance one another, so final outcomes are not much different from what simpler but completely specified nonpartisan theory predicts. Whether this alternative view is correct is, of course, an empirical question.

We agree that the central issue in evaluating a theory is whether its predictions are borne out by evidence, and we thoroughly address such evidence in this chapter. Nonetheless, it also seems perfectly appropriate to evaluate an assumption's plausibility in light of what we already know (see Fiorina 1995, 306), and thereby to raise questions *a priori* regarding the theory's implications. It is not as if we come to theory building with no knowledge of Congress. In that spirit, we mention a few points.

First, note how very strong Krehbiel's assumption must be to justify ignoring the effects of party in his theory. It is not enough to sustain his claim for the majority and minority organizations to balance each other

---

2. Another reason to draw this contrast is that Krehbiel's is not the only possible informational theory. It is *an* informational theory (see, e.g., Bianco 1998), in the same way that conditional party government is not the only possible partisan theory (see, e.g., Cox and McCubbins 1993).

on average.[3] Rather, they must balance their respective efforts vote by vote, issue by issue, and time after time. For example, if the majority party and the minority party each controlled the outcome on 50 percent of the votes or bills in a Congress—thereby yielding outcomes half the time close to the center of the Democratic Party and half of the time close to the center of the Republican Party—their impact would be roughly balanced. There would be no centrist outcomes, however, and ignoring party theoretically in such a circumstance would be entirely unjustified. We therefore take it to be Krehbiel's meaning that the parties counterbalance one another in each relevant instance, not just overall.

Perhaps of even more concern, in the light of available knowledge, is the fact that the assumption must mean parties balance over time. That is, imagine that the impact of the majority and the minority is roughly balanced at t_1 (for example, the 103d Congress). Then imagine that at t_2 (for example, the 104th Congress after the 1994 elections) the majority leadership is granted significant new powers over the agenda and in relation to its members, which greatly increases its influence over outcomes.[4] The assumption would assert that somehow, automatically, the minority party's influence over outcomes would also increase to balance out the increase by the majority. It would be an understatement to say that such a result would be implausible. Perhaps more to the point, we are aware of no evidence that reflects such a development, but we are aware of substantial evidence to the contrary. Note that whether the leaderships have consequential effects is not at issue; Krehbiel (as the quotation above demonstrates) believes they do. Rather the issue is whether these effects are symmetric in the ways we have discussed. Virtually all observers have concluded that the influence of the Republican majority leadership over the agenda and over GOP members was significantly increased, relative to the previous Democratic majority leadership, at the beginning of the 104th Congress. (See Aldrich and Rohde 1997–1998 for our discussion.) Yet we can find no evidence that would indicate a commensurate increase for the minority party leadership over the agenda and members between the two Congresses. A similar analysis can be made for the reform period

---

3. We want to make clear that we are specifically not contending that the assumption is untenable merely because parties occasionally have an asymmetric effect on outcomes. It is a separate question—one we will address in the context of the evidence we present—whether the impact of party is so rare and inconsequential that it can safely be ignored in the theory.

4. For argument and evidence that this is actually what happened at the outset of the 104th Congress, see Aldrich and Rohde (1997–1998).

in the House in the 1970s, when the powers of the majority leadership were strengthened (Rohde 1991). If this perception of what occurred is accurate, it would seem to present evidence contrary to the expectations of Krehbiel's theory.

What Is (and Isn't) Expected
Under Conditional Party Government?

Here we want to clarify and elaborate our view of some of the expectations of our theory. The aim of this clarification is to reduce the likelihood of misperceptions, especially those that might stem from a lack of specificity on our part. First, we do not expect party organizations to have an effect on choices or outcomes in every instance. As we have argued previously, not all issues are relevant to partisan interests, and the parties will not necessarily be active on all of those that are relevant. Partisan issues tend to be those that involve preference conflicts along partisan lines in the electorate, either among voters generally or among party activists in particular (Aldrich 1995, chap. 6). The higher the salience of the issue to those who are interested, the greater the likelihood that the congressional parties will be involved.[5] Yet issue salience alone is not sufficient to invoke the activity of the congressional parties. Such activity occurs only when the party will not win without it and when the party leaders think they would have a chance to win with it. In other words, party leaders would not try to induce their members to change their votes if they believed their side would win without them, nor would they do so if they believed they would lose even with the votes they could plausibly pick up. Our theory does not imply an omnipotent majority party, merely one that is efficacious and consequential under certain conditions.

That example offers the occasion for another clarification. We spoke about the effort of leaders to change members votes, and the quotation from Krehbiel implies that he sees such action—"bidding for pivotal votes"—as the only relevant party effect in this discussion. That is not our view. It is one potentially relevant activity, but at least as consequential are the majority party's influences on the agenda and procedures, which do not necessarily involve switching votes in any conventional sense. As we have sought to demonstrate elsewhere (especially Aldrich and Rohde 1997; 2000b), the majority party sometimes uses its powers to create legislative

---

5. Thus, because the theory only expects party effects on a subset of issues, any effort to test this theory relative to any other must be confined to the partisan agenda. Any test that does not do that is simply irrelevant.

packages that contain partisan elements that the full membership would not adopt if they stood alone. In such instances, the leaders need the members only to tolerate their actions, not necessarily to switch positions. In other cases, the leadership uses agenda tools to achieve partisan outcomes directly, without the necessity of members voting to support them. We will present evidence on these matters below.

Related to the previous point is another: just as vote switching is not the only relevant party effect, achieving nonmedian outcomes is not the only relevant partisan result expected within our theory. As the presentation of the theory of conditional party government has made clear from the beginning (Rohde 1991), the aim of the party leadership is to enact as much of the party's program as possible. Sometimes this goal involves trying to achieve a nonmedian result. At other times it involves trying to enact the floor median, when, without effective party intervention, a nonmedian result tilted toward the opposition would be the result. Such a result could occur when the opposition is trying to protect a previously enacted status quo on a policy. As Krehbiel (1998) has shown, one possible effect of pivotal politics is the maintenance of nonmedian policies, and vetoes and filibusters are, within a multimotivational partisan theory like ours, not the only relevant pivot points. Moreover, our theory does not argue that the median preference in the chamber is not important or consequential. "The chamber median exerts a powerful force, and it therefore takes an alternative powerful force to move outcomes away from it. We believe (and our theory expects) that parties can exert this kind of force on some issues on some occasions" (Aldrich 2000b). Regarding the achievement of nonmedian outcomes by the majority party, our theory contends (contrary to Krehbiel's theory) that such results are achievable in principle and that they will be achieved in practice frequently enough to make it important that we take them into account. It does not contend that nonmedian results will be achieved all the time or even that they will be the party's goal all the time.[6]

---

6. We should note, however, that when the condition underlying conditional party government is strongly satisfied, as in the 104th Congress (Aldrich and Rohde 1998), our expectation would be that nonmedian outcomes are likely to occur fairly frequently on high saliency bills. This is because *both* parties would be expected to develop partisan proposals that diverged from the median, and the majority would be expected frequently to couple their proposal with restrictions on the ability to amend them on the floor. The result would be that the floor would be presented with an ultimate choice *between* two nonmedian results.

We return to the matter of vote buying to make a further clarification about our theory. In his analysis of cosponsorship and discharge-petition-signing behavior in relation to a GOP-supported deficit reduction bill, Krehbiel (1995a) contends that partisan theories imply that party leaders will buy votes generally from within their own party because the "price differential" will be smaller for majority members. We discuss the empirical evidence in this article below in another context, but here address only the theoretical issue. We do not share Krehbiel's view about the theoretical expectation of partisan theories, at least as it relates to our theory. If majority party leaders wish to influence the outcome on a bill, they should seek to secure the support of members at the lowest cost. Under certain circumstances this might be members of their own party—either because of collective party interests or because the leaders can provide benefits such as committee assignments to their own members that they cannot offer to the minority. There is not, however, in our view any logical relationship between cost and majority/minority status of members near the median. For example, a majority party moderate in electoral jeopardy, may be inclined to vote with her district and against her party. The "price" for switching would have to be high to justify risking her seat. A minority member with approximately the same preference may be safe from challenge, with a correspondingly low price. Surely, the majority leadership would seek the vote of the minority member. Indeed, this result would seem to be the best from their point of view: they gain a vote without endangering the reelection of one of their vulnerable members. In our theory, the majority leaders want to achieve partisan outcomes. To that end, they seek votes from whatever source they can, at the cheapest cost, whether that means the then-majority Democrats' regular whip operation among moderate Republicans (Rohde 1991) or the GOP's routine whip contacts with the "Blue Dog" Democrats in the 104th and 105th Congresses.

Finally, we want to counter the contention by some other analysts that the theory of conditional party government is of dubious relevance because it implies that when the underlying condition is best met—that is, when the majority party is most homogeneous—there is the least need for majority party action because the majority, by virtue of having the most votes in the chamber, will win automatically. This view has never been a part of the theory, and we believe it to be a serious misunderstanding. We can illustrate this by citing two contrasting situations with real world referents. In the first case, the majority party is very large—two-thirds of the seats—but it is deeply split. This was the situation of the Democrats in the 89th Congress, 1965–1967. Despite the condition being poorly satisfied, the enormous majority makes party action unnecessary on most matters. In the second case, the majority party is very homogeneous, but small— for example, the Republicans in the 104th Congress. Here, because the generally high level of homogeneity, which affects the majority membership's willingness to grant power to their leadership, is not identical across issues, leadership action may well be crucial to victory on many issues. In our theory, a high level of homogeneity in the majority does not imply that leadership action is unnecessary.

Evidence on Majority and Minority Party Symmetry

In this section, we explore evidence that bears on whether the two parties are symmetric with regard to their impact on choices and outcomes, as Krehbiel's theory contends, or whether there is significant asymmetry that must be considered and taken into account. We focus on the construction of committees, including the selection of committee leaders, and on the tools that can help the majority to achieve nonmedian outcomes, including influences over members' choices and over the agenda. We also discuss some additional implications of majoritarian theory that we consider problematic.

Majority Advantage in Committee Construction: Composition and Assignments

In an article that challenged the partisan conception of legislative organization, Krehbiel (1993) analyzed data on committee composition. Specifically, he began by presenting data on party ratios on House committees in the 99th Congress, assessing the degree to which the distribution of seats between the parties on each committee approximated the distribution of membership in the chamber. He concluded (1993, 243) that the data illustrated a "well-known fact of committee assignments . . . that, with few exceptions, the party ratios that leaders negotiate closely approximate the partisan composition of the parent chamber." Krehbiel presented these data merely as a preliminary to other analysis, because he argued that little could legitimately be concluded from such composition data anyway. Our interest here is to explore the composition issue further, but before doing so, we offer a few words about the rest of Krehbiel's analysis.

Krehbiel wishes to test here what he asserts to be the implications of partisan theory against a nonpartisan majoritarian conception of the process.

He argues that partisan theories would expect that all committees would be stacked in favor of the majority party independent of its members' preferences, that is, over and above the seats that would be allocated by preferences alone. He then presents evidence to show that this is not the case. We will not address the point that the interest group data Krehbiel employs cannot legitimately be used as measures of preference for such analyses; that has been dealt with elsewhere.[7] Rather, here we note that we disagree with the premise of the analysis: we do not see the hypotheses he tested to be implied by any (and certainly not by our) partisan theory. All legislative parties, even those that are strongly homogeneous, contain varied preferences. To provide incentives for members to remain in a party, that party must provide opportunities for the members to achieve their personal goals. Further, the theory of conditional party government explicitly assumes that actors have a variety of motives. Therefore, in creating legislative organizations such as committees, the majority party has to take account of a variety of interests for leaders and rank-and-file members simultaneously.[8] Rather than expecting the majority party to try to extract partisan benefits from committee construction equally across committees and over time, the theory of conditional party government expects that parties will seek such advantages more often where the advantage is most desirable and when it is most necessary, and less often when these conditions do not hold. By most desirable, we mean that the majority would be more likely to try to gain partisan advantage on the committees that are most important to its agenda, and would be less likely to try it on committees that are less important. By most necessary, we mean that the party would be most likely to seek advantage in circumstances in which its program might be jeopardized without such advantage, and be less likely to do so when the program is not in jeopardy.

With regard to the distribution of member preferences on committees, the majority party (and probably both parties) would be most likely to try to stack with party loyalists those committees that are most central to its policy interests. In the House, that would be the "prestige" or "control"

---

7. There are at least two issues here. One is whether preferences can be assumed to be unidimensional and thus measured as such from interest group scores. We will deal with that issue below. The other question is whether one can infer interval measures of preference from roll call data alone. For an argument that this is not possible, see Marshall, Prins, and Rohde (1997, 16–17).

8. For a discussion of the interaction of these varied interests, see Marshall, Prins, and Rohde (1998).

committees: Appropriations, Budget, Rules, and Ways and Means.[9] Previous research has confirmed the expectation of partisan theories that higher levels of party loyalty were positively related to appointment to those committees (Cox and McCubbins 1993, chap. 7; Shepsle 1978; Sinclair 1981, 187; Smith and Ray 1983). Further, earlier work indicates that House Democrats and Republicans increased their leaders' control over committee assignments to give the leaders more influence over members (Rohde 1991, 24, 137). At the opening of the 104th Congress (1995–1996), the Republican leadership engineered the adoption of a new committee assignment system for the party that sharply increased the leaders' influence over assignments (Aldrich and Rohde 1997–1998). Speaker Newt Gingrich then used that system to influence which members were appointed to committees, particularly to Appropriations (Aldrich and Rohde 2000b). Given the predominant interest of party leaders in putting loyalists on the prestige committees, and given the fact that these are exclusive committees (they can be the member's only committee assignment), assignments to the other committees cannot be dominated by appointments of loyalists, unless the leaders are willing to allocate significantly more assignments across the board to more loyal members. This strategy would not be desirable, however, because it would reduce the incentive for less loyal members to remain within the party. Nor is there a clear policy-related incentive for the leaders to stack such committees under most circumstances. Thus, our theory would expect the assignment process to emphasize the appointment of party loyalists to the most important committees and to let self-selection (Shepsle 1978) dominate appointments to the other committees. The evidence we discussed above is consistent with those expectations.

Assignments, however, are not the only way to extract partisan advantage from the process of committee composition. The majority's assignment of "bonus" committee seats to itself—more seats than match the

---

9. There is a great deal of evidence to indicate the primary importance of these committees to parties and to members. See Rohde (1991, 27–28); Cox and McCubbins (1993, chap. 8); Deering and Smith (1997, chap. 3). In addition, Judiciary was particularly important to the Republicans at the beginning of the 104th Congress because a large proportion of the Contract with America was within its jurisdiction; the Commerce Committee also dealt with important issues on the party's agenda. The fact that Speaker Newt Gingrich violated seniority in appointing chairs on Appropriations, Commerce, and Judiciary is consistent with the expectations of our theory given these considerations (see Aldrich and Rohde 1997–1998).

chamber ratio between the parties, which Krehbiel addresses in passing—is another way. The pure majoritarian theory would expect no systematic variation across committees or across time with regard to the likelihood and degree to which the majority leadership would seek bonus seats. Our theory, on the other hand, has clear expectations in this regard. Majority party leaders should be more likely to create bonus seats on those committees that are most important to the party (the control committees), and when the context puts the party program in the most jeopardy, such as when the partisan division of the chamber is relatively close. As noted, Krehbiel (1993) had presented data on the 99th Congress, in which the Democrats held about 58 percent of the seats. With a comfortable majority, it is not surprising that the Democrats did not create bonus seats on most committees. However the three highest committees in terms of bonus seats—and three of the four on which the Democratic seat advantage exceeded one seat—were Appropriations, Rules, and Ways and Means, exactly what our theory would expect.

Data on one Congress, however, are not sufficient to conclude that the theory is supported, so we now present more systematic data. First, we consider bonus seats on three of the top committees (Appropriations, Rules, and Ways and Means) in all Congresses since World War II.[10] Table 3–1 shows the average bonus seats for the majority party on the three committees, overall and controlling for the percentage of majority seats in the House for the periods before and after 1978, the end of the reform period during which majority leadership powers were strengthened. The evidence shows that the number of bonus seats varies negatively with increasing majority seat percentage and positively with time. The majority party extracted more bonus seats when the chamber was closely divided than when it held a wide margin. In addition, the majority was more inclined (or able) to extract bonus seats after the majority party had strengthened its rules and the party had become more homogeneous (Aldrich and Rohde 1998). This pattern is what our theory would expect. On the other hand, there is no theoretical expectation of this systematic variation in majoritarian theory. Why would it occur?

Other systematic patterns can be seen by looking at data on all committees for the 103d, 104th, and 105th Congresses (see Table 3–2). Here

---

10. To simplify the presentation of the data, we do not include here data on the Budget Committee, a fourth top committee, because it did not exist during the entire period. All data on party ratios on committees displayed here were obtained from Nelson (1993) for 1947–1992. Data for subsequent years were taken from CQWR. (See p. 72 for publication abbreviations.)

Table 3–1

Majority Party Seat Advantage on Top Three Committees,
80th–105th Congresses

Congress	Percentage of Seats held by Majority				
	60%+	57.5–59.9%	55.0–57.4%	<55%	Total
80th–95th (1947–79)	−0.2 (6)	1.9 (2)	3.7 (4)	6.8 (4)	2.8 (16)
96th–105th (1979–99)	3.0 (3)	4.3 (4)	7.9 (1)	7.0 (2)	4.8 (10)
Total	0.1 (9)	3.5 (6)	4.6 (5)	6.9 (6)	3.6 (26)

Note: Each cell shows the average total number of seats taken by the majority party on the three top committees, more or less than what would be expected based on the number of the party's seats in the House. The number in parentheses is the number of Congresses in that category. For example, the bottom right cell indicates that the majority party averaged 3.6 bonus seats on the three committees across all twenty-six Congresses.

we can see comparisons across committee types and across contexts. In the 103d Congress, the Democrats held just under 60 percent of the seats. Because there was little reason to seek to create bonus seats on most committees, we see a pattern much like Krehbiel reports for the 99th Congress. While the bonus is positive on every committee except for Standards of Official Conduct (often called "Ethics"), which is the only committee constructed to provide equal representation for both parties, it exceeds one seat on only four committees, and the top three of them are the prestige committees. After the 1994 elections, however, the Republicans achieved majority status with a narrow 52.9 percent majority. Given that condition, plus a broad-based legislative program that sought major changes across the policy spectrum, we would expect GOP leaders to create bonus seats on more committees, while still putting the greatest emphasis on the control committees. And that is what we see. The average number of bonus seats in the 104th was approximately double that in the 103d, both overall and on the top committees in particular. The increase was smaller on the policy committees (important, but less so than the prestige committees) and smaller still on the less-consequential committees. Then in the 105th Congress, with a slightly narrower majority than the 104th, and with some divisions over policy increasing within the GOP majority, we would expect an even greater incentive to create bonus seats. The summary data show that the average number of bonus seats increased in every category, with the greatest increases being on the policy and the prestige committees.

All in all, this evidence provides strong support for the expectations of our partisan theory, and there is no theoretical justification for any of these occurrences within majoritarian theory. Why would they occur? In addition, we note that the minority party has no ability analogous to the major-

Table 3–2
Majority Party Seat Advantage on Standing Committees, 103d–105th Congresses

Committee[3]	103d Congress[1]			104th Congress[2]			105th Congress[3]		
	Maj. Seats	Expected Maj.	Maj. Bonus	Maj. Seats	Expected Maj.	Maj. Bonus	Maj. Seats	Expected Maj.	Maj. Bonus
Agric.	27	26.78	+0.22	27	25.92	+1.08	27	26.10	+0.90
Approp.	37	35.7	+1.30	32	29.62	+2.38	34	31.32	+2.68
Banking	30	29.75	+0.25	27	25.92	+1.08	29	27.67	+1.33
Budget	26	25.59	+0.41	24	22.22	+1.78	24	22.45	+1.55
Commerce	27	26.18	+0.82	25	24.33	+0.67	28	26.62	+1.38
D.C.	7	6.55	+0.45	—	—	—	—	—	—
Econ. & Ed. Opp.	24	23.21	+0.79	24	22.75	+1.25	25	23.49	+1.51
Gov. Reform	25	24.40	+0.60	27	25.92	+1.08	24	22.45	+1.55
House Over.	12	11.31	+0.69	7	6.35	+0.65	5	4.18	+0.82
Int. Relat.	26	24.99	+1.01	23	22.22	+0.78	26	24.53	+1.47
Judiciary	21	20.83	+0.17	20	18.52	+1.48	20	18.27	+1.73
Mer. Marine	28	27.37	+0.61	—	—	—	—	—	—
Nat. Sec.	34	33.32	+0.68	30	29.10	+0.90	30	28.71	+1.29
Post Office	14	13.69	+0.31	—	—	—	—	—	—
Resources	24	23.21	+0.79	25	23.81	+1.19	27	26.10	+0.90
Rules	9	7.74	+1.26	9	6.88	+2.12	9	6.79	+2.21
Science	33	32.73	+0.27	27	26.45	+0.55	25	24.01	+0.98
Small Bus.	27	26.78	+0.22	22	21.69	+0.31	19	18.27	+0.73
Standards	7	8.33	-1.33	5	5.29	-0.29	5	5.22	-0.22
Trans. & Inf.	37	36.30	+0.70	33	32.27	+0.63	40	38.11	+1.89
Vet. Affairs	21	20.83	+0.17	18	17.46	+0.54	16	15.14	+0.86
Ways/Means	24	22.61	+1.39	21	19.04	+1.96	23	20.36	+2.64

Average majority seat bonus (by committee type)[4]

Prestige	+1.09 (n=4)	+2.06 (n=4)	+2.27 (n=4)
Policy	+0.61 (n=6)	+1.06 (n=6)	+1.50 (n=6)
Constituency	+0.46 (n=8)	+0.74 (n=7)	+0.85 (n=7)
Unrequested	+0.03 (n=4)	+0.18 (n=2)	+0.30 (n=2)
(w/o Standards)	+0.48 (n=3)	+0.65 (n=1)	+0.82 (n=1)
All Committees	+0.54 (n=22)	+1.06 (n=19)	+1.30 (n=19)
(w/o Standards)	+0.63 (n=21)	+1.14 (n=18)	+1.38 (n=18)

1. Delegates are not counted in official ratios.

2. Delegates with party affiliations are counted in official ratios.

3. The committee names used are those that applied in the 104th Congress, except for the three committees that were eliminated before that Congress began.

4. Source of classification: Christopher J. Deering and Steven S. Smith, *Committees in Congress,* 3d ed. (Washington, D.C.: CQ Press, 1997).

ity's ability to create bonus seats. Therefore, we would have to believe that such seats would have no consequence in influencing legislative outcomes (we do not), or that the minority party has some compensating influence over outcomes to balance this ability (here, too, we do not), or we would have to conclude that this is relevant evidence against Krehbiel's theory (which, not surprisingly, is our conclusion).

Before moving on, we note some examples of the majority leadership's asymmetric capability with regard to another aspect of committee composition, namely, the ability to make ad hoc alterations in a committee in order to influence a particular policy outcome. These examples relate specifically to conference committees. Most conference committees are drawn from the senior members of the committee or committees with jurisdiction over the bill (Longley and Oleszek 1989). Occasionally, this practice conflicts with majority party interests about outcomes, but the majority leadership can take remedial action. For example, when the fiscal 1998–1999 State Department authorization bill was in conference, one House GOP conferee, Jim Leach of Iowa, third ranking member of the International Relations Committee, refused to sign the report for the leadership-supported version of the bill because he wanted more funding for the United Nations and opposed restrictions on family planning funds. Speaker Gingrich removed Leach from the conference committee, and replaced him with conservative Dan Burton of Indiana, who signed the report (CQWR 3/14/98, 673). Without this intervention, the bill would not have been reported.

Another kind of ad hoc manipulation of conference committee composition occurred on the 1998 highway bill.[11] The House had voted earlier in the year to allow a subsidy for ethanol to expire in two years. Concerned about the potential impact of such a move on GOP fortunes in farm districts in the 1998 elections, Speaker Gingrich decided to reverse the new policy and support an additional seven-year extension as proposed by the Senate. The problem was that the chairman of the Ways and Means Committee, Bill Archer of Texas, wanted to end the subsidy. Archer, following routine practice, recommended to the Speaker that he and Philip Crane of Illinois (second ranking on the committee) be appointed as conferees. Instead, Gingrich announced that he would appoint Archer, but not Crane. To cancel Archer's vote Gingrich appointed two pro-subsidy Republicans, one of whom was a freshman and the most junior member of Ways and Means. Gingrich said, "Archer exercised his prerogatives as

11. The account of this bill is drawn from WP 5/7/98, A4; RC 5/7/98, 10; and LEGI-SLATE NEWS 5/6/98, Article no. 49102.

chairman and I exercised mine as Speaker. . . . As leader of the overall party in the House . . . one of my jobs is to balance regional interests" (WP 5/7/98, A4). Thus, the previously adopted decision of the House majority was reversed by majority leadership action. The minority party had no analogous capability.

Majority Advantage in Committee Construction:
Committee Leadership

In addition to establishing committee ratios and making member assignments, the majority party has another important impact on committee composition. Beginning with the reform era of the 1970s, the majority party—first through the Democratic Caucus, later through the decisions of Speaker Gingrich—began to override the seniority norm and select certain committee chairs. In the early 1970s the Democrats adopted automatic votes on chair nominees at the beginning of each Congress (Rohde 1991, 20–23). After the 1974 elections the caucus exercised this power when they voted to replace three committee chairmen, all southerners, at least two of whom were far more conservative than the overall caucus. The power was similarly exercised a number of times in subsequent Congresses, putting Democratic committee chairs on notice. Research by Sara Crook and John Hibbing (1985) showed that these seniority reforms had an impact on the party loyalty of senior members. Democrats who occupied committee chairs or were close in seniority to committee chairs dramatically increased their level of party support relative to other members during the period 1971–1982. Focusing on a single important example, Rohde (1991, 75–76) presented data on the party loyalty of Jamie Whitten of Mississippi from 1955 to 1988. Whitten served as a senior subcommittee chair on Appropriations, and later as chair of the full committee.[12] His party loyalty went from being substantially lower than other southern Democrats to being higher than the average for *all* House Democrats by the middle of the 1980s. The Democrats adopted rules that were designed to make committee leaders more loyal and responsive to the party, and the evidence indicates that this is what happened.

When the GOP took over the House after the 1994 elections, they went even further in permitting the party to influence committee leadership. As the anticipated new Speaker, Newt Gingrich simply asserted the right to name committee chairs in violation of the seniority norm, and the

---

12. The Democratic Caucus also adopted automatic votes on Appropriations subcommittee chairs.

Republican Party acquiesced. On three committees that were vitally important to the GOP agenda—Appropriations, Commerce, and Judiciary—Gingrich passed over the senior Republican to appoint a more junior member who would do a better job from the leadership's point of view. Indeed, on Appropriations the Speaker went down to fifth-ranking Bob Livingston of Louisiana for his choice. Accounts of legislative action in the 104th and 105th Congresses are replete with examples of chairs of these three (and other) committees being induced by the leadership to change legislation because of an implied or explicit threat of possible removal from their committee leadership positions.[13] For example, in 1995 the Commerce Committee passed a major telecommunications bill by a vote of 38–5 (see Aldrich and Rohde 1997, 12). Shortly after the vote, under orders from the party leadership, Chairman Thomas Bliley of Virginia announced that the bill would be changed even though he had supported it. On various appropriations measures in 1995, the intervention of the leadership was even greater. On the Labor-Health-Education bill, conservative Republicans wanted to include a "rider" (legislation in an appropriations bill) that would prohibit organizations that received federal funding from lobbying (Drew 1996, 261). Livingston was strongly opposed to including this provision and told the Speaker so. After his discussion with Gingrich, he returned to the committee and indicated that the provision would have to be included. He said that the rider "had such import that the leadership determined we should take it." Later during consideration of the bill, one of the subcommittee chairs objected to the inclusion of the rider. Livingston responded that "the Chair is very sympathetic" to the argument, but "it has been a leadership decision to move ahead with this initiative."

Evidence from both Democratic and Republican majority regimes indicates that the parties changed their rules and practices to give party structures influence over the tenure of committee chairs. They did so to make the chairs more responsive to the wishes of the majority party, which in turn would have consequences for legislative outcomes that the party cared about. There is considerable evidence, some referenced above, that the chairs' behavior did indeed change. There is also some evidence that policy outcomes were different as a result. Krehbiel has said in various works (for example, 1991, 115, regarding committee assignments) that he focuses more on outcomes than on the processes that produce them. We do not believe that such a disjunction is appropriate; moreover, we have evidence that bears both on behavior (of parties and of chairs) and

---

13. See, for example, Aldrich and Rohde 1997; 1997–1998; 2000b; Drew 1996; Maraniss and Weisskopf 1996.

on outcomes (the party processes that were adopted). As noted, the majority parties changed the way they select committee chairs because they believed the new procedures would alter behavior and affect outcomes. Otherwise the changes would make no sense. Further, the evidence indicates that the chairs changed their behavior toward being responsive to the party. If the rules changes did not alter the incentives of the chairs, the changes in behavior make no sense. If the majority party leaders did not perceive a connection between changes in the chairs' behavior and outcomes, their continued efforts to influence the chairs would make no sense. In the first section of this chapter we pointed out the necessity of making sense of both behavior and outcomes; we conclude here that the majority parties believed that their impact on outcomes had been enhanced.

This discussion brings us back to the point raised above about the time factor of the assumption about symmetric effects between the parties. From one point in time to another, majority parties changed their procedures regarding chair selection. There is direct evidence that chairs' behavior changed as a result. There is indirect (and some direct) evidence that these events increased the majority party's influence over outcomes. Where then is the corresponding evidence that between the same points in time the minority party's influence over outcomes also was enhanced, as the majoritarian theory implies? What powers does the minority party have that counteract those of the committee chairs who are made more responsive to their party? As far as we can see, there is no such evidence. The influence of the majority party was increased asymmetrically, without any counterbalancing increase for the minority.

Achieving Nonmedian Outcomes: An Instance Where We Can Be Certain

We have indicated that our theory has implications for both behavior and outcomes, and that in at least some instances the majority party achieves nonmedian outcomes. Therefore, it seems important to provide evidence in this connection—that is, to show that some policy outcomes diverge significantly in the direction of the majority party away from the median preference on the floor.[14] As Krehbiel (1998, 170) notes, demonstrating this divergence is difficult, because it is hard to measure the location of

---

14. For some such evidence on the 100th and 104th Congresses, see Aldrich and Rohde (1996).

outcomes and preferences and the relationship between them.[15] Even so, we can provide evidence of at least one certain instance of achievement of a nonmedian outcome through party action, additional evidence that the outcome in numerous instances depended solely on the preference of the leader of the majority party, and other evidence that indicates either that a nonmedian outcome was likely and/or that the majority's influence over the outcome was asymmetric to that of the minority. We turn to the first of these points.

The unequivocal example of a nonmedian result involved the majority leadership's scheduling powers during floor consideration of the fiscal 1996 Veterans-HUD appropriations bill. A coalition of Democrats and fifty-one GOP moderates had joined together to produce an unexpected 212–206 victory on an amendment to strike legislative provisions restricting the regulatory activities of the Environmental Protection Agency. Three days later the leadership scheduled a second vote on the amendment. This incident illustrates three different aspects of the majority leadership's agenda power for which the minority party leadership has no parallel capabilities. First, the ability to schedule a second vote—to have a second chance—rests solely with the majority leadership. Second, and in this case more important, the timing of the vote belonged to the majority. The leadership had been trying to switch GOP votes without success. They noticed, however, that when they resumed consideration of the bill on Monday, July 31, a number of Democrats were not yet back in town from the weekend. In the evening, when they were sure that the Democrats had not returned, they called for a second vote. Not one Republican defector switched to the leadership's side, but because of the absences the new vote was a 210–210 tie, which defeated the amendment. A third scheduling power was used; as noted earlier, when the Republicans were unsure of their vote count, they pulled the bill from the floor, resuming consideration when they were more certain (Drew 1996, 266–67). Most important for our purposes here, victory for the GOP position was also a defeat for the majority-preferred outcome. The 210 yes votes, added to the eight Democrats who voted yes the first time but were absent for the second vote, made up a majority of all members (CQWR 8/5/95, 2367).

15. We should note here, however, what should be already apparent to the readers of this chapter, or to anyone who has read even one of our previous works: Krehbiel's following claim—that the only evidence that has been offered for the predictions of conditional party government is high rates of party voting—is completely false.

A nonmedian outcome resulted from the asymmetric powers of the majority party leadership.

Achieving Nonmedian Outcomes: The Speaker and the Majority Party's Preference

In this section we focus on three examples (although many similar cases could be cited) in which we cannot be sure that a nonmedian result was achieved, but we can be sure that the outcome was determined solely by the powers and preference of the Speaker. We can also be certain that the powers were held by the Speaker and were not balanced by countervailing powers in the minority party or its leadership. Each example has two common salient features: a floor vote was scheduled on a matter that was important to the majority party and the majority's preferred outcome was losing when time for the vote ran out. The first instance is the vote on passage of the budget reconciliation bill in 1987, an important measure for both parties (see Rohde 1991, 117–18). When the customary fifteen minutes ran out, the margin stood at 205 to 206 against. Speaker Jim Wright held the vote open, over vociferous GOP objections, while Democratic whips scoured the Capitol for a switchable member. They eventually persuaded Jim Chapman, D-Texas, to change his vote, and Wright gaveled the vote closed with a 206–205 Democratic victory.[16]

The second instance occurred on the fiscal 1997 budget resolution (CQWR 6/15/96, 1654). When time had expired, the majority's position was losing 201–212. The Democrats were calling for closure, while Gingrich and other GOP leaders went around the floor seeking to persuade recalcitrant Republicans. Gradually they made progress, which resulted in a 216–211 victory. The final example came the following year, on the District of Columbia appropriations bill, which included a controversial GOP plan to provide subsidies for private school tuition. In that case, with the nays ahead, Gingrich kept the vote open for more than half an hour, until the party secured the switches for a 203–202 win.

As we indicated, we cannot be sure in each case whether the nonmedian position eventually prevailed, although, if our earlier conjecture is correct, it is likely that both positions in each example were nonmedian. What is certain, however, is that asymmetric majority powers determined the outcome.

---

16. It is worth noting that at the beginning of the next Congress, Speaker Wright intervened to secure for Chapman an appointment to the Appropriations Committee (Rohde 1991, 108).

Imagine in each instance that only one thing was changed: the Speaker presiding was replaced by the minority floor leader. In each instance, this different presiding officer would have ended the vote at the moment the time expired, and the outcome would have been reversed. In each example, the outcome depended only on which position the majority party leadership favored, and on the majority's complete control over when the time for voting ended. Here again we see the impact of a power held by the majority party for which the minority has no equivalent.

Asymmetric Partisan Capabilities: Influencing Members' Choices

As the examples in the previous section seem to indicate, one way the majority party may have a disproportionate impact on outcomes is that it may exert more influence on members choices than the minority party. The majority may control a greater proportion of valuable resources to use as positive or negative incentives or perhaps what the majority controls has greater value than the minority equivalents. In fact, we argue that both are true (Aldrich and Rohde 1997). We have discussed these capabilities, along with concrete examples, in virtually all of our previous work and will not repeat them here. Rather, we want only to draw these features to the reader's attention and to provide a few more recent examples.

One concerns the majority's more valuable resources. We discussed the Speaker's ability to select committee chairs beginning in 1994. Subsequent events indicated that this change was not a one-time thing. For example, Bob Smith of Oregon retired from the House in 1994, after six terms. The GOP candidate won the seat, but was then involved in a scandal and forced to retire. To persuade Smith to run again for the House in 1996 and help the Republicans maintain their majority, Gingrich promised him that, if he won, he would be made chairman of the Agriculture Committee (Barone and Ujifusa 1997, 1186). This offer came even though, by tradition, Smith had lost all committee seniority by retiring. Furthermore, the majority leadership's influence seems to extend to subcommittee chairmanships as well. In 1994 Gingrich intervened to secure subcommittee chairs for two freshmen, skipping over more senior Republicans (Aldrich and Rohde 1997–1998, 552). In another case analogous to the inducement offered to Smith, Gingrich encouraged a potential GOP candidate in North Carolina to run by promising him a subcommittee chair if he won (Duncan and Lawrence 1997, 1078). In all of these cases, the majority leadership was able to offer committee leadership positions to bring about desired behavior. Even if the minority party leadership had analogous powers over

Democratic leadership positions on committees—and they do not—it seems clear that members would not regard the minority ranking positions to be as valuable as the chair positions held by the majority.

The majority leadership also can influence members' choices on legislation by promising side payments in that bill or another. For example, on the 1998 budget resolution, GOP leaders secured the vote of Rep. Jo Ann Emerson, R-Mo., by promising her an $8 million flood control project for her district. Gingrich also promised to secure additional defense funding in a subsequent bill to pick up other votes (WP 6/15/98, 1, 22). The majority leadership is much better able to make credible commitments for trades across bills than is the minority. We offer additional examples of ways the majority has greater influence over members' choices when we discuss control of the agenda.

Asymmetric Partisan Capabilities: Majority Leadership Advantage from A to Z

Further evidence of the majority party's asymmetric influence over choices and outcomes, as well as another example of the majority achieving a non-median result, comes, ironically, from Krehbiel's (1995a) analysis of cosponsoring and discharge-petition behavior. The bill in question was the 1993 deficit-reduction proposal dubbed the "A to Z Spending Plan," after the initials of its two major sponsors, Robert Andrews, D-N.J., and Bill Zeliff, R-N.H. The proposal was overwhelmingly supported by Republican members and their leadership and vigorously opposed by Democratic leaders and most of their members. Democrats used their majority control to keep the bill bottled up in committee, even though the number of cosponsors exceeded a majority of all members of the House. (One of Krehbiel's central hypotheses, which he concludes to be supported, is that cosponsorship is a preference-based phenomenon like roll call voting, governed by electoral forces, so we follow him in taking the cosponsorship position as the "true" exogenously determined preferences of the members.) Supporters of the A to Z bill sought to force floor consideration of it by starting a discharge petition. The Democratic leadership, on the other hand, tried to use the tools at their disposal to influence the choices of members—to induce them not to sign the petition. Krehbiel terms this behavior "waffling."

Three significant hypotheses follow from Krehbiel's majoritarian theory that can be addressed with the evidence in this chapter. These hypotheses are contrary to the expectations of our conditional party government theory, so the evidence is particularly useful. They are (1) the majoritarian position should prevail—that is, the choice of the median member should be the outcome; (2) more specifically, party action should have no net effect on members' choices; and (3) the majority party should not be able to change the outcome. Our theory contends that, because this is a party-relevant issue, the majority leaders should be likely to influence members' choices disproportionately, switching more supporters to their side than the minority can move in the opposite direction. Further, such an ability will, in some cases, enable the majority to shift the outcome in their favor, at times achieving a nonmedian outcome opposite to the exogenously determined majority preference. The evidence from the analysis of the A to Z proposal is, in all respects, consistent with our theory and opposite to the implications of Krehbiel's majoritarian theory. The position supported by the Democratic leaders gained support disproportionately (see Krehbiel 1995a, 914, for examples of the devices they used). More members switched toward them (cosponsors who refused to sign the discharge petition) than went the other way. As a result, the position supported by the majority preference failed. The majority-favored (median) position did not prevail, and the outcome switched to that favored by the majority party leadership.[17]

Asymmetric Partisan Capabilities: Influencing the Agenda

In addition to, and perhaps more important than, the majority party's greater resources to influence members' choices is the majority's asymmetric influence over the agenda of the House. We have already touched on some aspects of this in our discussions of second votes on the same issue, the choice of vote timing, and the decision on whether to hold open or close off a vote in progress. There are, however, many other aspects of this capability. The lion's share of the empirical analysis in our previous work has dealt with this matter, and we will not try to reproduce it here.[18] As with the discussion of influencing members, we touch on just a few points and offer some additional examples.

In addition to the powers already mentioned, the majority leadership can decide which bills to take up and when. This power is a considerable

---

17. On a separate point, in his analysis of waffling behavior Krehbiel concludes that party has no effect on members' choices over and above that of preferences, assuming (as we discussed earlier) that the majority should be buying votes only from their own members. A reanalysis of this question with improved data indicates that significant party effects are present on this score as well. See Binder, Lawrence, and Maltzman (1998).

18. The most extensive treatments are in Aldrich and Rohde (1997; 1997–1998).

bargaining tool; the leaders may be able to secure a member's compliant behavior on one bill by promising to bring up (or not bring up) another. The minority has no parallel ability. In addition, the control over timing can be crucial. The majority can schedule a bill it favors at the most felicitous time or bring up a measure at the worst time for the minority.[19] The leadership also can withdraw bills from the schedule or the floor when difficulties arise. For example, when the leaders were uncertain whether they had enough votes for an amendment they favored, they pulled the bill until they had a more secure count (Aldrich and Rohde 1997, 18). Minority members have no parallel strategic flexibility; if things go awry for them on the floor, they must just suffer through.

In our view, the most important majority leadership agenda powers revolve around the control of the Rules Committee. Before the reform era, the Rules Committee was an independent center of power and competed with the party leaderships. As a result of successive rules changes, committee leaders and its members from both parties are now appointed by the respective party leaders and serve at their pleasure. The result is that the Rules Committee has become an arm of the majority party leadership. Martin Frost, D-Texas, a member of Rules, confirmed this point. Frost was responding to a reporter who noted that Rep. David Dreier, R-Calif., the new Rules chair in the 106th Congress, had some policy disagreements with his party leaders. Frost said, "None of that really makes any difference. . . . Whoever is the top member on Rules executes whatever the party's game plan [is]. That's what the job is all about." (RC 4/30/98, 32)

Given the central place of this committee in our theoretical thinking, we have dealt with it extensively elsewhere. Here, we deal mainly with some general points, emphasizing that the Rules Committee can be an important tool for the leadership, first, by shaping the content of bills and, second, by creating special rules.

As the theoretical discussion at the beginning of this chapter indicated, multidimensionality underlies our conception of the legislative process in the House, and that multidimensionality gives potential leverage to the majority party. One significant role for the Rules Committee is shaping the content of omnibus legislation, such as reconciliation bills.[20] Whatever else is true of the full legislative agenda, these bills are unquestionably

---

19. See the discussion of gun control in the 104th Congress in Aldrich and Rohde (1997, 18).

20. For a discussion of the marked increase in the use of such bills, see Sinclair (1997).

multidimensional. They are packages of issues, often largely created by majority leadership decisions. The leaders choose which provisions are included or left out of the package and then direct the Rules Committee to carry it out. Because the majority leaders control the committee, they control the decisions (see Aldrich and Rohde 1997, 16–17, for examples). The minority leadership has no parallel capability. Thus, the majority leaders can shape the bill to their party's advantage, often including policies that the chamber majority would not pass individually. The power also gives the leaders great bargaining leverage; they can agree to changes when necessary and enforce those changes. This does not mean that they will always be successful; sometimes some of the majority's members defect, endangering passage. But the majority always controls the shaping of the package, surely a significant advantage.

As important as this ability to shape bills may be, the more ubiquitous role of the Rules Committee is to set the terms and procedures for floor debate on individual bills, which our theory asserts can be used to partisan advantage. The debate on the partisan use of Rules has been vigorous. Krehbiel (1991, 1997, 1997b) has argued that there is no solid evidence for partisan effects. Douglas Dion and John Huber (1996, 1997) have contended that there is such evidence. Note the applicability of the earlier discussion about the relevant portion of the legislative agenda. That is, we should expect to find party effects on that subset of legislation that is important to the majority party, and where party action is necessary to achieve success. We should not expect to find it on legislation that is not on the party's agenda or on bills where the party expects to be successful without any special intervention.

Research by other scholars bears directly on this matter. Barbara Sinclair (1998) offers an extensive theoretical and empirical discussion of the partisan use of special rules that is compatible with our argument. For evidence she examines rules on major legislation in recent Congresses. She notes that Krehbiel's conception of restrictive rules—that is, rules that constrain amending activity or other choices—is that these rules are used as incentives to committees to be informative, and that his theory predicts that they will be granted more on consensual rather than partisan bills. Partisan theories, on the other hand, see a manipulative role for restrictive rules, and expect that they would be used more on partisan legislation. Sinclair found that restrictive rules were much more likely on bills characterized by partisan division in the committee of jurisdiction and on bills in which the party leadership was involved. In another study, Greg Thorson and Tasina Nitzschke (1998) examined bills reported from committees by a roll call vote from 1981 through 1994. They found that bills reported by a partisan vote were more likely to receive a restrictive rule. Thus, both studies, with different empirical bases, found that restrictive rules are more probable on measures that divide the two parties, exactly what our theory would expect.[21]

The next point grows out of our detailed analysis of appropriations politics in the 104th Congress compared with earlier Congresses (Aldrich and Rohde 2000b), which has since been extended to the 105th Congress (Marshall, Prins, and Rohde 1998). It relates to the use of legislative riders in appropriations bills. The Republican leaders decided to use these devices as vehicles for accomplishing their party's agenda to change government policies. Such legislative riders violate House rules. Unless a special rule grants specific protection, any single member can delete those provisions by raising a point of order. Thus, the point noted earlier—that the majority leadership controls the Rules Committee and can decide which riders are protected and which are not—is especially relevant here. House rules against legislating on appropriations bills also apply to efforts to attach amendments to them. If the majority party supports a rider in the bill or a floor amendment to create one, it can block any changes in that rider by protecting it in a special rule but not protecting the amendment. If both a policy status quo supported by the minority party and a policy change proposed by the majority party are nonmedian outcomes, but the majority proposal is even a little bit closer to the median than the status quo, the majority can sustain its nonmedian outcome by using this asymmetric protection. The minority cannot offer an alternative proposal that is closer to the median because such a proposal is not protected by the special rule. Thus, we have the potential irony that, if the majority proposal is in the bill and is protected, but no amendments are protected, the *open* rule is a deliberate and specific majority party manipulation of the agenda (see Aldrich and Rohde 2000b).

This point highlights a more basic one. We strongly support the kind of quantitative general analyses of special rules of the type discussed above, but we also think that such analysis needs to be supplemented by consideration of the specifics of individual bills. We have sought to do that in our work. Without such detailed consideration, the kind of manipulation and partisan advantage that is possible through an open rule would not be apparent.

---

21. In another study (Aldrich and Rohde 1996) we show that partisan votes on special rules and on the underlying bill are strongly related on matters on the majority party's agenda.

In this connection, we reiterate our conception of the theoretical foundation of the partisan exploitation of special rules. We have discussed, here and in earlier work, some of the ways the majority party can benefit by imposing restrictive rules and using them to achieve nonmedian outcomes. The question that naturally follows is why would a chamber majority support such rules? Krehbiel's majoritarian perspective predicts that they will not. If the rule would produce an outcome different from the preference of the floor majority, the expectation is that the majority would vote down the rule and substitute a different one. How then does our theory predict a different result? Summarizing our view, there are at least three avenues leading to support for partisan restrictive rules (with myriad variations), which might be labeled *conspiracy, inducement,* and *contextual self-interest.*

Conspiracy springs from the view that members can hold conflicting electoral and policy motivations. Conditional party government theory explicitly assumes that legislators can have both types of goals. Krehbiel's theory is not explicit with regard to members' motivations; indeed, he says (1995b, 5) that he is "agnostic about the sources of what we regard as primitive and exogenous preferences over x"—in other words, over outcomes. As with most agnosticism, such a position is fine if it has no negative consequences, but we think this one does. That is, what can we expect members to do if they have both electoral and policy motives, and those motives push them in different directions? For example, what if a southern Democrat in the late 1980s was faced with a bill to which the GOP planned to attach an antiabortion amendment? The members' constituents favored such an amendment, but she personally opposed it. If faced with the actual choice, she might risk her seat and vote "nay" or go with the district and vote "aye." In our theory, however, she would have a third (and preferable) choice: vote for a party-sponsored restrictive rule that deprived the Republicans from offering such an amendment in the first place. That way she could achieve her desired policy without endangering herself electorally.

Inducement simply refers to the kind of situation we discussed before: a member is faced with a vote on a rule that will lead to a bill and a policy outcome the member does not prefer. Leaders, however, can offer side payments—either rewards or punishments—that can induce the member to support the rule anyway. The discussion of the results in Krehbiel's A to Z analysis, as well as a number of our own examples, illustrates cases of success, although the majority leadership does not always prevail. Indeed, under both party majorities in the last twenty years, partisan restrictive rules failed a number of times, but there were many more successes. The parties also can enhance the leaders' capabilities in this regard. For example, after a few party failures on rules, a GOP representative proposed in a petition to the Republican Conference that a member's failure to support the party position on procedural matters be taken into account when determining whether he or she should be permitted to hold committee or subcommittee chairs. One of the first signers of the petition was Speaker Gingrich (RC 6/22/98, 1).

Finally, *contextual self-interest* recognizes the multidimensionality of many policy situations. Like a bill, a rule may be a package that enhances some things the member wants very much while also protecting some things he opposes. In principle the member could try to vote down the rule, but doing so might endanger what he supports and wants most. The rule package may be acceptable as a means of guaranteeing that the most valued provisions are protected. Each of the three avenues to restrictive rules we have discussed here (and there are others) could be a basis for sustaining a restrictive rule with a majority party bias. In combination, they offer solid grounds on which to expect such rules in the appropriate circumstances.

Some Problematic Implications of Majoritarian Theory

Most of our discussion to this point has presented arguments or evidence on behalf of our theory or to counter criticisms of it. In this section, we deal with some implications of the majoritarian analysis that we see as problematic and on which we can bring evidence to bear. The first of these is the majoritarian theory's unidimensional perspective. We believe we can demonstrate the weakness of its predictive power.

The median position's dominance comes from the assumptions of single-peaked preferences and sincere voting.[22] Given those assumptions, the median will win because that position will get more votes than any alternative. Unfortunately for majority party leaders, even in one dimension, the situation is often not that simple. They are sometimes faced with a unified opposition party on one side and a recalcitrant fringe element in their party

---

22. Single-peaked preferences is the assumption that the desirability of an option (on a spatial line) to a member decreases as the option moves farther from the member's most preferred position, and this is true for all members simultaneously. Sincere voting is the assumption that a member will always vote for the closer alternative, regardless of the strategic context.

on the other. The fringe element, recognizing that the minority party will vote no on a proposed rule or bill, also threatens to vote no unless concessions are made to their position—that is, unless the measure is moved away from the median toward them. So, for example, with a Republican majority, GOP leaders may have to contend not only with solid Democratic opposition, but also with the potential defection from a contingent of their party's "hard right" members.

In some instances, this pattern may be a result of real multidimensionality, with the GOP conservatives deciding on a different dimension from the Democrats. In other cases, it may be strategic voting by the conservatives because they are not sufficiently satisfied with the final result. Sometimes it may be a combination. In any event, situations like these are not captured by the unidimensional model, but they represent the real bargaining problems the majority leadership faces. The leaders must be concerned with producing a legislative record for the party to run on in the next general election so that it can hold its majority. Extreme members of the party can exploit this interest of the leaders to extract concessions on specific bills, moving the outcome toward the right. Sometimes the moderates and the leaders must acquiesce in a nonmedian result (which they might or might not prefer) in order to get a bill passed at all.

This multidimensionality is not just theoretical speculation. There is evidence that such situations occur and that they usually occur on high saliency bills. One example from the 105th Congress involved the rule on the 1997 supplemental appropriations bill designed to provide disaster relief to midwesterners and money for Bosnian peacekeeping.[23] Democrats opposed the rule because of a dispute over the Women, Infants, and Children Program and over restrictions on the Bosnian mission. The opposition within the GOP apparently revolved around the conservatives' general displeasure with the Republican leadership rather than specific elements of the appropriations bill, although those things also had an effect. For example, Minority Whip Tom DeLay of Texas believed that a pledge to him about the rule had been broken, and a group of conservatives were angry about an environmental vote the previous week. The rule was voted down 229–193, with the Democrats opposed 185–13, and the GOP in favor 180–43. The one Independent member was also opposed.

To shed light on the point at issue, we divided the membership into four groups: within each party, members were categorized according to

---

23. This account is drawn mainly from Bradley (1997).

whether they stood to the right or left of their party's median on the Poole-Rosenthal NOMINATE scores for that Congress. Because there is virtually no overlap between the parties on these scores (Aldrich and Rohde 1998), they yield four sets of representatives that can be distinctly ordered from left to right. Figure 3–1 shows the proportion of each group that voted yes on the rule. We see a clear "ends-against-the-middle" pattern. Democrats were against the rule, but the more moderate group yielded a slightly higher proportion of support than the more liberal group. Among Republicans, on the other hand, the more conservative side of the party included a noticeably higher proportion of opponents than the more moderate group. Thus support did not monotonically increase across the ideological spectrum.

We are not in a position to provide an exhaustive analysis of all votes in order to assess precisely how frequently this phenomenon occurs. We can, however, show that the vote just described was not an isolated event. It seems that such events might be more likely to occur (and have greater impact) on close votes. We therefore examined each final passage roll call and each roll call on a special rule that was decided by twenty votes or less from 1995 through 1997. There were five votes that appeared to illustrate the phenomenon of interest (see Table 3–3). Three involve special rules (reinforcing our earlier arguments about partisan manipulation of the agenda through rules), and two are final passage votes. In each instance, the right wing of the GOP provided less support than the more moderate

Figure 3–1 "Ends-Against-the-Middle Voting," Supplemental Appropriations Rule, 1997

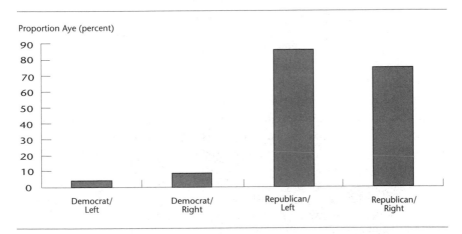

Table 3–3
"Ends-Against-the-Middle Voting," 104th and 105th Congresses

Roll Call	Party/Faction			
	Dem./ Left	Dem./ Right	Rep./ Left	Rep./ Right
Rule, Interior appropriations bill 7/12/95	12.2%	9.9%	90.4%	56.9%
Rule, minimum wage and small business tax 5/22/96	0	0	100	87.9
Budget Resolution conference report 6/12/96	0	4.2	94.7	88.9
Rule, House committee funding 3/20/97	0	0	100	90.4
Supplemental appropriations conference report 6/5/97	3.1	28.7	91.7	77.2

Note: The faction indicates the member's position on the Poole-Rosenthal Nominate scores relative to her/his party median. Thus, Dem./Left indicates Democrats to the left of the Democratic median. Each cell gives the percentage of those members (excluding nonvoters) who voted aye.

Republicans, with the result that the party-supported outcome was either endangered or defeated. Thus, there is evidence that ends-against-the-middle voting does occur and can undermine the pull toward the center that is inherent in the unidimensional model.[24]

Another problem to consider is empirical evidence that bears on the supposed dominance of the floor median and on the supposed lack of net party effect. The evidence relates to the election of the Speaker in the House. Majoritarian theory assumes that the House is a majoritarian institution in which parties do not bias results and that the Speaker is the leader of the whole House rather than of the majority party. If these assumptions are true, majoritarian theory would expect that the person elected Speaker would hold a position in the middle of the policy spectrum. Furthermore, if the majority party does not nominate the floor median for Speaker, the minority would have a pure strategy response of nominating someone at

24. We cannot, however, present data on the other important aspect of this phenomenon—those cases where the GOP right threatened to defect in this fashion, and the Republican leadership chose to accommodate them in advance.

the median from either party to be its choice. Finally, under majoritarian theory there is no reason to expect that the winning candidate is more likely to come from the majority party than from the minority party, except for the greater number of majority members. In contrast, partisan theory would expect each party to nominate someone near the median position of the party for Speaker and for the majority party to win the election in every case.

Regarding the outcomes, readers need no presentation of evidence. As everyone who studies Congress knows, the person selected as Speaker is invariably a member of the majority. Regarding the nominees of the two parties, we draw on the Poole-Rosenthal NOMINATE scores again to assess the evidence since World War II. Table 3–4 presents the party and floor medians, the score for the minority leader (their Speaker nominee), and a score for the Speaker.[25] In four of the twenty-six Congresses, the position of the Speaker is closer to the floor median than to his party's median; in four it is closer to the party median but between the two; and in eighteen cases the Speaker's position is more extreme than the party median![26] Within the minority party, there are two instances where the leader is closer to the floor median, fourteen where he is between the medians but closer to the party's, and ten instances where he was more extreme than the party median. In summary, with regard to outcomes, the result implied by the majoritarian theory never occurred; and, with regard to party nominations, partisan theory was correct in forty-six cases, while majoritarian theory was correct in six.

---

25. In most Congresses there is no position measured for the Speaker. Where this number is available, it is based on very few votes and is not very dependable. Therefore, we use the score for the Speaker from the last Congress before he became Speaker. Because, as Poole and Rosenthal (1997) show, members' positions tend to be stable over time, this procedure would seem to offer a relatively good approximation. We note that if we were to use the actual ratings of the Speaker in those Congresses where we have them instead of these surrogate scores, our conclusions would be completely unchanged.

26. The four instances of the Speaker being closer to the floor median were the four consecutive Congresses from the 101st through the 104th—Tom Foley's three terms as Speaker and Gingrich's first. The former may have more to do with Jim Wright's resignation as Speaker and the unwillingness to divide the party under those circumstances. There certainly were doubts among Democrats at the time about the desirability of Foley as Speaker (see Rohde 1991, chap. 6). Note that we used Foley rather than Wright as the Speaker in the 101st; otherwise that would have been one more correct case for our theory.

Table 3–4

Party Leadership Positions and Floor Median Comparisons,
80th–105th Congresses

Congress	Speaker's Position	Majority Party Median	Floor Median	Minority Party Median	Minority Leader's Position
80th (1947–49)*	.351	.354	.186	.204	-.316
81st (1949–51)	-.316	-.271	-.05	.346	.311
82d (1951–53)	-.316	-.226	.071	.343	.270
83d (1953–55)*	.270	.340	.124	-.208	-.305
84th (1955–57)	-.305	-.235	.079	.331	.230
85th (1957–59)	-.305	-.245	.075	.305	.189
86th (1959–61)	-.305	-.267	-.041	.290	.289
87th (1961–63)	-.523	-.247	.021	.273	.273
88th (1963–65)	-.523	-.258	.028	.267	.257
89th (1965–67)	-.523	-.264	-.093	.24	.241
90th (1967–69)	-.523	-.257	.054	.225	.232
91st (1969–71)	-.523	-.259	.035	.216	.223
92d (1971–73)	-.286	-.236	.011	.210	.214
93d (1973–75)	-.286	-.236	.022	.209	.205
94th (1975–77)	-.286	-.240	.166	.208	.205
95th (1977–79)	-.346	-.221	-.082	.210	.195
96th (1979–81)	-.346	-.212	-.058	.242	.195
97th (1981–83)	-.346	-.233	0.0	.259	.299
98th (1983–85)	-.346	-.232	-.056	.287	.299
99th (1985–87)	-.346	-.242	-.035	.320	.283
100th (1987–89)	-.232	-.256	-.053	.331	.275
101st (1989–91)	-.274	-.529	-.292	.228	.240
102d (1991–93)	-.274	-.425	-.203	.416	.415
103d (1993–95)	-.274	-.438	-.236	.388	.386
104th (1995–97)*	.435	.693	.386	-.460	-.53
105th (1997)*	.435	.580	.290	-.560	-.279

*Indicates Republican control.

Note: The scores run from +1.00 (most conservative) to –1.00 (most liberal).

One Step Closer to Outcomes

As we have stressed, both our theory and Krehbiel's two theories focus on outcomes. However, direct evidence on outcomes is rare because it is difficult to devise dependable systematic measures. (One attempt to do so is Aldrich and Rohde 1996.) In closing here, we want to return to some results about outcomes. They do not, unfortunately, deal with evidence on final outcomes, but they do relate to final actions of the House, which are at least proximate to final outcomes. This analysis pursues the theoretical point about relative frequency of party victory that we made earlier. We think these data will help us to evaluate the accuracy of the implications of the contending theories.

The majoritarian theory sees the unidimensional case (with the dimension specific to each committee's jurisdiction) to be a reasonable approximation of reality. If that is true, and if there is no net effect from parties, there would be no reason to expect that the final passage coalition on a bill should be more likely to be built from one end of the spectrum than the other. Take, for example, the seven-member legislature in Figure 3–2, in which all Democrats are to the left of all Republicans, thus strongly satisfying the condition in conditional party government. By the majoritarian view, there is no reason to expect that Coalition B, made up only of GOP members, would be more likely to prevail than Coalition A, made up of all Democrats and the most moderate Republican. Conditional party government theory, on the other hand, would expect the majority party to be able to exploit its asymmetric advantages, and therefore to be on the winning side much more often than the minority party.

We can use data on floor votes on final passage of bills to assess these contrasting expectations. Table 3–5 shows which party won on all such votes that were decided by a party unity roll call, meaning majorities of each party opposed to the other. The results are overwhelming. The majority party supported and the minority opposed 622 of the 664 bills, or about 94 percent. One possible objection to our argument is that it does not consider the location of the reversion point as the alternative to each bill. In other words, it does not consider the status quo that would obtain if the bill did not pass. We do not find this argument persuasive within the context of majoritarian theory. Under that theory's conditions, both parties should recognize that the status quo (if nonmedian) cannot prevail, so each should propose options at or near the median, with the vote being between those options in effect. Moreover, to seriously analyze these data in terms of the likely locations of the status quo (given that

Figure 3–2 Unidimensional Choice and Floor Coalitions on Bills

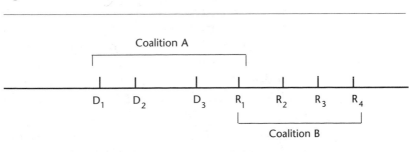

Table 3–5
Who Won on Final Passage of Bills, 83d–105th Congresses
(party unity votes only)

Congress	% Democratic	% Republican	Total N
83d (1953–55)	9.1%	90.9%	11
84th (1955–57)	75.0	25.0	8
85th (1957–59)	64.3	35.7	14
86th (1959–61)	88.0	12.0	25
87th (1961–63)	100.0	0.0	28
88th (1963–65)	94.4	5.6	36
89th (1965–67)	100.0	0.0	46
90th (1967–69)	88.9	11.1	27
91st (1969–71)	76.5	23.5	17
92d (1971–73)	69.2	30.8	13
93d (1973–75)	96.4	3.6	28
94th (1975–77)	91.5	8.5	59
95th (1977–79)	93.5	6.5	46
96th (1979–81)	100.0	0.0	36
97th (1981–83)	92.0	8.0	25
98th (1983–85)	93.8	6.3	48
99th (1985–87)	97.3	2.7	37
100th (1987–89)	100.0	0.0	41
101st (1989–91)	97.1	2.9	34
102d (1991–93)	na	na	na
103d (1993–95)	na	na	na
104th (1995–97)	1.6	98.4	64
105th (1997)[a]	4.8	95.2	21
Total	—	—	664
Success Under Democratic Majorities	93.1%	6.9%	—
Success Under Republican Majorities	3.1%	96.9%	—

a. The 105th Congress includes 1997 only.

actual measurement is not feasible) would require far more space than we can devote to it.

We can, however, use a second best option by confining our analysis to appropriations bills, where the reversion point is zero spending, and so the problem of the location of the status quo is irrelevant.[27] Those data are displayed in Table 3–6. As one can see, partisan appropriations roll calls are more likely to come from more recent Congresses (see Aldrich and Rohde 2000b for a discussion of the reasons), but the pattern of the outcomes is the same. The majority party prevailed on nearly all of the votes.

27. Zero is the reversion point only in the formal sense, but that is the only thing that is relevant in terms of the expectations of the majoritarian theory.

Table 3–6
Who Won on Final Passage of Appropriations Bills,
83d–105th Congresses (party unity votes only)

Congress	% Democratic	% Republican	Total N
83d (1953–55)	100.0%	0.0%	1
84th (1955–57)	—	—	0
85th (1957–59)	100.0	0.0	1
86th (1959–61)	50.0	50.0	2
87th (1961–63)	100.0	0.0	1
88th (1963–65)	100.0	0.0	6
89th (1965–67)	100.0	0.0	4
90th (1967–69)	66.7	33.3	3
91st (1969–71)	100.0	0.0	3
92d (1971–73)	—	—	0
93d (1973–75)	100.0	0.0	2
94th (1975–77)	100.0	0.0	5
95th (1977–79)	100.0	0.0	5
96th (1979–81)	100.0	0.0	5
97th (1981–83)	100.0	0.0	5
98th (1983–85)	100.0	0.0	14
99th (1985–87)	100.0	0.0	11
100th (1987–89)	100.0	0.0	10
101st (1989–91)	100.0	0.0	7
102d (1991–93)	na	na	na
103d (1993–95)	na	na	na
104th (1995–97)	0.0	100.0	18
105th (1997)[a]	16.7	83.3	6
Total	—	—	109
Success Under Democratic Majorities	97.6%	2.4%	—
Success Under Republican Majorities	8.0%	92.0%	—

a. The 105th Congress includes 1997 only.

Some Evidence Regarding the President

One of the major reasons that the first political parties formed in the United States was to coordinate policy and actions across the separated powers of the branches of government (see, for example, Aldrich 1995). To put it simply, the term is "parties-in-government," not "parties-in-Congress." Indeed, the president is leader of his party, no matter how strong or weak his powers might otherwise be. While some Speakers, such as Newt Gingrich, are national as well as congressional party leaders, they assume that role because they lead the party not headed by a president. In this section, we look briefly at the president's role in terms of the analysis undertaken elsewhere in this chapter.

To do so, the first question to ask is this: Where does the president stand—as party leader—in comparison to the parties in Congress? One way to look at this question is to examine where he stands on the major (liberal/conservative) dimension on the scores as estimated by the Poole-Rosenthal technique. Keith Poole and Howard Rosenthal provide such estimates in two ways. For presidents who served in at least one chamber of Congress, we can look at their votes in that body as one way to measure their stances. Poole and Rosenthal (1997) provide evidence that, on average, members do not change their estimated position over time, suggesting that perhaps estimates based on earlier votes are not irrelevant. However, these measures may be far removed in time from the service as president. The extreme case is George Bush, who had completed his time in Congress more than two decades before he won the presidency.

A second basis for such measures is to estimate the position of a member of Congress who voted for the position advocated by the president on all measures supported by the president. By inference, this is the position that would have been estimated for the president had he been able to vote in Congress. This procedure has several advantages: it can be measured for all presidents; it is based on bills sufficiently important for the president to go on record about them; and it is a timely measure.[28] From a partisan perspective, we might imagine that the bills that go into the creation of these estimates are disproportionately those that define the position of the president's party—a sort of annual "platform"—and that differentiate it from the opposition party. Thus, we might expect that the consistent presidential supporter would appear more extreme than one who voted on all measures, including those less important to the parties. Those who are skeptical about the relevance of party might argue that the president is better understood as the leader of the nation, responsible to and responsive to the preferences of the entire electorate. Therefore, a nonpartisan perspective would, if anything, anticipate that the consistent presidential supporter would be at the position of the median voter, which should be similar to the position of the median member of Congress. A partisan perspective, conversely, would anticipate the consistent supporter would be located away from the center in the direction of the president's party.

---

28. John Zaller provided us with a variety of measures of the president's overall stance (personal communication), including the two Poole-Rosenthal–based measures. The other measures do not have congressional positions estimated, and therefore cannot be used for the purposes of the current analysis. By way of partial validation, the presidential support–based measure is strongly correlated with each of the other measures (.8 and above).

Five postwar presidents served in Congress and therefore have both measures (actually a sixth, Truman, did as well, but the presidential support measure is unavailable for him). Each of the five has a more central (nearer to zero, in absolute value) position based on their actual voting in Congress than from the estimate based on bills supported as president. Reporting the congressional vote–based measure first, Kennedy was estimated to have a score of −.274, compared to a Kennedy supporter–based score of −.532. The scores for Johnson are −.273 and −.419, respectively. For Nixon the two figures are a very similar .222 and .282, while for Ford they are .218 and .252. Finally, for Bush, the two estimates are .149 and .462. These first-cut comparisons suggest that it is plausible to argue that the president took positions on party-oriented bills, perhaps making them party-related, or accentuating their partisan basis, because he proposed or endorsed them.

Truman has only a congressional voting–based score, and that is −.254. The only scores available for the remaining postwar presidents are support-based scores. They are .261 for Eisenhower, −.478 for Carter, and −.370 for Clinton. All of these scores can be compared to those for the floor and party medians and the two party leaders in the House for the 80th through 105th Congresses in Table 3–4.

No matter which of the two measures is used, the estimates suggest that the president is a party leader, or at least articulates a partisan rather than a national median stance. By either measure the presidential position was never closer to the House floor median than to the median of his party. Indeed, more often than not, the president was more extreme than his party. Eisenhower and Clinton were the only two presidents who supported policies that were more moderate than their party was, on average, in the House. All other presidents were more extreme than their congressional party by the support measure, and mostly (all but Truman and Bush) by the actual vote measure.

To the extent that the Poole-Rosenthal measures can be considered plausible estimates of an individual's ideal policy preferences, presidents are clearly, even extremely, partisan. This perspective is consistent with evidence that can be garnered from Krehbiel (1998) concerning the presidential veto. He presents data from which he seeks to estimate the relative pull of the president versus party on members of Congress. One of the most striking features of his data, however, is the distribution across presidencies, from Truman through Clinton and the 103d Congress.

What the data show is that presidents of the same party as the Congress are rarely challenged when they use the veto. Eisenhower during the 83d Congress and Kennedy and Johnson throughout their administrations

never faced an attempted veto override. Carter was challenged twice, and
Truman ten times when he presided over a unified government. Clinton
vetoed no legislation during the 103d Congress. Challenges were much
more common when the House and president were held by different parties. The counts are Truman 9 (during one divided Congress compared
to two unified Congresses), Eisenhower 11, Nixon 21, Ford 29, Reagan
16, and Bush 22. That is, under unified control, there were 14 challenges
to a presidential veto, while under divided control—the House and president from different parties—there were 108 such challenges, a ratio of
7.7 to 1 compared to only a 2 to 1 ratio of divided to unified Congresses.
The data do not permit us to judge the Truman administration, but for
the rest, there was an even greater disproportion in the number of successful overrides. Of the thirty-one successful veto overrides from the 83d
through 103d Congresses, only two occurred when the president and
House were held by the same party. About 94 percent of presidential
vetoes were sustained under unified control, while nearly 30 percent were
overridden under divided control. This evidence further supports the view
that parties have a substantive impact on the legislative relationship
between Congress and the president.

With regard to the presentation of evidence, it is appropriate and useful that we close this section by focusing briefly on the impeachment of
President Clinton. As the matter approached a floor vote in late December 1998, some moderate Republicans sought a middle ground—censure
of the president—that would have permitted the House to express its disapproval without impeachment. Some moderate GOP members, such as
Amo Houghton of New York and Mike Castle of Delaware, took the lead
in the House. Outside Washington, the censure option received public
support from prominent party leaders, including former senator Bob
Dole, Gerald Ford, and William Weld, the former governor of Massachu-
setts. It was also preferred by majorities of respondents in polls throughout the impeachment proceedings.[29] That course was, however, vigorously resisted by Republican House leaders, especially Tom DeLay, and by
the most conservative members of the Republican Conference. Although
the leadership had publicly pledged that they would not pressure members to vote a certain way on impeachment, and that House Republicans

---

29. See, for example, the ABC News/*Washington Post* polls conducted December 12–13, 1998, which showed respondents opposed to impeachment 58 percent to 41 percent, against removal 61 percent to 38 percent, and for censure or
reprimand by 59 percent to 37 percent. The poll results are available on the *Washington Post's* Web site, *www.washingtonpost.com*.

would be permitted to vote their conscience, it quickly became clear that the censure option was off the table, no matter what the members' consciences dictated. "DeLay and Livingston have said publicly they would take a dim view of any Republican who refused to back up the leadership in blocking a floor vote on censure" (Pianin and Merida 1998, A22). On the floor, the crucial point was reached on a vote to table (kill) a Democratic effort to alter the impeachment resolution to permit a vote on censure. The motion to table passed 230–204, with only two Republicans and four Democrats crossing party lines.

We cannot be certain that the censure option was the floor median, but it seems plausible given the efforts of moderate Republicans and the fact that only twelve net Republicans would have had to prefer censure to impeachment. Moreover, one can ask why, if the GOP leadership did not fear that the censure option would pass if it were in order to vote on, did they deny members the option. In any event, the situation offers an example of the *possibilities* of agenda manipulation by the majority leadership of the kind we discussed above: if the floor median policy is not permitted to be offered as an option for choice, a nonmedian outcome must necessarily be the result.

Conclusion

As we stated at the outset, we have sought to amplify the theory of conditional party government and to present relevant evidence on an important issue. Our central theme, juxtaposed with the work of Keith Krehbiel, is that the majority party has asymmetric influence over members' choices and over policy outcomes relative to the minority party. To most actors in the political world, as well as to most students of Congress, this is not a novel idea. In observing Congress, we see that one of the constants is the struggle of the minority party to replace the current majority and of the current majority to remain in power. Would these members struggle so if they did not believe that outcomes are different depending on which party is in the majority? Certainly the evidence we have presented would seem to indicate that they are right. We have repeatedly cited instances of decisions that members have made that would not make sense unless the majority had an asymmetric impact on choices or outcomes. Even on the more mundane aspects of policy, majority status seems to matter. As Barry Rundquist and Thomas Carsey's (1998) analysis indicated, the majority members are the principal beneficiaries on distributive issues. There are, moreover, indications that other actors have come to the same conclusion.

For example, Gary Cox and Eric Magar (1998) documented a shift in corporate and trade donations away from incumbent Democrats and toward incumbent Republicans after the GOP victory in 1994, controlling for other influences. Why would donors make these decisions unless they believed that majority status made a difference in outcomes?

In our view, there is a general point to be made here. Rational choice theories are theories about individual decision making and (sometimes) the aggregate consequences. Whatever else a particular theory may bear on, it has implications about individuals' choices. A rational choice theory that is successful at predicting broad aggregate patterns but unsuccessful at predicting individual-level behavior is deficient. Moreover, if observed individual behavior is *inconsistent* with the theory's predictions—if that behavior is illogical or makes no sense in terms of the theory—then that theory must be regarded as falsified regardless of the aggregate results it achieves. We have sought to devise and present a theory that accounts for both behavior and outcomes. The evidence appears, at least broadly speaking, to be consistent with that conception.

We acknowledge the research assistance of Brad Gomez of Duke University and Jamie Carson, Charles Finocchiaro, Bryan Marshall, Roger Moiles, and Brandon Prins, all fellows in the Political Institutions and Public Choice Program at Michigan State University. Thanks are also due to Keith Poole for making available NOMINATE scores and congressional roll call data through his Web site. We also appreciate comments on an earlier version of this chapter from Geoffrey C. Layman and Michael D. McDonald.

Note: Much of the discussion of events and quotations from members and other participants are taken from accounts in *Congressional Quarterly Weekly Report, National Journal, Roll Call, Washington Post,* or *The Hill*. These sources are cited as CQWR, NJ, RC, WP, and Hill, respectively, and the individual articles that are the sources do not appear in the list of references.

CHAPTER 4

Congress, the President, and Party Competition via Network News

Tim Groeling and Samuel Kernell

In their chapter, "Congress, the President, and Party Competition via Network News," Tim Groeling and Samuel Kernell add a new perspective to the analysis of partisanship and its impact on national institutions. While most analyses of national politics focus on what Groeling and Kernell refer to as "deeds," such as votes, bills passed, and vetoes, the analysis in this chapter examines partisan warfare in "words." Systematic research on partisan talk tends to focus on political campaigns, but political discourse does not stop when the campaign is over. To convey political messages to the public, politicians issue press releases, make speeches to all kinds of groups, appear on television and radio talk shows, and distill their rhetoric into "sound bites" in hopes of getting on the evening news programs. The absence of systematic research on political discourse seems to assume that politicians' efforts to present a policy or political message publicly are just a by-product of conflict over government actions. But because politicians with so many demands on their scarce time invest so much effort into developing and conveying these messages, it is reasonable to see—and analyze—political talk as purposive behavior in its own right. Politicians engage in such activities not out of vanity but as political strategy aimed at achieving a policy goal. Consequently, there is a partisan component involved.

Groeling and Kernell focus on one part of the strategy: efforts to convey a coherent policy message on the network news. Yet their analysis significantly expands our understanding of presidential-congressional relations by incorporating political talk into the conventional model of party action. They note that political parties in America face special institutional obstacles resulting from the separation of powers—presidents and members of Congress serve different constituencies and face different pressures and constraints. Consequently, even congressional members of the president's party may at times present their own version of a party position. Furthermore, in the United States, where the First Amendment to the Constitution protects a free press, a party's team efforts to present a coordinated message can be thwarted by an independent news media that has its own priorities, professional standards, and routines regarding the news it gathers and reports.

Groeling and Kernell's analysis shows that, given the obstacles resulting from the separation of powers, there is indeed competition within each of the parties to define the party's message, and it is difficult for a party to speak with one voice. The authors show that delivering a coherent party message is further complicated because party leaders must communicate through the news media, independent actors guided by their own professional norms and priorities. To avoid engaging in a messy internal battle of words that may harm the party, leaders try to guide public talk in the form of consistent criticism of the opposition party. Divided government may increase a party's ability to communicate a coherent message because it allows members to focus on attacking the opposing party.

———

In the spring of 1992 House minority leader Newt Gingrich, R-Ga., met with Republican president George Bush to discuss party strategy for the upcoming November election. Well before the party conventions, national polls showed Bush locked in a tight race with Bill Clinton and Ross Perot. Meanwhile, congressional Republicans were trying to break out of their seemingly permanent status as the minority party in the House of Representatives. The purpose of the meeting was to discuss Gingrich's proposal that the president join with Republicans in Congress in offering the American public a comprehensive conservative program of action. Some of Gingrich's ideas reminded Bush of former president Ronald Reagan's agenda—a massive tax cut, deregulation, and a constitutional amendment to balance the budget. Other proposals, such as term limits for members of Congress and time limits for eligibility for federal welfare, were new (Seelye, Engelberg, and Gerth 1995).

Bush looked over the conservative manifesto and quickly decided he wanted none of it. One can easily see the strategic problem Gingrich's conservative program posed for the president. Perot's appeal among moderate voters had initially vaulted him into first place in the polls. Clinton, a so-called new-style Democrat with few allegiances to the traditional core of the Democratic Party, was free to roam toward popular Republican issue positions. If Bush shifted to the right and formed a common front with congressional Republicans on Gingrich's proposal, the Contract with America, he might alienate moderate voters and deliver them into the hands of his opponents.

The meeting ended cordially but resolutely. For the next two years, the Contract with America stayed under wraps as the House minority leader awaited the 1994 midterm elections. Had Bush won reelection in 1992, he and Gingrich might well have had the same conversation in the spring of 1994, and this time, the lame-duck president might have endorsed the contract. Had he not, however, one can hardly imagine how Gingrich and his congressional allies could have attracted sufficient public attention to have the contract serve as a viable platform for Republican challengers trying to unseat the Democratic majority. So, perhaps Bush's defeat helped set the stage for the contract's debut. The same can be surmised for President Clinton's nearly disastrous first two years in office. Clinton was the least popular president to take his party into midterm elections since polls began gauging presidential approval in the 1930s. A more propitious moment could hardly be imagined for Gingrich to propose a sharp departure from the administration's policies—policies that by party association also belonged to the Democratic majority in Congress.

With the financial resources of his political action committee, GOPAC, Gingrich and his congressional allies spent the fall of 1993 recruiting, training, and fund raising for dozens of Republican challengers who had pledged allegiance to the contract. A surprisingly large number of them won, and the Republican Party took control of both chambers for the first time since it rode into office on Dwight D. Eisenhower's coattails in 1952.

In organizing the campaign around the contract, Gingrich briefly moved congressional Republicans as close to a parliamentary party as has ever been assembled in a nonpresidential election year. In office, they continued their parliamentary behavior. In February 1995 Gingrich, the newly elected Speaker, received prime-time network coverage to present his legislative agenda in response to the president's State of the Union message. In subsequent months, the Speaker conducted far more scheduled press briefings than did President Clinton. Acting on a self-proclaimed electoral mandate for the contract, the new majorities proceeded to pass many of its provisions and to confront the president with enrolled bills. Some (farm subsidy program reform, for example) were dutifully signed into law; some were vetoed. Others, such as welfare reform, were hijacked on the way to the White House and made the president's own legislation.

If in 1994 politics served policy, the reverse was equally true, particularly in the second session of the 105th Congress, as both sides assumed policy stances designed to put them on their best footing for the 1996 presidential election. In late 1995 partisan confrontation replaced any semblance of cooperation. Presidential vetoes (and veto messages) proliferated.

Congressional Republicans escalated the confrontation by attaching antiabortion and balanced budget riders to "untouchable" appropriations legislation. Twice at the end of the year, the government shut down when Clinton vetoed continuing spending legislation that contained provisions from the contract. Clinton vetoed an appropriations bill in November 1995 and immediately toured the country to explain his position. Meanwhile, the Democratic National Committee launched ads attacking the Republicans as intransigent ideologues. Within weeks, public opinion swung solidly behind the president and against Gingrich and Senate majority leader Robert Dole, the front-runner for the Republican presidential nomination. The confrontation ended in early 1996, and with it any chance to enact major provisions of the contract.

The rise and fall of the Contract with America shows national politicians competing on two distinct levels—*deeds* and *talk*. Systematic research on party competition in Washington focuses almost exclusively on deeds. There is no shortage of research analyzing topics such as the extent to which party members in Congress vote together in committees and on the floor (Collie 1985) and presidents' decisions to exercise the veto (Cameron 2000) and to nominate appointees to the federal departments (Krutz, Fleisher, and Bond 1998). Systematic research into partisan political *talk*, however, tends to be reserved for election campaigns. Naturally, partisan chatter is ubiquitous; Woodrow Wilson called it the "atmosphere of politics." The talk that one hears every evening on the national news tends to be regarded as static caused by the everyday friction of contending partisan forces within Congress and between Congress and the White House. But as the politics of the contract made clear, public debate over policy barely subsided after the 1994 election. Holed up in their separate institutional bastions, Democrats and Republicans engaged in partisan warfare both in deeds (legislation, votes, and vetoes) and talk. They behaved as if each battleground would decide the 1996 presidential election.

In this chapter, we examine partisan political rhetoric more carefully—not as the by-product of conflict over government actions, but as purposive behavior in its own right. Modern politicians give speeches, issue news releases, and otherwise conduct the public's business in front of television cameras not from vanity but from strategy.[1] We begin the next section by incorporating political talk into the conventional model of party action. In addition to the normal problems of collective action, the separation of

---

1. The most dangerous place to stand in Washington, as a familiar quip informs us, is between a politician and a network news camera.

powers poses special problems for U.S. political parties, as Gingrich experienced firsthand in his meeting with President Bush. In addition to these internal problems, parties face a major external obstacle in their attempts to communicate with the public. The news media have their own priorities regarding the kinds of news they gather and the way they report it. A model of party talk in Washington must, therefore, take into account modern news practices and, more important, how these practices influence the parties' and individual politicians' communication strategies.

After developing a model of partisan talk, we systematically examine the manner in which such talk was aired on national network evening news broadcasts during a four-year period, 1992–1995. Altogether, we identified more than 7,500 news stories, containing more than 10,000 political evaluations, that satisfied our criteria for analysis. These data allow us to delineate the structural and strategic characteristics of partisan talk in the news and assess their intended effects on the electorate.

The Basic Party Model

The conventional view of American politics regards politicians as independent office-holding entrepreneurs. They decide on their own to enter public life and do so by filing a petition of candidacy. They succeed or fail largely through their own efforts to raise money and wage effective campaigns. In office they stake out positions on issues and engage in constituency service to strengthen their prospects of reelection and the possibility of moving to higher office. Whether by cause or effect, America's independent office-holding politicians are not nearly so loyal to their political parties as are their counterparts throughout Europe and in other strong party systems.

Yet, despite their self-reliance, U.S. politicians have always found reason to associate themselves with a political party. They do so despite the costs of having to conform to the party's collective agreements and the risks that the party's actions will be unpopular back home. Politicians accept these liabilities because they derive substantial benefits from their partisan affiliation, not the least of which is economical communication with the constituency. No matter how diligently they practice constituent service, they know that a sizable share of the electorate will elude them. Party labels offer an efficient way to advertise a politician's stand on issues to a dispersed and inattentive constituency.

A stable, consistent party image is essential if it is to provide a valuable cue for voters and thereby serve politicians. Ideally, it will communicate perfectly the candidate's position on issues. Where the match is close, the candidate can run a cheap and effective campaign simply by advertising the party label. When the party image diverges significantly from the constituency's preferences, however, the candidate must compensate by distinguishing his or her position from the party. The latter is both costly and fraught with risks. Consequently, all politicians find themselves at one time or another trying to influence their party's decisions to bring them in closer accord with the preferences of their constituents.

Deeds and Talk as Defining Party Labels

Both deeds and talk are subject to conflicting pressures as members compete to define the party message. Those who lose this competition are tempted to defect from the party's stance in order to align themselves more closely with their constituency. Long-standing institutional mechanisms have evolved to facilitate deal making and enforce agreements. A political party need not have a consensus to produce a clear and consistent legislative record.

Unlike deeds, talk is a kind of party-defining activity that resists collective action. Surprisingly few opportunities are available for a party to speak with a unified voice. Party conventions issue platforms, committees report to the parent chamber, the president reports on the state of the nation, but these mechanisms are infrequently available and imperfectly designed for expressing party sentiment. Instead, most partisan talk takes the form of individuals expressing their own preferences. Senator A says something provocative on the Senate floor; a colleague issues a press release joining or disputing the statement; others show up on the Sunday talk shows to stake out their position; and a lucky few end up in front of a network news camera.

In addition, party members can always circumvent their fellow partisans' wrath by "leaking" information through informal "off the record" conversations with news reporters. Although parties might be expected to promote a party line and discourage individual defections from the party position, there is little evidence that they do so in concert, and even less that they succeed. Gag rules are foreign to Congress, and even in the more hierarchically organized White House, presidents' efforts to impose them have proven notably unsuccessful. One can see the problem: there are numerous opportunities for individuals to stake out positions on issues but few occasions for a party to speak with a single authoritative voice.

Political talk exposes a potential Achilles' heel of party action. There is simply too great a temptation for members to defect and too little means for the collectivity to prevent it. Moreover, news reporters earn their livings by encouraging defections. Not only can reporters directly reward defection, but the U.S. legal system shields their sources, the defectors, from disclosure.

Partisan Talk as News

Very little of politicians' talk is directly consumed by the citizenry. Most of it is delivered as a condensed, highly edited package called news. One study (Sigal 1973) found that talk is just about all that political news is—talk in the form of statements, interviews, press releases, reports, testimony, and the like. Past research has been more interested in the decision rules the news media follow in selecting, editing, and transmitting partisan talk than in their mediating effects on politicians' efforts to communicate a consistent party message. Nonetheless, these rules deserve brief consideration here because they reveal the extent to which the news media's participation in political communication must be taken into account (Gans 1980; Paletz and Entman 1981).

The pecking order of sources, a favorite subject of research on news coverage of politics, provides the first decision rule (Balutis 1976, 1977; Robinson and Appel 1979; Tidmarch and Pitney 1985). The presidency wins hands down, at least during the twentieth century (Kernell and Jacobson 1987), and the Senate edges out the House of Representatives (Hess 1986). Both institutional and individual politicians' newsworthiness rankings reflect the institutional authority of the sources. Those who control decisions naturally enjoy greater access to the news media. A secondary consideration, according to some research based on interviews with journalists and their editors, is the celebrity status of the source. "The Senate gets more coverage than the House," explain Michael Robinson and Kevin Appel (1979, 415), "because the Senate contains fewer heads."

A second purported decision rule encompasses various forms of news bias. Other things being equal, the press prefers to criticize politicians. Presidents cry foul more than most and have attracted more systematic research, which offers qualified support for their claims (Brody 1991; Groeling and Kernell 1998; Kuklinski and Sigelman 1992). Congress fares a little better. Coverage is mostly neutral, but when it is not, it tends to be negative (Tidmarch and Pitney 1985). A third related decision rule is that the media prefer conflict and controversy to cooperation and consensus. In early 1995 Speaker Gingrich dressed down the press corps for refusing to cast a bipartisan meeting with President Clinton in a favorable light. After announcing that the recently elected Republican Congress looked forward to working constructively with the Democratic president, a reporter asked, "What do you think it [bipartisanship] will break down over?" Gingrich responded, "You just heard the leaders of the Republican Party say that the Democratic president today had a wonderful meeting on behalf of America; we're trying to work together. Couldn't you try for twenty-four hours to have a positive, optimistic message as though it might work?" (See Cappella and Jamieson 1997, 3–5.)

Analysis of Partisan News, 1992–1995

The compound effect of a political party's limited influence over its members' talk and politicians' limited control over what talk gets transmitted to the electorate as news poses serious problems for party teams as they attempt to fashion and communicate a coherent message to the electorate. Even when party members enjoy relative comity and agreement on goals, news reporters still search for and find internal dissension. Political parties in America must work within the constraints imposed by the Constitution's separation of powers, so that even when Congress and the presidency are controlled by the same political party, politicians frequently find themselves working at cross-purposes. Differences in constituency, electoral calendar, and constitutional responsibilities preordain a certain level of internal party disagreement. All may have influenced President Bush's decision to reject Gingrich's Contract with America platform.

In addition, the separation of powers makes divided party control of government possible. Although divided government virtually guarantees greater levels of interparty conflict, its effects on the ability of party members to communicate a consistent party image is less clear. One can easily see how divided party control would create a common target and allow an internally diverse, if not divisive, party to unify its message. But here, too, forces promoting defection are present. Frequently, reaching compromise means that a president from one party negotiates policy agreements with the leaders of the opposition majority in Congress and, in the process, marginalizes his fellow partisans in Congress. Often, this scenario results in public dissension as some of the president's partisans in Congress distance themselves from the agreement. Similarly, rank-and-file members of the congressional majority will sometimes publicly reject their leaders' compromises with the president.

In this chapter we investigate the ability of national politicians in separate institutions to communicate consistent party images via the news media. After finding that partisan messages vary greatly in consistency, we search for causes among both the structural—such as party control of Congress and the presidency—and the more transient features of Washington politics.

Our Data: Network Evening News Broadcasts

The news content data reported here were collected by the Center for Media and Public Affairs (CMPA). From 1992 to 1995 CMPA coders watched 55,289 evening news stories broadcast by the three major television networks. The stories were timed and scored according to whether they mentioned Washington political actors (Congress, the president, the administration, and, during the transition period, the president-elect) as sources or subjects. CMPA refined the measurement by distinguishing extensive coverage from incidental coverage. The former includes only those stories in which a Washington actor received twenty seconds or more of coverage. Figure 4–1 reports the share of time devoted to these stories for the three networks compared to the time available for all news stories.

Figure 4–1 Political Story Time Compared to the Time Devoted to All Stories

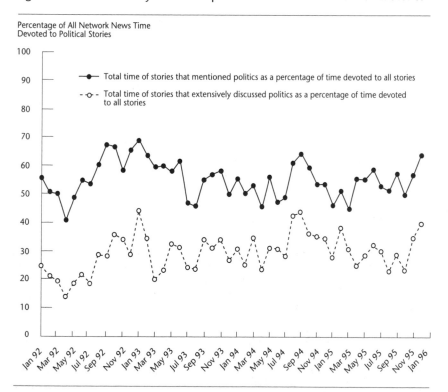

Percentage of All Network News Time
Devoted to Political Stories

—●— Total time of stories that mentioned politics as a percentage of time devoted to all stories

- ○ - Total time of stories that extensively discussed politics as a percentage of time devoted to all stories

Political news of the type that interests us here varies substantially from month to month, but in no month was less than 40 percent of network news time devoted to stories containing at least incidental coverage of these national actors. The volume of extensive coverage varies from a low of around 15 percent of all news time to a high of about 45 percent.[2]

Most news stories contain multiple, diverse elements, with various partisans offering sometimes contradictory opinions about one or more targets. This diversity renders analysis at the story level difficult and subject to arbitrary coding decisions. To solve this problem we followed CMPA's practice of further breaking down stories into their constituent evaluations. An evaluation is a statement made up of "words or phrases which convey an unambiguous assessment or judgment about an individual, an institution, or an action."[3] We included only those evaluations that are rich in partisan information. Specifically, we limited our data to evaluations for which both the source and subject, or target, can be clearly associated with a political party. Of CMPA's 22,927 evaluations of political figures from 1992 through 1995, about 2,000 targeted the "federal government," and another 10,000 involved clearly nonpartisan or ambiguously partisan figures, such as journalists, scholars and other specialists, foreign sources, interest group representatives, and people-on-the-street. Limiting our analysis to positive and negative assessments by and about unambiguous partisans yields a dataset of 10,404 evaluations. These represent the kinds of partisan talk that send the clearest and strongest cues to the electorate about the policy positions of the political parties.[4] More-

---

2. The variation becomes even more extreme if we examine the content of the lead story on the network news. The monthly percentages of time devoted to extensive discussions of politics vary enormously, from around 20 percent of lead story time in April 1992 to more than 80 percent in January 1993 and August 1994. Stories mentioning political actors also vary enormously, from about 35 percent in January 1995 to nearly 100 percent in December 1992.

3. Using evaluations (for example, a single evaluation of a political figure, rather than an entire sound bite or story) as its unit, CMPA can gather more nuanced information than would otherwise be possible. A single evaluation can have only one valence (positive or negative) and magnitude, thus avoiding the coding pitfalls of stories or sound bites containing contradictory or balancing comments. CMPA coding guidebook, filename TRACK1.BOK, August 1997, 120.

4. It is important to note that our dataset excludes a large amount of partisan communication and rhetoric. For example, Republican criticism of health care reform would not be included unless that criticism was directed at a particular political actor or institution. However, what our dataset loses in volume it makes up for in clarity: the cases that remain are in some sense extreme cases where strategic politicians have

over, each evaluation conforms to a standard syntax—source, type of message, and target—suitable for statistical analysis.

Classifying partisan talk in this way yields the four different types of party messages diagrammed below. Consistent signaling occurs when politicians commend the actions and preferences of fellow party members (X) or when they criticize those of the opposition (Y) politicians. A discrepant message arises either from internal criticism or from favorable assessments of the opposition. We shall refer to the former as "dissension" and the latter as "bipartisanship." Whatever the virtues of bipartisanship, they muddle party images and make it more difficult for citizens to distinguish Democratic and Republican positions on the issues.[5] Yet, dissension is potentially even more destructive. Where bipartisanship allows for two internally coherent political parties to converge on some issues, dissension can only raise questions about where the party stands on issues and, as a consequence, corrode the value of the party label in voting. With these evaluations, we can assess how consistent partisan talk is and begin to identify the structural and strategic circumstances that strengthen or weaken the ability of political parties to signal constituents through the news.

A Typology of Stories
(S is the source of a message, T is the target of the message, and M + or – indicates whether the message was positive or negative.)

Positive consistent	Positive discrepant
$\longrightarrow$	$\longrightarrow$
$S_x \qquad M^+ \qquad T_x$	$S_x \qquad M^+ \qquad T_y$
Negative consistent	Negative discrepant
$\longrightarrow$	$\longrightarrow$
$S_x \qquad M^- \qquad T_y$	$S_x \qquad M^- \qquad T_x$

(*continued*) chosen not to take a moderate path and have instead clearly supported or opposed another actor.

5. It can be argued that discrepant evaluations about splits or disputes within parties might offer superior information or gain greater credibility through a costly action. However, such information makes a voter's choice between parties more difficult. A related issue is that, on a particular policy, parties could have an incentive to strategically encourage the public's uncertainty about the party's true median position. However, if politicians want to present a more moderate policy

Does the Public Receive Consistent Political Messages?

Table 4–1 shows us that the great majority of the evaluations, 77 percent, are consistent, but negative. Rather than the classic image of a party team proposing and defending a policy platform, most consistent talk takes the form of criticism of the opposition. Moreover, among discrepant messages, negative evaluations—arguably the most damaging for defining a party image—predominate. Network news programs are about three times more likely to broadcast dissension than bipartisanship. Bear in mind, too, that as networks combine these individual evaluations to form stories, they increase the likelihood that the viewer will encounter discrepant messages interspersed among the consistent talk. Indeed, 42 percent of all stories from which we drew evaluations contained discrepant party evaluations.

Whether the prevalence of negative evaluations (59 percent of all messages) in modern partisan talk accurately represents what politicians are saying about one another or reflects a sampling bias by the news media cannot be distinguished with these data. Whatever the processes that produce it, partisan rhetoric includes a strong dose of discrepant information.[6]

Table 4–1
Consistent and Discrepant Evaluations, by Party

	Consistent		Discrepant		
	+	−	+	−	Total
Democrats	24%	21%	3%	12%	60%
	(2,547)	(2,141)	(263)	(6,205)	
Republicans	10%	21%	3%	5%	40%
	(1,081)	(2,233)	(364)	(521)	(4,199)
Total	35%	42%	6%	17%	100%
	(3,628)	(4,374)	(627)	(1,775)	(10,404)

Note: Entries are the cell's percentage of total evaluations, with raw numbers in parentheses.

(continued) position than their peers, they could do so by stating the position rather than criticizing their fellow partisans. By virtue of its concentration on evaluations of actors, our dataset consciously excludes such individual position taking.

6. Note that our dataset presents evaluations of officeholders, not candidates. Democratic totals probably understate the level of consistent evaluations because they do not contain evaluations of Clinton or other Democrats until after the 1992 election. Similarly, Republican evaluations of these same candidates are excluded. But evaluations of Bush by both parties are included, as are evaluations of Clinton during the transition.

Are Separation of Powers and Divided Party Control to Blame?

Above we identified two political features that might prompt politicians to criticize fellow partisans: the constitutional separation of powers and divided party control of the executive and legislature. We can assess the effects of each by monitoring the direction of rhetorical traffic. To obtain this information we break out the distribution in Table 4–1 according to the institutional affiliations of the sources and targets. The results are shown for Democrats and Republicans in Tables 4–2 and 4–3, respectively.

Overall, politicians evaluate their same branch party colleagues more favorably than they do their fellow partisans in the other branch. With a favorable to unfavorable ratio of nearly 6 to 1 on internally directed messages, both the Bush and Clinton administrations came about as close to achieving the nirvana of successful self-promotion as one is likely to find in American politics. Considering that the president appoints the other administration officials who are doing much of the talking and that he can fire them, it is not surprising that they all make happy talk. Neither centralized recruitment of members nor hierarchical supervision apply to Congress, and it shows in their much more modest success in partisan boosterism, where consistent-positive messages exceed negative-inconsistent evaluations by less than a 2 to 1 margin.

Nevertheless, even this modest level of party consistency represents an accomplishment when compared to party talk across the branches. By a 7 to 4 ratio both Bush and Clinton were subjected to more criticism than praise by their own party in Congress. Presidents are more generous, but the main difference is that they prefer to ignore their party rather than criticize it. They

Table 4–2
Evaluations by Democratic Sources

	Democratic Targets		Republican Targets	
	Democratic Congress	Clinton Administration	Republican Congress	Bush Administration
Democratic Congress Consistent	245	420	833	209
Democratic Congress Discrepant	142	716	104	11
Clinton Administration Consistent	77	1,805	825	274
Clinton Administration Discrepant	58	338	97	51

Table 4–3

Evaluations by Republican Sources

	Republican Targets		Democratic Targets	
	Republican Congress	Bush Administration	Democratic Congress	Clinton Administration
Republican Congress Consistent	718	47	478	1,703
Republican Congress Discrepant	318	71	23	330
Bush Administration Consistent	1	311	38	13
Bush Administration Discrepant	2	49	1	10

Note: In Tables 4–2 and 4–3, the presidential administrations include both the president and their administrations as sources and targets. Additionally, the Clinton administration includes evaluations made by the Democratic campaign in 1992 (but not evaluations of the Democratic campaign, for which the data are unavailable).

spend their time instead criticizing the congressional opposition.[7] Clearly, the separation of powers limits the ability of party politicians to deliver consistent, reinforcing messages to the public.

To test the effects of divided party control of Congress and the presidency on partisan signaling, we must add a time dimension. Although our data are limited to four years, they cover several combinations of government control: 1992, a Republican president with a Democratic Congress; 1993–1994, unified Democratic government; and 1995, a Democratic president and a Republican Congress. These differences allow us to test whether institutional control alters the volume and type of partisan rhetoric in the news. In Figure 4–2 we can observe substantial changes in the consistency and volume of evaluations by Democrats. In 1993 and 1994 the majority Democratic Party primarily transmitted messages about itself—mostly self-praise but also significant levels of dissension—while largely ignoring the out-of-power Republicans. With the Republican ascendancy to majority status in 1995, the target shifted, and Democrats united in transmitting consistent-negative rhetoric.

Figure 4–3 suggests that the loss of institutional power in 1993 translated into a diminished presence for Republicans in national news. With Democratic majorities in both houses of Congress and a Democratic pres-

---

7. Whatever the parties' capacity for self-criticism, there are few signs of bipartisanship in these figures. Only the Bush administration's evaluations of Clinton hint at discrepant positive evaluations, but bear in mind that all of these evaluations of Clinton occurred during the transition after his November victory.

Figure 4–2 Consistent and Discrepant Democratic Evaluations

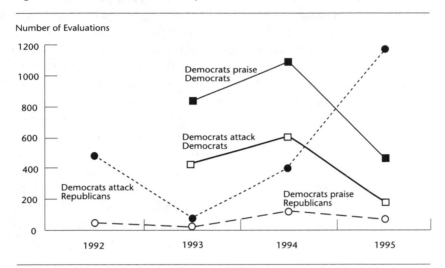

Note: 1992 does not contain Democratic Party presidential candidates as targets.

Figure 4–3 Consistent and Discrepant Republican Evaluations

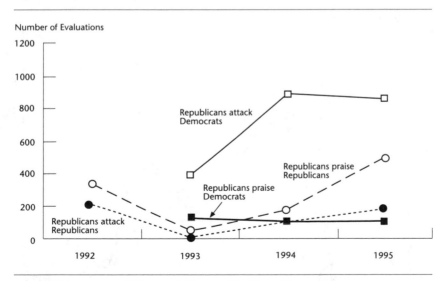

Note: 1992 does not contain Democratic Party presidential candidates as targets.

ident, Republican messages, especially the efforts at self-promotion, filled
news editors' wastebaskets. Unlike the Democrats, whose most common
categories of rhetorical statements consisted of positive and negative self-
evaluations, the vast majority of Republican success in communicating
partisan messages took the form of attacks on the Democrats. Because the
Republicans could not control the outcome of policy decisions, network
news showed little interest in their stances.

In 1994 the Republicans' fortunes changed in degree, if not kind. In addition to increased exposure for their own self-evaluations, their role as critic
of the Democratic unified government mushroomed, more than doubling
their previous year's total. In 1995 critical evaluations of Democrats diminished slightly as the Republicans began concentrating on intraparty boosterism. Political talk emanating from the new Republican majority consisted of
mutual support among members more than any other time in our dataset.

Figure 4–4 brings the same trends into sharp relief by displaying

Figure 4–4 Consistent and Discrepant Democratic Evaluations, Stacked
Percentages

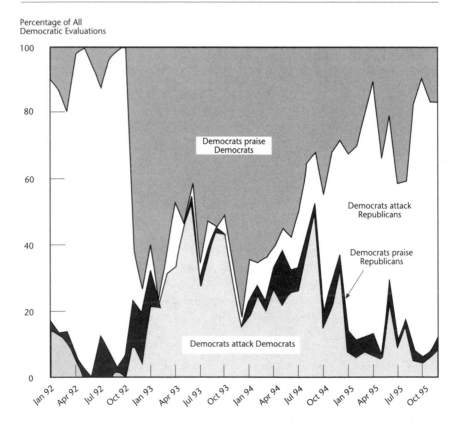

monthly percentages of consistent and discrepant evaluations. After the 1992 election, Democratic targeting of the Republican Party faded to insignificance until late 1994. In the meantime, most of the Democratic statements were self-directed, with periods of intense intraparty criticism. Figure 4–5 provides the same monthly data for the Republicans. The Republicans generated much less intraparty criticism once President Bush left office in 1993. And while 1994 signaled an increase in the Republican ability to put forward and support their own party, criticism of the Democrats remained a large part of their communication with the public.

The flow of partisan messages from Washington corresponds to our expectations. Under unified party control, the majority party controls public policy. Accordingly, the internal competition to commit the party to a particular course of action shifts attention away from the irrelevant

Figure 4–5   Consistent and Discrepant Republican Evaluations, Stacked Percentages

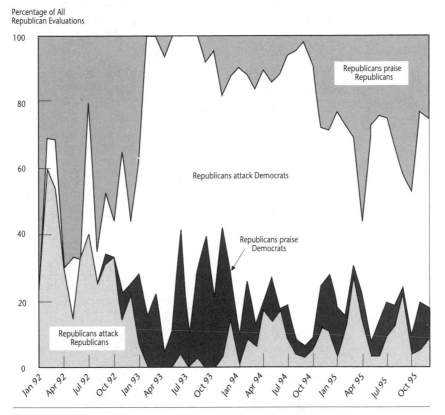

Note: 1992 figures do not include evaluations of Clinton or other Democratic presidential candidates.

opposition to the preferences of fellow partisans. Divided control, conversely, dampens these centrifugal tendencies and prompts partisans to sharpen differences between themselves and their opponents through consistent-negative messages.

To What Extent Does Partisan Talk Follow Politics in Washington?

Party control of Congress and the presidency clearly account for much of the variation we observe in the consistency with which national politicians convey partisan messages. However, this is not the whole story. One can imagine myriad local and transient circumstances that would at times prompt politicians to tone down criticism of the opposition or turn it against members of their own party.[8]

To measure the relation between politics in Washington and the flow of partisan messages to the nation via news, we turn to two often-used measures of partisanship in congressional roll call voting. The first, party unity, comes from Congressional Quarterly's annual vote analysis of party support scores.[9] Basically, this index measures the cohesion of a legislative party on those votes where majorities within each party oppose each other. The second is CQ's presidential support score, which measures the level at which partisans support presidential initiatives. Figures 4–6 and 4–7 display the consistency of party rhetoric (either negative or positive) against these two measures.

In Figure 4–6, the annual measure of both party voting and talk hover near or slightly above 75 percent. This congruence breaks down completely in Figure 4–7, when rhetoric is paired with support of the president's position in roll call voting. In their statements in the news, the president's partisans in Congress oppose the president more often than they

---

8. Against the expectation that partisan talk reflects partisan deeds, we must also consider a variant of the null hypothesis that the volume of conflictual rhetoric is less sensitive to politics than to the taste of a news media that favors conflict.

9. CQ defines party unity votes as "recorded votes that split the parties, with a majority of voting Democrats opposing a majority of voting Republicans. Members who switched parties are accounted for." The party unity support score reflects the "percentage of party unity votes on which members voted 'yea' or 'nay' in agreement with a majority of their party. Failures to vote lowered scores for chambers and parties." From "For the Record," *Congressional Quarterly Weekly Report*, January 3, 1998, 33.

Figure 4–6 Congressional Party Unity in Votes and Talk

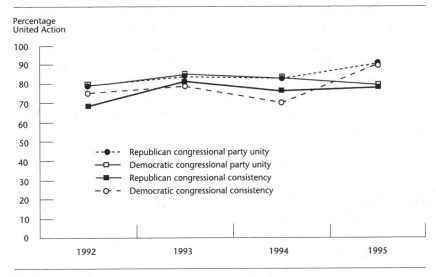

Note: Consistency includes only congressional sources and targets.

Figure 4–7 Congressional Support of the President in Votes and Talk

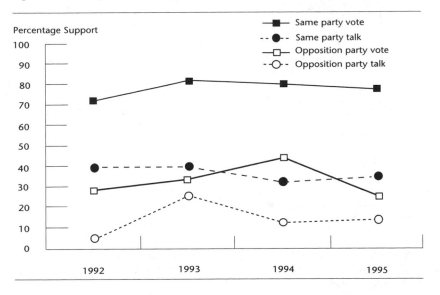

support him. However, in their voting the president's partisans in Congress actually support their president's position about 75 percent of time. The disparity is less for opposition party members, but they, too, vote with the president more than would appear based on their public statements. These differences correspond with the earlier finding that consistent messages flow more heavily within the branches than across them.

To examine this pattern more carefully we have disaggregated the annual percentages in Figure 4–7 for the Clinton administration into monthly series and estimated the relation between legislative support for presidential initiatives and the net volume of favorable messages directed at Clinton by members of Congress. In Table 4–4 these two series are related with each other, albeit weakly. Moreover, the negative intercept is consistent with the different plateaus of support displayed in Figure 4–7.

One potential explanation for these swings lies in the president's approval rating, which research has shown to be closely related with his congressional party's electoral fortunes (Campbell 1993; Kernell 1977; Tufte 1975). To test whether politicians in Congress might have monitored the president's public standing before deciding which kinds of messages to propose (and the news media in deciding which to transmit), we collected monthly Gallup job approval data for Clinton.[10] The relationships between average monthly presidential approval ratings and net pos-

Table 4–4

Congressional Net Evaluations of Clinton as a Function
of Presidential Support Scores in Roll Call Votes

	Presidential Support by Democratic Members of Congress in the News	Presidential Support by Republican Members of Congress in the News
	Coefficient (Standard Error)	Coefficient (Standard Error)
Intercept	−36.69*** (13.63)	−42.13*** (6.39)
Presidential Vote Support	0.35** (0.17)	0.35** (0.16)
	Adj. R^2 = .10	Adj. R^2 = .11

Significance level: ***at .001; ** at .05.

10. We exclude Bush from this analysis because of the short time he appears in our sample, and because data on Bush are limited to his status as a candidate and as a lame duck.

itive evaluations show congressional Democrats' consistent (hence favor-able) presidential assessments to have been significantly related to both the president's overall level of support and recent changes in that support.[11] Moreover, when Democrats controlled the Congress, they were signifi-cantly more critical of Clinton in these news-based messages than in 1995, when they entered the opposition.[12] Republicans, by contrast, appear to have been indifferent to President Clinton's standing in the polls (see Table 4–5).

Table 4–5
Congressional Net Evaluations of Clinton as a Function of His Popularity

	Presidential Support by Democratic Members of Congress in the News	Presidential Support by Republican Members of Congress in the News
	Coefficient (Standard Error)	Coefficient (Standard Error)
Intercept	−56.12*** (15.95)	−3.85 (38.95)
Presidential Approval (t-1)	1.11*** (0.33)	0.80 (0.81)
Change in Approval (t)	1.64*** (0.45)	−0.07 (1.10)
Democratic Congress	−6.97** (2.83)	−7.24 (6.84)
	Adj. R^2 = .40	Adj. R^2 = .00

Note: t-1 refers to the previous month's presidential approval; t indicates the current month's change in approval.
Significance level: *** at .001; ** at .05.

---

11. Note that as in the previous same party regressions, consistent evaluations are the same as positive evaluations of fellow partisans, while discrepant evaluations are negative. Also note that the dummy variable for Democratic control of the presidency is a constant because Clinton was the president for the entire period of these regressions.

12. These findings conform to a common view among Washingtonians that the fortunes of the minority party in Congress are bound to the success of their pres-ident. As analyst Mark Shields said about Democratic support for Clinton during his impeachment, "The Democrats grasped a central truth and that is when your party owns the White House, your party is defined by your president. Like it or not. And they decided that it was important to hang together." *The News Hour with Jim Lehrer*, February 12, 1999, PBS Television.

Conclusion

Comparing the peculiarities of the American political system with a classical party model of government is a favorite pastime of political scientists. The paragon of responsible party teams similarly provides us a standard with which to assess the ability of America's political parties to agree on and promote coherent policy commitments and emit clear, informative signals to the electorate. The other chapters in this volume suggest that during the 1990s the Democratic and Republican parties became more coherent and programmatic and, as the party theory of government predicts, so have the voters. Barbara Sinclair finds that institutional changes in the House of Representatives make it easier today for party leaders to plan and pursue a set of policies with a reasonable expectation that they will not be hijacked in the standing committees, the Rules Committee, or on the floor. John Aldrich and David Rohde's representation of "conditional party government" offers an explanation for these institutional reforms in the growing ideological consensus in both political parties. Gary Jacobson shows us that voters are more consistently sorting themselves into the political parties according to their own ideologies to a greater extent than at any time in the last half century. Yet, America's political parties still fall well short of attaining their intended promise. Policy commitments remain ambiguous and fluid; members in positions of institutional authority—from presidents to committee chairs—frequently exercise their prerogatives of office with little apparent regard to a coherent policy agenda. Only during the brief heyday of the Contract with America did party politicians in Washington begin to defer to a party program.

Scholars in search of party government have previously concentrated on policy decisions: roll call voting, presidential appointments and vetoes, conference reports, floor amendments, and the like. In this chapter, we have lumped all of these decisions and activities together under the rubric *deeds* to distinguish them from another important form of party behavior, *talk*, which, aside from election campaigns, has received less scholarly attention. As we suspected, the structural barriers to coherent party action appear especially formidable in limiting party politicians' ability to communicate a consistent party message through talk. While presidents mostly ignore their partisans in Congress, those partisans mostly criticize their party's president in the news. But the forces interfering with coherence are pervasive and undermine party government within these separated institutions as well as across them. Once a party becomes a congressional majority, it starts broadcasting a cacophony of negative, discrepant messages. The low point in our brief data series came in 1993 and 1994, when the Democratic Party controlled the White House and both chambers of Congress.

Our findings consistently indicate that coherence is more achievable through negative commentary about the opposition. When the opposition controls one or both of the branches, it becomes a convenient target. Whatever the internal disagreements over policy, party members can find common advantage in attacking the opposition. Moreover, this strategy corresponds to the preferences of the news media that have final control over which party messages are transmitted to the public. This point introduces a profound irony of American politics, at least within the realm of partisan talk: political parties send the most coherent signals via the news when they enjoy the least control over government policy. Conversely, at each stage of taking control of government—winning the White House and attaining majority control of the House and Senate—they turn their sights inward and, before an attentive news media, compete with one another to define the party's program.

The authors wish to express appreciation to the Center for Media and Public Affairs for access to the data, and to Meena Bose, Daniel Ponder, and Steven Weatherford for their comments on an earlier version of this chapter.

CHAPTER 5

Continuity and Change
in Civility in the House

Kathleen Hall Jamieson and Erika Falk

Kathleen Hall Jamieson and Erika Falk's chapter, "Continuity and Change in Civility in the House," carries forward the analysis of words by documenting the frequency of uncivil words spoken by House members on the floor. Although breaches of civility on the House floor are unusual, they became more frequent during the first session of the 104th Congress. Jamieson and Falk discuss the importance of rules to foster civil discourse in Congress. They also provide a useful historical perspective, observing that the current tendency for the members to act in an uncivil manner toward one another is not new. Indeed, early in the nation's history, there were numerous incidents of extreme incivility. Rules adopted to promote civil discourse generally had the desired effect, and breaches of civility declined until recently.

Analysis of two indicators of uncivil speech on the House floor—words ruled out of order and demands that words spoken on the floor be taken down—shows a sharp rise in the first session of the 104th Congress. The authors identify several possible causes of the heightened conflict over spoken words, including (1) the change in party control (other peaks have occurred during similar periods); (2) the Democrats' loss of agenda control for the first time in forty years, which necessitated a frustrating adjustment for them; (3) the Republicans' difficulty in adjusting to majority status, when they found that managing the legislative agenda requires skills different from those usually exercised by the minority; and (4) the increasing ideological polarization between the parties.

I n *The American Commonwealth* (1888), Lord Bryce notes that "no high qualities of statesmanship are expected from a Congressman" (187). But he also said, "To get on in American politics one must be civil and pleasant" (144). Although most people would accept these statements, there is little agreement about when members of Congress stopped being civil and pleasant or when the norm of comity began to erode. Indeed some contend that the House is now more, rather than less, civil than it was in earlier times. At various points in the past, distinguished congressional leaders lamented the demise of the good manners of an earlier era. One scholar attributes such an observation by Sam Houston, a senator from 1846 to 1859, to the crankiness of old age! "On one occasion," writes Llerena B. Friend, "he seemed to show his age—he would be sixty-four—when he complained of the noise and informality in the Senate and of the change in that body from the decorum of twenty years before" (1954, 247).

Other distinguished members of Congress have defended the institution against its detractors. For example, Speaker Champ Clark, who served in that position from 1911 to 1919, wrote in his memoirs that "every evil-disposed person in the land can find some slander to utter about the American Congress. If the House takes time enough to discuss an important measure, these slanderers savagely assail it for being too slow. If the House puts in overtime and hurries a bill through, these same malignants fiercely denounce it for sending half-baked measures to the Senate" (1920, 194ff).

Others are more specific in pinpointing moments that eroded trust between the parties and the confidence that each was prepared to act in the higher interest of the country and the institution in times of need. Some identify the late 1960s as a turning point. "As tensions grew over Vietnam, norms of courtesy and institutional patriotism were honored more in the breach; by the early 1970s, the idea that antisocial or anti-institutional behavior should be ostracized or punished in any significant way was dismissed" (Ornstein 1990, 14).

Others see fracture points appearing in and expanded by abuses of power by those of the other party. Naturally, those points are different for each party. For Democrats, one such moment occurred in 1989, when Republicans led by Rep. Newt Gingrich of Georgia ousted the Democratic Speaker, Jim Wright, on ethics charges. For Republicans, a comparable abuse of power occurred in 1985, when the Democrats voted to seat Democrat Frank McCloskey rather than Republican Richard McIntyre after a disputed election in the Eighth Congressional District in Indiana. Recalls a participant, "Most people in the House now just refer to it as the 'Bloody Eighth'" (Penny and Garrett 1995, 180). As the vote approached, reports a participant, Republican moderate Pat Roberts "warned that this election could poison relations for years to come. 'You're going to win here,' Roberts told the committee, 'But you're losing by tearing the fabric of this place. If you worry folks like me, we're in serious trouble.'" "The

committee action infuriated Republicans," recalls former representative
Tim Penny of Minnesota, "who began tying up legislative business in
protest" (Penny and Garrett 1995, 181). "Every House Republican who
was in the House at that time believed that election was stolen," recalls
Vin Weber, another former representative from Minnesota. "There isn't a
single one that thought this was a legitimate process and that we just lost"
(Penny and Garrett 1995, 181).

The tension created by that vote affected relations between the parties
and within the Democratic ranks. Only 19 of the 252 Democrats in the
House voted with the Republicans to declare the seat vacant so that a special election could be held. Of these, only one, Rep. Ron Mazzoli, D-Ky.,
delivered a floor speech justifying his vote. "It took from 1985 until well
into the early 1990s for some guys who were involved with that to even
talk to me," Mazzoli recalled (Penny and Garrett 1995, 183).

An alternative but not necessarily incompatible view of congressional
civility holds that it rises and falls, with the changes driven by an interaction of individuals and events. History is marked by moments in which
words that seem mild by today's standards were strongly condemned. For
instance, the House voted its first formal censure in 1832, when Rep.
William Stanbery was punished for saying, "The eyes of the Speaker are
too frequently turned from the chair you occupy toward the White
House" (Ornstein 1995, 776).

When current members suggest that civility has declined, they mean in
comparison to the recent, not the remote past. As a cursory survey of the
past ten or twenty years confirms, the Congresses of that period do not
approach either the level of vituperation or violence of their eighteenth-
and nineteenth-century ancestors. In 1839 Michel Chevalier observed
that discussion in Congress "is an animated exchange of arguments of
every caliber and degree, of contradictory resolutions mixed with applause
and hisses, of exaggerated eulogies and brutal invectives" (Chevalier
[1839] 1961). Among those known for their mastery of invective was a
man who served in the House after completing his term as president. Of
John Quincy Adams, Rufus Choate observes, "He has peculiar powers as
an assailant, and almost always, even when attacked, gets himself into that
attitude by making war upon his accuser; and he has, withal, an instinct
for the jugular and the carotid artery, as unerring as that of any carnivo-
rous animal" (quoted in Stimpson 1952, 66).

Only recently has deadly physical violence been unthinkable because
instances of it exist only beyond living memory. But violence did persist
into the twentieth century; in 1902 two senators were censured for engaging in a fistfight on the floor (Bacon 1995, 2064). And later Congresses

have produced a number of instances in which members threatened to punch someone or engaged in shoving or tie pulling.

One such occurrence came just before the July Fourth recess in 1985. "As members of one party were accusing the other of 'shortcounting' votes in procedural matters, a livid House Majority Leader . . . stepped down from the rostrum and confronted the two of them." That leader, "a former Golden Gloves boxer, threatened to punch" two members of the other party in the mouth. Although he later apologized, "hard feelings from the incident lasted until after the recess and led to a near fist fight" between a Democratic and Republican member, "who shouted epithets at each other from across the aisle" (Winneker 1995, n.p.).

There have been disruptions within party ranks as well. In a caucus during a late night session in 1989, two members "got into a shoving match that nearly escalated" before another member "broke it up" (Winneker 1995, n.p.). In 1996 the ranking member on a committee threw a handful of papers in front of the committee chair from the other party, "stalked out of the committee room and yanked on the necktie" of another member of the majority (Grove 1996, B-1). Nor was that the only moment in recent times in which members shoved each other. One member "administered a stiff shove" to another, "prompting a general melee and an urgent summons to the Capitol police" (Grove 1996, B-1).

By contrast, former Democratic Speaker Tip O'Neill recalled that the meanest thing Speaker John McCormack had ever been heard to say about a colleague was "I hold him in minimal high regard" (O'Neill 1987, 120). So, have times changed? Writing in 1963, Charles Clapp observed, "Public disparagement of colleagues is strongly discouraged; it is not the way to play the game. Personal attacks are sharply censured and members seldom invade the congressional districts of colleagues of another party to campaign against them. Democrats reacted strongly to the action of one House Republican in sending letters into the district of a Democratic colleague criticizing the latter for apparent inconsistencies between a stated position and a vote" (1963, 18).

Unmentioned in many accounts of incidents of incivility are two facts. First, more often than not the perpetrators apologize publicly for their breach of decorum. For example, on November 20, 1995, a member rose to address the House for one minute and said:

> Mr. Speaker, Friday evening the gentleman [X] directed an inappropriate remark at me for which he subsequently apologized. Unfortunately, I responded to that remark in an even less appropriate way by forcing [X] to leave the House floor with me and then instigating a physical confrontation

outside the doors. I acted in a way that is unbecoming a Member of the Congress.

If this were an athletic ring, a top gun Navy fighter pilot the size of [X] would certainly have made for a fair fight of it. But we are supposed to be engaged in a battle of ideas, demonstrating to the American people and other countries how we settle our differences in a nonviolent way.

[X] deserves an apology from me. I hereby offer one. (141 Cong. Rec. H13360, 1995)

Second, the day in and day out norm of Congress is, if not cordial, at least civil. Demands to "take down" the words of another member are rare; still more unusual are rulings that words should be taken down. Similarly, although members are more likely nowadays than in more remote times to call another member a liar, that ascription is still rare.

Because the taking down process is the formal mechanism the House uses to censure inappropriate discourse spoken on the floor, it is that measure we use to answer the following questions: Has the level of civility in the House changed in the past half century? If so, when and why? Answering these questions requires an understanding of the House rules governing decorum in the chamber.

The rules that govern a Congress are adopted at the beginning of its first session. The process commits the membership to precepts—some centuries old, others new—that determine the formal context within which the deliberations of the body will take place in the coming two sessions. Historians have recognized the role that the rules can play in creating a climate conducive to action or inaction, comity or contention. From 1800 to 1828, for example, "Contentiousness was encouraged by Senate and House rules which gave higher precedence to raising questions than to deciding them and which guaranteed almost total freedom from restraint to the idiosyncratic protagonist" (Young 1993, 141).

By adopting the rules at the beginning of a new Congress, the membership voluntarily limits the range of rhetoric acceptable on the floor. When members wonder why they cannot call another member a liar or a hypocrite even if the evidence justifies the label, the answer is not simply that the rules of the House forbid it; rather, it is that the membership has voluntarily agreed by vote that these are the rules under which the House will operate during that Congress. Among other things, the rules caution a member not to call another a liar even if she or he is not telling the truth, not to impugn another's integrity even if the actions invite it, and not to call someone a hypocrite even if she or he deserves it. These boundaries are designed to create a climate conducive to deliberation. Central to the ability to deliberate is the presumption of mutual respect.

The rules are not engraved in granite but have instead "been greatly modified in the last quarter century. Voting practices have changed; debate has become more structured; reliance on special orders of business has replaced the use of more traditional methods of considering legislation on the floor," writes William Holmes Brown, who served as House parliamentarian from 1974 to 1994 (1996, vii).

In 1992, for example, "The tough criticism such candidates received during one-minute and Special Order speeches on the House floor during the 1992 election season led the Speaker to announce to the House his intention to expand the protections of decorum restraints to all candidates for the Presidency" (Nickels 1995, 6). The ruling applied to nominated candidates for both the presidency and vice presidency (138 Cong. Rec. H9299, 1992).

The Origin and Function of House Rules

Article 1, Section 5, of the U.S. Constitution gives Congress the power to govern itself: "Each House may determine the rules of its proceedings, punish its Members for disorderly behavior, and with the concurrence of two-thirds, expel a Member." In his *Manual of Parliamentary Practice,* Thomas Jefferson observes, "It is very material that order, decency, and regularity be preserved in a dignified public body" (1868, n.p.). The presence of uniform, agreed-upon rules and procedures creates a legislative atmosphere subject neither to "the caprice of the Speaker" nor to the "captiousness of the members." The rules make it less likely that a member will be censured for language that seems uncivil to the hearer but incisive to the speaker. The House adopted rules of decorum on April 7, 1789. House precedents are summarized in *The House Rules and Manual* of each Congress as well as in works by House parliamentarians.[1]

House rules specify that a member

1. "Shall confine himself [or herself] to the question under debate, avoiding personality" (Rule XIV, Clause I). Avoiding personality is taken to mean arraigning or impugning the motives of members (Jefferson 1868, 171).

---

1. See *Cannon's Procedure in the House of Representatives* (1949), *Deschler's Procedure in the U.S. House of Representatives* (1974), *Cannon's Precedents* (1936), *Deschler's Precedents* (1977), and William Holmes Brown's *House Practice: A Guide to the Rules, Precedents and Procedures of the House* (1996).

2. "A Member, officer, or employee of the House of Representatives shall conduct himself [or herself] at all times in a manner which shall reflect creditably on the House of Representatives" (Rule XLIII, Clause 1).

3. A member may say that what has been said by another is untrue but not that the representation is deliberate or intentional (Rule XLIII, Clause 1). The word *lie* is, as a result, unacceptable.

4. "Debate may . . . not include characterizations of Senate action or inaction, other references to individual Members of the Senate, or other quotations from Senate proceedings" (Rule XIV, Clause 1). In the early 1990s the House rules were amended to allow for some general discussion of Senate legislative action, but members are still forbidden to characterize those actions or inactions.

5. Members may not use "offensive words against the character of the House, or impeaching the loyalty of a portion of the membership" (Jefferson 1868, 170). Drawing on a practice in the English House of Commons, Thomas Jefferson (1868) in Section 368 of his *Manual* prohibited the use of "indecent language against the proceedings of the House."

6. When speaking, members do not refer to each other by name or in the second person. The proper reference is "the gentleman from" or "the gentlelady from."

Rules and procedures are important because they "provide stability, legitimize decisions, divide responsibilities, reduce conflict, and distribute power" (Oleszek 1989, 5). The House rules give the chair the authority and responsibility for maintaining decorum. Rule I, Clause 2, states, "He [or she] shall preserve order and decorum, and, in case of disturbance or disorderly conduct in the galleries, or in the lobby, may cause the same to be cleared." Members too have power to assist in the process of preserving decorum. Rule XIV, Clause 4, gives the Speaker or any member the power to call to order a member who has "transgressed" the rules: "It is . . . the duty of the House to require its Members in speech or debate to preserve that proper restraint which will permit the House to conduct its business in an orderly manner and without unnecessary and unduly exciting animosity among its Members or antagonism from those other branches of the government with which the House is correlated."

The rules of the House and the precedents interpreting them are designed to create a climate conducive to deliberation. Accordingly, they circumscribe what a member may say about those involved in the legislative process: other members of the House, members of the Senate, the Speaker, the president, and those nominated for president or vice president.

By dampening tensions, the rules of the House and Senate increase the likelihood that the best ideas of each party will be heard whether or not they are incorporated into legislation. The rules themselves and the presence of a nonpartisan parliamentarian decrease the likelihood that the party or ideology of the chair will dictate the chair's rulings.

While a demand to take down words is pending, for example, "the Speaker has the right to refuse to recognize parliamentary inquiries" or a "unanimous consent request that a Member be allowed to proceed for one minute" (Michel 1993, 7). By curtailing a member's right to speak until it is determined whether the offending words will be struck from the record, the rules also dampen the likelihood that the tensions will escalate. The process of taking down the words focuses the House's attention on the nature of inappropriate discourse; striking words from the *Congressional Record* expresses collective disapproval; requiring the consent of the body before the offending member is permitted to reenter the day's debate establishes a formal mechanism for reincorporating into the deliberative community those who have breached decorum.

This process also minimizes the likelihood that a person attacked will respond in kind. By focusing debate on the topic under consideration rather than on the advocates themselves, the rules depersonalize the discourse of Congress. So, for example, speakers do not address each other but rather the chair ("Mr. Speaker"); they speak of each other as representatives of a state ("the gentlewoman from") not as spokespersons for a party or a position; the person recognized by the chair determines whether, if, and to whom to yield the floor.

The Logic of the Taking Down Process

The taking down process is an elaborate rhetorical ritual used to mark conduct that transgresses the rules, to elicit acknowledgment of the transgression from the offender, and, if that is not forthcoming, to open the option of punishing the behavior and lack of repentance by depriving her or him of the floor for the rest of the day. When a member "transgresses" the rules, the

> Speaker shall, or any Member may call him [or her] to order; in which case
> he [or she] shall immediately sit down, unless permitted, on motion of
> another Member, to explain, and the House shall, if appealed to, decide on

the case without debate; if the decision is in favor of the Member called to order, he [or she] shall be at liberty to proceed, but not otherwise; and, if the case requires it, he [or she] shall be liable to censure or such punishment as the House may deem proper. (Rule XIV, Clause 4)

House Rule XIV, Clause 5, took its current form in 1880:

If a Member is called to order for words spoken in debate, the Member calling him [or her] to order shall indicate the words excepted to, and they shall be taken down in writing at the Clerk's desk and read aloud to the House; but he [or she] shall not be held to answer nor be subject to the censure of the House therefore, if further debate or other business has intervened.

The procedure to take down words is specified in Section 368.

The taking down process makes institutional sense only if the chair is perceived as evenhanded and consistent and the members of both parties are presumed to share an interest in maintaining comity. By contrast, if the members of each party treat the taking down process as a partisan act, the process becomes a meaningless exercise that will inevitably produce a result consistent with the wishes of the majority party. Depending on what suits its interest, the majority party can successfully appeal any ruling of the chair or table any motion to appeal a ruling. If a member of the minority objects to striking the words, the majority has the votes to strike. In this scenario, any ruling by the chair against the words of a member of the minority would be upheld and any against a member of the majority voided. The request that the member be permitted to proceed in order can be politicized as well.

The taking down process is most effective when the offending member recognizes what was unparliamentary about the statement, asks unanimous consent that the words be withdrawn, apologizes to the person whose integrity has been impugned, and does not hold a grudge against the person who demanded that the words be taken down. The process is least effective when the person demanding that words be taken down is from the other party, the person whose words have been challenged does not understand why, the chair does not provide a clear and compelling explanation, the opportunity to apologize is foreclosed, and the request to permit the member to proceed in order is denied. The first scenario reduces tension, while the second magnifies it. The first invites understanding; the second invites payback. The first instructs the House and the members in the norms of appropriate discourse, but the second is simply punitive.

The Speaker has the option to respond to a request that words be taken down by asking whether the challenged member wishes to seek unanimous consent to withdraw the words. The chair can also ask that a member reconsider the request that words be taken down. When these moves are successful, the chair minimizes the amount of time spent on the exchange and cuts off avenues that would otherwise magnify tension. When accepted, the request to withdraw words also constitutes an acknowledgment that they may have been inappropriate.

Tracking Incivility Through the Taking Down of Words

Tracking civility or the lack of it assumes access to an accurate record of what has been said on the floor. For a number of reasons, that assumption is problematic. Until the 104th Congress, the *Congressional Record* did not faithfully reflect what had happened on the floor. Members were able to alter the *Record* "usually," wrote *Roll Call*, "to preserve an illusion of total decorum in Congress" ("A Real Record" 1993, n.p.).[2] For example, two members got into a shouting match during the debate over the Family Planning Amendments Act in April 1993, and one yelled at the other, who was trying to interrupt him, "You had better not do that, ma'am. You will regret that as long as you live. Who do you think you are?" What appeared in the *Record* was, "I will say to the gentlelady, for whom I have the greatest respect, I would hope that she or any other Member not try to cut off another Member when a serious matter like this is to be resolved here in the proper House" (Barr 1995, A15). Because the taking down process that results in a ruling *is* recorded, we view it as the most reliable measure of the institution's own perception of breaches in decorum on the floor.

To determine whether debates on the floor of the House have become more uncivil, we charted demands to take down words and rulings on words taken down from 1935 through 1998. This was done by copying the reports on words taken down from the House Journal appendices, checking that record against the one gathered in two Congressional Research Service reports by Ilona Nickels and one report by Republican leader Bob Michel (1993), and conducting a computer-based search of the *Congressional Record* from 1985 to 1998. Figures 5–1 and 5–2 document the findings.

---

2. The same is true of the Senate. When a senior senator told another to "shut his own mouth," he was able to excise the statement from the *Record*.

Figure 5–1 Words Ruled Out of Order, 1935–1998

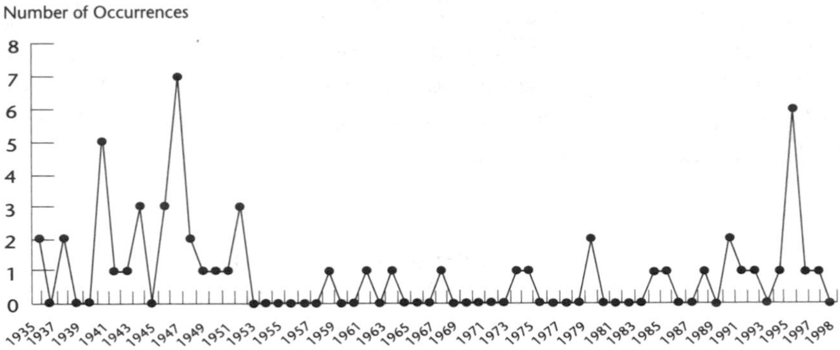

Number of Occurrences

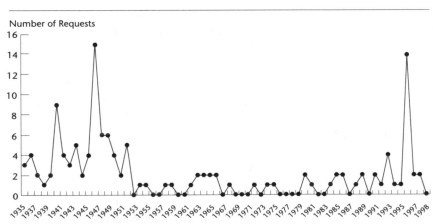

An analysis of demands to take down words and of words ruled out of order from 1935 to 1998 suggests that incivility was higher in the period from 1935 to 1951 than in the period from 1980 to 1998, that the interim was relatively quiet, and that incivility peaked in 1946 and 1995. Each of those times corresponds roughly to a change in control in the House and Senate when the White House was held by the other party. By these measures (words taken down, words taken down that go to a ruling), the first session of the 104th Congress was less civil than its recent predecessors.

An analysis of the instances of words taken down reveals that some situations are more likely to produce incivility than others. These include the

Figure 5–2 Requests to Take Down Words that Resulted in a Ruling from the
            Chair, 1935–1998

Number of Requests

situation mentioned above—a change in control of Congress that creates a divided government—incidents in which the minority feels abused or the majority obstructed, and occasions when members (or a member in a leadership position) are being investigated on ethics charges.

Because the 104th was the first Congress in forty years with both houses controlled by Republicans, it represented a dramatic alteration in roles for both the Democrats and the Republicans. "A great many Democrats remained in shock over the very concept of having lost control, which they thought they were entitled to by divine right" (Jamieson 1997, 22), a veteran congressional reporter noted. It was obviously difficult for those who had power to be without the staff support and agenda control to which they had been accustomed. Similarly, the Republicans "didn't do well at assuming power" (Jamieson 1997, 22). And the task of managing a legislative agenda required a set of skills different from those usually exercised by the minority.

When the House has been in the hands of one party for a long time, members of that party may fail to empathize with the frustrations of the minority. Speaker Sam Rayburn's seventeen-year tenure was interrupted twice by Republican majorities, reminding the Democrats of how it feels to be the minority party.

The Republican majority surprised many by guaranteeing the minority the right to include instructions in motions to recommit, banning proxy voting in committees, and promising to provide more open rules. But, stung by their reversal in role and status, the Democrats responded by adopting the tension-producing tactics they had found so offensive when the Republicans wielded them, including raising parliamentary objections and demanding roll call votes.

One other dynamic played a role in the spike of moves to take down words—a Democrat in the White House confronting a highly partisan House led by Newt Gingrich, a person not highly regarded by the new minority. The 104th was more ideologically polarized than the 103d in part because many of the fifty-two seats lost by Democrats in the House had been held by moderates.

The freshman class of the 104th was elected on appeals similar to those that brought the Watergate classes into power. Indeed, thirty-five were first-time elected officials. By the 104th, the Watergate generation of Democrats had assumed the leadership of their party, pitting two reform driven, anti-establishment groups against each other. By contrast, the 83d Congress (1953–1954), which put the executive and legislative branches in the hands of the Republicans, did not produce an escalation in instances of taking down words largely because the Democratic minority was led by individuals ready to join with Republican moderates in service of President Dwight D. Eisenhower's agenda.

The spike in 1946 suggests as well that context affects deliberations in the House. It was a tumultuous year in U.S. politics: FDR was dead; World War II had ended, bringing thousands of U.S. military personnel home from overseas; and President Harry S. Truman was under siege. Following a divisive debate over price controls and strikes by railroad and mine workers, the Republican campaign of 1946 produced a majority in both houses in 1947, creating a face-off between Congress and the president. In addition, 1946 was the beginning of the cold war, a fact reflected in the taking down of phrases such as *communist line, enemies of our country, subversive,* and *red-baiting tactics.*

The patterns revealed by a charting of the requests to take down words and requests that led to a ruling, however, indicate that those who believe that incivility has been on an upward curve since the Vietnam War are, at least by this measure, mistaken. The charts suggest as well that the House is a resilient and self-correcting institution. In the second session of the 104th the measures return to the range of earlier years. The reason is straightforward. Faced with reelection campaigns, neither party could afford an unproductive second session. In this sense, Lord Bryce was correct when he observed that to get along in politics, one must be civil.

CHAPTER 6

Presidential Agenda Setting in Congress

George C. Edwards III and Andrew Barrett

In their chapter, "Presidential Agenda Setting in Congress," George C. Edwards III and Andrew Barrett look at the president's ability to set the congressional agenda, and they identify a paradox concerning this central aspect of presidential-congressional relations. Presidency scholars routinely declare that setting the agenda is an important—perhaps the most important—presidential power. However, only a little systematic empirical work has been undertaken to document this assertion, and some of the studies indicate that the president's ability to influence the congressional agenda is quite limited.

Setting the congressional agenda is important because items not under consideration have no chance to pass; that is, getting his proposals on the agenda is a necessary condition for the president to succeed in the legislative arena. But even if the president is able to get his proposals on Congress's agenda, a more important question is whether they succeed; in other words, is setting the agenda a sufficient condition for success?

In their study, Edwards and Barrett identify major legislative proposals from 1953 to 1996 and determine whether the proposal was a presidential or congressional initiative. They find that the president almost always gets his legislative items on the agenda. These proposals, however, must compete with congressional proposals for agenda space. Overall, presidential proposals make up about one-third of the congressional agenda. But party control of Congress and the presidency make a difference: under unified government, presidential initiatives comprise about half of the congressional agenda. Presidential agenda items are also more likely to pass under unified government. Compared to congressional agenda items, the president's proposals are more likely to pass both chambers than congressional initiatives because his proposals are more likely to get attention in both chambers. Yet there is a substantial gap between proposing and winning—less than half of the agenda ultimately passes.

At the core of every president's legislative strategy is getting his most important proposals on the congressional agenda. Attaining agenda status is a necessary prelude to Congress's consideration of a bill and to the president's affecting public policy. Influencing the policy agenda—the set of issues that receive serious attention by policymakers—has long been viewed as one of the most important sources of political power and has attracted steady attention from scholars (Anderson 1975; Baumgartner and Jones 1993; Cobb and Elder 1983; Downs 1972; Flemming, Wood, and Bohte 1997; Jones 1994; Kingdon 1995; Light 1991; Peters and Hogwood 1985; Walker 1977; Wood and Peake 1998).

The White House must obtain agenda space for its proposals in order to build momentum and obtain congressional commitments of support for them. It is to the president's advantage for Congress to use his proposal as the starting point in marking up a bill (McKelvey 1976). Having the president's proposal on the agenda makes his bargaining position known to members of Congress and provides him a greater chance to define the terms of debate and thus the premises on which members of Congress make their decisions (Edwards 1989, 206–9).

In addition, the White House wants to ensure that its proposals compete favorably with other proposals on the agenda. If presidents cannot focus Congress's attention on their priority programs, the programs will get lost in the complex and overloaded legislative process. Moreover, presidents and their staff have the time and energy to lobby effectively for only a few bills at a time, and the president's political capital is inevitably limited. As a result, presidents wish to focus on advancing their own initiatives rather than opposing or modifying the proposals of others. Thus, the White House not only wants its initiatives to be on the congressional agenda but also prefers to have fewer congressional initiatives with which it must deal.

For decades, scholars have maintained that the president has a significant—indeed, the most significant—role in setting the policy-making agenda in Washington (see, for example, Huntington 1973). John Kingdon's careful study of the Washington agenda found that "no other single actor in the political system has quite the capability of the president to set agendas . . . the president can single handedly set the agendas, not only of people in the executive branch, but also of people in Congress and outside the government" (1995, 23). Frank Baumgartner and Bryan Jones, in their broad examination of agenda setting, concluded that "no other single actor can focus attention as clearly, or change the motivations of such a great number of other actors, as the president" (1993, 241). Jon Bond and Richard Fleisher argue that "the president's greatest influence over policy comes from the agenda he pursues and the way it is packaged" (1990, 230).

Even scholars who have cautioned against acceptance of a presidency-centered view of government have recognized the importance of agenda setting to the presidency (Moe and Teel 1970). George Edwards (1989), for example, argues that agenda setting has the potential to be one of the president's most important strategic powers. Like Edwards, Charles O. Jones (1994, 181) is skeptical of the president's ability to set the policy agenda easily. Nevertheless, Jones concludes that the president has "significant influence" in agenda setting.

Despite the consensus among scholars about the president's influence on the policy agenda, little systematic empirical work has been done to measure the president's impact on the congressional agenda, as opposed to studies of the president's influence at the final stage of the legislative process. The most prominent work on the president and agendas is that of Paul Light (1991), who examined the president's domestic agenda from the Kennedy administration to the Reagan administration. Although he provides a solid descriptive and quantitative study of the agenda-setting process, his analysis centers on the process by which a president sets his own agenda, not the role the president plays in setting the congressional agenda. Cary Covington, Mark Wrighton, and Rhonda Kinney (1995) address the impact of presidential agenda setting in Congress, but are concerned with the president's success on roll call votes on his agenda issues rather than his effectiveness in influencing the congressional agenda or the relative success of presidential and congressional proposals. Wayne Steger (1997) also compares the success of the president's agenda items on the floor to that of legislation proposed by others.

More recent research has challenged the president's preeminence in agenda setting. Dan Wood and Jeffrey Peake (1998) and Edwards and Wood (1999) have found that the president usually has limited influence on the agendas of both the media and Congress. Although these works do not focus explicitly on the president's legislative agenda, they raise questions about scholars' assertions regarding presidential influence.

Therefore, we have suggestive but inconclusive and contradictory findings regarding a central aspect of presidential-congressional relations. If we are to understand presidential leadership of Congress, we need to know (1) the president's success in obtaining agenda space for his most significant proposals; (2) the extent to which these proposals make up Congress's agenda; and (3) the conditions, if any, in which the president is most likely to dominate the congressional agenda. In addition, underlying the conclusions regarding the president's influence in agenda setting is the implication that agenda setting matters. Do presidential proposals have a greater chance of passing than legislation proposed by others? To answer these questions, we must first think more rigorously about agenda setting in Congress.

Theorizing About Presidential Agenda Setting: Some Hypotheses

One of the paradoxes in the literature on presidential-congressional relations is the contrast between the conclusions of scholars that presidential influence on votes to pass legislation is marginal (for example, Bond and Fleisher 1990; Edwards 1989; Jones 1994) and their agreement with other scholars that the president is a powerful influence in setting Congress's agenda. If these conclusions are correct, the forces that affect Congress's decisions about its agenda must differ from those that affect decisions on final passage of legislation.

At the floor stage of the legislative process, the most important influences on congressional voting are party, ideology, and constituency (Bond and Fleisher 1990; Edwards 1989). These factors are largely beyond the president's control, especially in the short run. The president's legislative skills have little impact at this stage of the consideration of legislation (Bond and Fleisher 1990, chap. 8; Edwards 1989, chap. 9).

The burdens of leadership are considerably less at the agenda stage. On the floor, the president must try to influence decisions regarding the political and substantive merits of a policy. At the agenda stage, in contrast, the president has only to convince members that his proposals are important enough to warrant attention. To do so the White House can use three principal sources of influence: *service, incentives,* and *persuasion.*

The most direct type of influence a president can assert on the congressional agenda is to sponsor legislative proposals. The president provides a *service* by giving Congress a starting point for the consideration of legislation. Richard Neustadt observes that "Congressmen need an agenda from outside, something with high status to respond to or react against. What provides it better than the program of the president?" (1960, 6–7). In addition, a proposal's identification as coming from the president helps members of Congress decide which among the thousands of bills introduced in each session deserve consideration. The president does not have to influence Congress to allow him to provide this service. Instead, Congress has invited or directed by statute the president to take the lead on the budget, the economy, national security, the environment, and other major areas of public policy (Sundquist 1981, chap. 6). Congress's needs become the president's leverage. But there is more involved here than the service of the "chief clerk." A presidential proposal also signals Congress what the president wants or perhaps what he is willing to settle for, valuable political information for the legislative battles to come.

A second way for a president to influence the congressional agenda is to speak out in favor of an initiative. By doing so, the president may draw enough attention to the issue that members of Congress feel the need to do something about it. The president is especially likely to go public on his most important legislative proposals. To provide an *incentive* for Congress to act, the president must influence what the public thinks is important. We are just beginning to understand presidential influence on public opinion, but Jeffrey Cohen (1997) found that presidents' State of the Union messages do seem to influence the public's policy agenda (views of the most important problem), although not for a sustained period of time.[1]

Finally, the president may influence the congressional agenda by personally contacting members of Congress, especially party leaders or committee and subcommittee chairs, and *persuading* them to act on a particular initiative. In addition, the president does not want congressional leaders to offer competing proposals or proposals that would force the administration into taking unpopular stands. For reasons that are well understood, congressional leaders are typically susceptible to following the president's lead (Taylor 1998), but only if they are members of the president's party (Edwards 1989, chaps. 3, 5). There is no reason to expect that opposition party congressional leaders will find the president's arguments compelling.

Despite the president's advantages in influencing the congressional agenda, Congress is quite capable of setting its own agenda (Taylor 1998). The public expects Congress to take the initiative, and members of Congress have strong electoral incentives to respond. Thus, when President Jimmy Carter sent a full legislative program to Congress, it had to compete for agenda space with congressional initiatives. As a presidential aide put it, "Congress was scheduled up before most of the items arrived" (Light 1991, 54). Most of the major legislative actions of the 1980s were congressional initiatives (see, for example, Calmes 1986, 2647).

---

1. Cohen also found that more substantive policy rhetoric did not influence the public's agenda.

Agenda setting is of interest to scholars and practitioners alike because it is an early and critical stage in the policy-making process. Ultimately, our concern with presidential agenda setting in Congress revolves around its impact on the outcomes of the legislative process. Do the proposals the president initiates and for which he succeeds in obtaining space on the congressional agenda have a greater chance of passage than other proposals?

There is some reason to think they do. Presidents play an important role in the legislative process. The bills they initiate should have a greater chance of becoming law than the bills members of Congress initiate.[2] In the first place, they are unlikely to be vetoed. Edwards, Barrett, and Peake (1997) found that a substantial portion of the potentially significant legislation that did not pass failed because of vetoes or the threat of a veto. Of the important bills passed in postwar Congresses, identified by David Mayhew (1991, 1995), only eleven were passed over a president's veto. The president's role in the final stage of the legislative process magnifies his importance in the overall process.

In addition, congressional proponents of any bill must contend with the bicameral nature of the U.S. Congress. They must pass a bill not only in the chamber in which they serve but in the other chamber as well. If we are correct regarding the president's advantages in agenda setting, we should find that the president's proposals are more likely than congressional initiatives to achieve agenda status in *both* houses. So, even though he does not dominate the legislative process, the president is the single most important actor in the process (Bond and Fleisher 1990; Edwards 1989; Jones 1994). He adds persuasive potential on behalf of his initiatives that is not present for other legislation.

Several hypotheses follow from our theorizing about presidential agenda setting. Because of the president's advantages in influencing the congressional agenda, it follows that we should expect that *the president's most important proposals almost always find a place on the congressional agenda*. Equally important, because the service the president provides Congress is useful to whichever party is in the majority and because the incentives the president uses to encourage members to consider his proposals apply across party lines, it follows that *the president should succeed in obtaining agenda status for his major proposals no matter which party controls Congress*. Thus, the president may lose a large percentage of the

---

2. It is important to note that we are examining bills the president *initiates* rather than bills he just supports. There is a significant difference between the two. Presidential initiatives are part of the president's program, legislation he can claim as his legacy.

votes on which he takes a stand at the final stage of the legislative process, but he almost always "wins" at the agenda-setting stage.

Given Congress's ability to set its own agenda, however, it also follows that the president will not dominate Congress's agenda of potentially significant proposals. Instead, *the president's proposals will make up a modest portion of the congressional agenda of significant proposals.*

As noted earlier, presidents not only want Congress to consider their proposals but also want to limit the competing proposals with which they must deal. One implication of Congress's ability to set its own agenda is that the extent to which the president's proposals comprise the congressional agenda varies. The president's ability to influence the legislative process depends to a large degree on the partisan makeup of Congress (Bond and Fleisher 1990; Edwards 1989). As his party's leader, the president should be more successful in influencing the congressional agenda when his political party is in the majority in Congress. It is the majority, especially in the House, that has the ultimate power to control the agenda.

Conversely, when the president's party is in the minority in Congress, the majority party leadership has little incentive to defer to him. Instead, it has substantial incentives to develop its own proposals to counter the president's as well as proposals in areas in which the president opposes legislative action. It is here that the congressional majority may try to appeal to the public on behalf of its own agenda and perhaps embarrass the president by forcing him to oppose popular measures. In addition, the president may act strategically and not provide drafts of proposals because of fear that the majority party will exploit these proposals as a focus of criticism. Some examples of such strategic behavior include the Clinton administration's lack of specific proposals on welfare reform in 1995 and on Social Security financing reform in 1999.

This line of thinking raises questions about how divided government affects agenda setting. Typically, research on divided government has focused on its influence on the passage of significant legislation, with some authors finding that the legislative process continues to move forward regardless of whether the government is divided (Jones 1994; Mayhew 1991) and others reporting that divided government inhibits the passage of important bills (Edwards, Barrett, and Peake 1997; Kelly 1993a, 1993b). No one has examined systematically the impact of divided government at earlier stages of the legislative process, especially on agenda setting.

Because of the importance of party leadership to agenda setting, it follows that *when the president belongs to the majority party in Congress, presidential initiatives constitute a larger percentage of the bills on the congressional agenda than when the government is divided.* Conversely, when the president belongs to the minority party, we expect to find a larger percentage of congressional initiatives on the congressional agenda than when the government is unified.

A related concern is the variability of presidential agenda setting within a term of office. All the presidents in our study have been weakened by their party's losses in midterm congressional elections, which emboldens the opposition party in Congress under divided government to make policy initiatives (Jones 1994, 292). In addition, the White House may run short of time, energy, and ideas as the president's term runs its course (Light 1991, 17–18, 40–46, 102). Therefore, we expect to find that *the congressional agenda consists of a larger percentage of presidential initiatives during the first two years of a presidential term than during the third and fourth years.*

Once on the congressional agenda, presidential initiatives have the advantage of the president's persuasive resources behind them and are not subject to the president's veto. We therefore expect that *presidential initiatives are more likely to become law than are congressional initiatives.*

This influence is mitigated by party circumstances. Presidential initiatives in times of divided government typically face significant opposition in Congress. As we said, we expect these initiatives to make up a smaller portion of the congressional agenda than when the government is unified. It is also reasonable to expect that presidential initiatives are less likely to pass either or both houses when they face a Congress dominated by the opposition party. Therefore, we expect that *the bills presidents initiate are more likely to pass under unified government than under divided government.*

Collecting the Data

To investigate presidential agenda setting and its consequences for potentially significant legislation, we first had to determine (1) what constitutes a presidential initiative; (2) the agenda of each house of Congress; (3) potentially significant legislation on the agenda; and (4) bills that passed and those that did not among the potentially significant legislative proposals on the congressional agenda.

Our first step was to identify presidential initiatives. To do so, we searched through the relevant volumes of Congressional Quarterly's yearly *Almanacs,* yearly congressional reviews in the *New York Times* and *Washington Post,* and relevant commentaries on Congress during the forty-four years from 1953 through 1996. We were especially alert to the possibility that the absence in any source of extensive treatment of an initiative resulted from its failure to achieve agenda status in Congress. It is unlikely that a presidential proposal of potentially significant legislation would not have been mentioned in at least one of these sources.

Our search for presidential initiatives was more extensive than that of researchers whose purposes differed from ours. For example, Mark Peterson (1990) limited his study to a sample of the domestic legislation listed in CQ's Presidential Box Scores from 1953 to 1984.[3] Patrick Fett (1992) examined only bills mentioned by the president in 1977 and 1981, potentially overlooking initiatives that did not receive presidential mention.

Regarding the composition of the congressional agenda, we adopted the decision rule of Edwards, Barrett, and Peake (1997) that if a committee or subcommittee held hearings on a bill, we counted it as being on the congressional agenda. This decision rule is similar to Mayhew's suggestion that "for any Congress, an agenda could be assembled for research purposes out of proposals that make it to the 'much talked about' stage" (1991, 36).

To decide whether legislation was significant, we focused on bills that had or, if they had passed, would have had the most impact on public policy. Several thousand bills are introduced each Congress, and hearings may be held on hundreds of them, but only a small percentage of these bills represent potentially significant changes in existing law.

Mayhew limits his analysis to "important" legislation that he identified in making two sweeps through recent history (1991, chap. 3). Edwards, Barrett, and Peake (1997) follow a similar approach, agreeing with Mayhew that "innovative and consequential" are at the heart of what most political observers mean when they term legislation "important." We can combine Mayhew's (1991, 1995) lists of significant legislation that passed with Edwards, Barrett, and Peake's (1997) list of potentially significant legislation that failed to pass to create a master list of potentially significant legislation on the congressional agenda.[4]

---

3. Because CQ stopped publishing the box score after 1975, Peterson applied similar criteria to that previously employed by CQ to create his own box scores for 1976 through 1984.

4. Some proposals made both by members of Congress and the president are symbolic gestures to satisfy constituents or to make rhetorical points. Edwards, Barrett, and Peake (1997) omit such bills from their list of potentially significant legislation. This meets our needs as well, because our concern is with the agenda status of legislation that the president seriously proposed rather than legislation that failed to achieve agenda status because no one, including those who proposed it, ever took it seriously.

From those lists we omit treaties and the four failed Supreme Court nominations in the Edwards et al. list (Mayhew did not include nominations), because our purposes are different from theirs. We are primarily interested in investigating the president's influence on the congressional agenda and the competition for agenda space. Because treaties and nominations can be proposed only by the president and acted upon only by the Senate, they are not useful tests of agenda setting. Such measures virtually always achieve agenda status and cannot be compared to similar proposals by members of Congress.

There were a total of 865 potentially significant, seriously proposed bills during the 1953–1996 period.[5] We then coded each piece of potentially significant legislation as either a presidential or a congressional initiative, a task made easier by our initial identification of presidential initiatives. If the president introduced the original draft bill or a detailed set of proposals that formed the basis for congressional hearings or other congressional action, the bill was coded as a presidential initiative. Congressional initiatives are bills introduced by members of Congress without a request from the president and without the assistance of the White House in the drafting process.

Whoever initiated the consideration of an issue in Congress was credited with the proposal, even if the original legislation was subjected to substantial alteration. In agenda setting (as opposed to final passage), whoever decides what is debated is more important than who wins the debate. For example, in the 90th Congress, President Lyndon Johnson introduced a bill to ban age discrimination in employment. The version of the bill that Congress passed contained only portions of the president's proposal, but

---

5. Within each Congress, these bills represent different issues so that a similar bill in the House and in the Senate in one Congress is counted only once. In a few cases the coding of bills was hampered by the use of omnibus bills. To determine which bills to include when multiple bills were combined into larger omnibus bills, we examined their components to see if they merited inclusion in our data set. As a result, we included three bills in our data set for the 103d Congress that eventually were part of the 1993 Omnibus Budget-Reconciliation Act. We also included the entire act because it represented a major departure in fiscal policy. At various points in the legislative process, Congress considered each of these bills on their own merits. In the 104th Congress, under similar circumstances, however, we included three bills that were eventually combined into a larger budget reconciliation bill, but we excluded the reconciliation bill itself. Without the provisions from the other three bills, the reconciliation bill did not warrant inclusion on its on merits.

it was his initiative that led Congress to consider the issue. If two substantially different proposals that dealt with the same issue were introduced at approximately the same time, the proposal that Congress acted upon (and which usually was reported) was included in this study and the initiator of that proposal was given credit.

In some cases, it was impossible to determine who initiated action on an issue for several reasons: the president and Congress simultaneously proposed legislation; the president originated a bill in one house and a member of Congress initiated a similar bill in the other house at about the same time; or the president and a member of Congress proposed different bills that the relevant committee combined into one measure. Because of such problems, thirty bills were excluded from the analysis.[6] Of the remaining 835 bills, 287 were coded as presidential initiatives and 548 as congressional initiatives.

To determine whether a bill passed, we examined the bills on the agenda that became law by the end of each Congress. We did not use individual years or sessions because a bill's failure to pass in the first session of a Congress is neither determinative of the eventual outcome nor critical to the bill's impact.

Analyzing the Data

In analyzing the data, we hoped to answer four questions central to understanding the president's role in congressional agenda setting: (1) Is the president successful in obtaining agenda space for his initiatives? (2) How much of Congress's agenda is made up of presidential initiatives? (3) Under what conditions are presidential initiatives most likely to comprise a large percentage of the congressional agenda? (4) Are presidential initiatives more likely to pass than congressional initiatives?

---

6. Examples of initiatives proposed by both the president and members of Congress include (1) the Area Redevelopment Act of 1961, which was introduced by Sen. Paul H. Douglas, but written with the assistance of Kennedy staff members; (2) legislation to tighten drug regulation following the thalidomide tragedy, introduced by President John Kennedy, which was eventually superseded by a similar congressional proposal; and (3) legislation concerning public financing of congressional elections, introduced by President Carter on March 22, 1977, even though a similar bill had been introduced March 16 in the House by Rep. Phillip Burton and in the Senate by five senators on March 7.

Presidential Success in Securing Agenda Space

We have hypothesized that the president's advantages in influencing the congressional agenda will result in the president's most important proposals almost always obtaining a place on the congressional agenda, no matter which party controls Congress. Below is a list of presidential initiatives that did *not* receive at least a hearing in a committee or subcommittee from 1953 to 1996. We were able to identify only seven such measures over the period of our study.

To overhaul the nation's unemployment compensation system
      (1963–1964)
To create a national health insurance and health plan (1971–1972)
To create health block grants (1975–1976)
To create a government energy corporation (1975–1976)
To create child nutrition block grants (1975–1976)
To limit where busing for school integration is required (1975–1976)
To dismantle the Department of Education (1981–1982)

President Gerald Ford made four of these proposals. Unfortunately for him, in the period just after the Watergate scandal, Congress was in no mood to accommodate the president. *The results are clear: the president can almost always place potentially significant legislation on the agenda of Congress.* Indeed, from 1935 to 1996 the president obtained agenda status for 97.6 percent of his legislative initiatives!

Although the items in the list above do not allow us to infer either that the president dominated the congressional agenda or that his legislation ultimately passed, they do show that Congress is at least willing to give the president a hearing on his major legislative initiatives. Whatever success the president may achieve at later stages of the policy-making process is built on his success in obtaining a place on the congressional agenda for his proposals.

At first glance our results may seem somewhat inconsistent with Peterson's (1990, 151–59, 182–84) findings that Congress was "inactive" on 14 percent of "major" proposals, on 16 percent of the "most consequential" proposals, and on 20 percent of "large/new initiatives" (the proposals overlap). The differences in the findings result from different pools of legislation and potentially significant legislation and different definitions of congressional action. In addition to focusing on only a sample of domestic legislation during the 1953–1984 period, Peterson also used less restrictive criteria for inclusion as "major," "consequential," or "large/new" (1990, 323–24, 327) than did Mayhew and Edwards, Barrett, and Peake in their selection of significant and potentially significant legislation. Equally important, Peterson's study did not focus on agenda setting per se, so his definition of "inaction" includes instances of one house of Congress taking no action, even if the other did, and instances of a measure not reaching the floor of the parent body (82–83), even when hearings were held. This definition well served his purpose, which focused on outcomes, but it does not well represent agenda status. Therefore, it is not surprising that he found somewhat larger levels of inactivity than we did.

Fett (1992) examined *all* bills mentioned by the president in 1977 and 1981 and found that less than 20 percent came to a vote. His research differs from ours in that he did not limit his study to potentially significant legislation, nor did he focus on legislation obtaining agenda status. He also did not determine what happened to a bill during the second year of a Congress.

Presidential Proposals' Composition of the Congressional Agenda

Given the legislature's ability to set its own agenda, we have hypothesized that the president will not dominate Congress's agenda of potentially significant proposals but instead will provide only a modest portion of the congressional agenda of significant proposals. To investigate the degree of presidential dominance of the congressional agenda requires comparing the numbers of presidential and congressional initiatives on Congress's agenda. Table 6–1 presents an overview of the 825 different bills on the congressional agenda.[7] The data show that the president initiated an average of 12.7 potentially significant bills per Congress that achieved agenda status in at least one house of Congress from 1953 to 1996. Members of Congress, on the other hand, initiated an average of 24.7 potentially significant bills per Congress. Based on these numbers, the president initi-

---

7. This table excludes the seven presidential initiatives listed on page 120 and three congressional initiatives that did not receive a hearing in either house. These three bills proposed permitting manufacturers to fix the minimum retail prices of their national brand goods (1965–1966); amending the Constitution to abolish the electoral college (1971–1972); and exempting 90 percent of businesses from Occupational Safety and Health Administration restrictions (1979–1980).

Table 6–1

Number of Potentially Significant Presidential and Congressional Initiatives

Congress	Years	Presidential Initiatives	Congressional Initiatives	Total Bills	Percent Presidential
83d	1953–54	9	14	23	39.1%
84th	1955–56	6	16	22	27.3
85th	1957–58	11	17	28	39.3
86th	1959–60	4	17	21	19
87th	1961–62	24	11	35	68.6
88th	1963–64	21	19	40	52.5
89th	1965–66	30	22	52	57.7
90th	1967–68	19	15	34	55.9
91st	1969–70	16	23	39	41
92d	1971–72	17	37	54	31.5
93d	1973–74	17	39	56	30.4
94th	1975–76	15	40	55	27.2
95th	1977–78	19	21	40	47.5
96th	1979–80	17	18	35	48.6
97th	1981–82	11	25	36	30.6
98th	1983–84	10	25	35	28.6
99th	1985–86	5	27	32	15.6
100th	1987–88	2	35	37	5.4
101st	1989–90	8	31	39	20.5
102d	1991–92	4	31	35	11.4
103d	1993–94	15	22	37	40.5
104th	1995–96	0	40	40	0
Total Bills		280	545	825	33.9%
Average Bills/ Congress		12.7	24.7	37.5	

ated an average of 33.9 percent of the total number of potentially significant bills on the congressional agenda.

Most bills were acted on in both houses, but 47 presidential initiatives and 152 congressional initiatives attained agenda status in only one; therefore, the N for the total number of bills (825) is greater than that for either chamber. Table 6–2 shows that presidential initiatives made up 35.4 percent of the 725 agenda items in the House and a virtually identical 35.5 percent of the 726 agenda issues in the Senate.

As we hypothesized, the president does not "dominate" the congressional agenda. Although we will see that there is substantial variance around the mean, presidential initiatives, on average, make up just a little more than one-third of the congressional agenda of potentially significant legislation. Members of Congress initiate most of the potentially significant legislation on the congressional agenda.

Table 6–2
Presidential and Congressional Initiatives in the House and Senate

	Presidential Initiatives	Congressional Initiatives	Total Bills	Percent Presidential
House	257	468	725	35.4%
Senate	256	470	726	35.3

Variance in the Composition of the Congressional Agenda

The data in Table 6–1 show that there is considerable variance around the mean in the extent to which presidential initiatives comprise the congressional agenda. What explains this variance? We have hypothesized that presidential initiatives will make up a greater portion of the congressional agenda under unified government than under divided government. We also expect that presidential initiatives will constitute a larger percentage of the bills on the congressional agenda in the earlier years of a president's term.

The Impact of Divided Government. In Table 6–3, we can see that the president initiates an average of 24 percent of the potentially significant legislation on the House agenda under divided government and 56.7 percent under unified government. In the Senate, the results are similar: the president initiates 24.1 percent of the potentially significant legislation under divided government but 47 percent under unified government.[8] There is little question, then, that the president initiates a much larger percentage of the bills on the congressional agenda under unified government than under divided government. (To determine whether the observed difference between sample proportions in our tables could occur by chance in the populations from which the samples were selected, we used the methods described by George Bohrnstedt and David Knoke [1988, 198–200] regarding significance testing with proportions.)

When the president belongs to the majority party in Congress, either his fellow partisans are more willing to defer to him in setting the congressional agenda or both the president and his party's congressional leaders

---

8. The difference between the percentage of bills the president initiates under unified government in the House and in the Senate can be attributed to the three sessions of Congress in which the Republicans controlled the Senate during the 1980s. Unlike Democratic presidents who initiated a large number of bills under unified government, President Ronald Reagan initiated only a small number of bills in the Republican-controlled Senate.

Table 6–3
Impact of Divided Government on Presidential Initiatives

	House					
Party Control	Presidential Initiatives	Congressional Initiatives	Total Bills	Bills Per Congress	Percent Presidential	
Divided	113	358	471	33.6	24.0%	
						t=8.84*
Unified	144	110	254	31.8	56.7	

Chi-Square: 77.3 (p<.05)
*significant at .01 probability level

	Senate					
Party Control	Presidential Initiatives	Congressional Initiatives	Total Bills	Bills Per Congress	Percent Presidential	
Divided	90	283	373	33.9	24.1%	
						t=6.54*
Unified	166	187	353	32.1	47.0	

Chi-Square: 41.7 (p<.05)
*significant at .01 probability level

want to pursue similar agendas based on shared partisan preferences. Thus, as we hypothesized, the president is in a far better position to set the congressional agenda if he has a partisan advantage in Congress. We should also note, however, that even when the president is a member of the minority party, he still is able to play a significant role in congressional agenda setting. White House initiatives account for about one-fourth of the congressional agenda under divided government.

Because all but one of the cases of divided government in this study consist of a Republican president and a generally more liberal and activist Democratic Congress, it is possible that the difference between presidential initiatives under divided and unified government results from comparing nonactivist Republican presidents during divided government with activist Democratic presidents during unified government. This hypothesis can be rejected for two reasons.

First, during the three sessions of Congress of the Reagan administration in which the White House and the Senate were controlled by the Republicans and the House by the Democrats, the president proposed an average of 8.3 initiatives in the unified Senate and only 5.7 in the divided House. In other words, the president was 46 percent more likely to initiate proposals in the chamber controlled by his co-partisans than in the chamber controlled by the other party.

Second, the experience of the Clinton administration under divided government supports our argument. Under unified government in his first two years in office, Clinton proposed a number of significant pieces of legislation, including major health care reform, a crime bill, and the North American Free Trade Association agreement. Confronted with the Republican 104th Congress and its Contract with America, Clinton made no significant proposals in his next two years in office, as we see in Table 6–1. A more definitive test of the hypothesis must await additional cases of Democratic presidents facing Republican Congresses.

The Impact of Time Within a Term. We also hypothesized that the congressional agenda will consist of a larger percentage of presidential initiatives during the first two years of a presidential term than during the second two years. In Table 6–4 we compare the time periods.[9]

Table 6–4
Impact of Time Within Term on Presidential Initiatives

	House				
Time Period	Presidential Initiatives	Congressional Initiatives	Total Bills	Percent Presidential	
First Half	150	215	365	41.1%	
					t=3.16*
Second Half	107	253	360	29.7	

Chi-Square: 10.3 (p<.05)
*significant at .01 probability level

	Senate				
Time Period	Presidential Initiatives	Congressional Initiatives	Total Bills	Percent Presidential	
First Half	153	225	378	40.5%	
					t=3.11*
Second Half	103	245	348	29.6	

Chi-Square: 9.4 (p<.05)
*significant at .01 probability level

9. As a result of the unusual circumstances surrounding the Kennedy assassination during the 88th Congress and President Richard Nixon's resignation during the 94th Congress, we investigated whether including these terms changed the results. They did not.

As the data in Table 6–4 demonstrate, there is some support for the contention that presidential initiatives make up a larger percentage of the congressional agenda during the first half of a president's term. The differences are eleven percentage points in each chamber, and they meet the conventional standards of statistical significance.

Because we have found that divided government influences presidential initiatives, we must control for its effects here. We can see in Table 6–5 that in both the House and Senate the hypothesized impact of the period within a presidential term occurs only under conditions of divided government. Under unified government, both the White House and Congress offer fewer initiatives in the second half of a term. Congressional ini-

Table 6–5
Impact of Time Within Term and Divided Government on Presidential Initiatives

	House				
Time Period	Presidential Initiatives	Congressional Initiatives	Total Bills	Percent Presidential	
First Half Unified	89	76	165	53.9%	
					t=1.22
Second Half Unified	55	34	89	61.8	
First Half Divided	61	139	200	30.5	
					t=2.83*
Second Half Divided	52	219	271	19.2	

Chi-Square: 85.1 (p<.05)
*significant at .01 probability level

	Senate				
Time Period	Presidential Initiatives	Congressional Initiatives	Total Bills	Percent Presidential	
First Half Unified	105	122	227	46.3%	
					t=.38
Second Half Unified	61	65	126	48.4	
First Half Divided	48	103	151	31.8	
					t=2.80*
Second Half Divided	42	180	222	18.9	

Chi-Square: 48.2 (p<.05)
*significant at .01 probability level

tiatives decrease more rapidly than do those of the president, however, so the percentages of the congressional agenda reflecting presidential initiatives increase slightly rather than decline.

Under divided government, the president also decreases the number of his initiatives, but Congress substantially increases its already high level of initiatives in the second half of a presidential term. This increase may be due to the congressional majority's positioning itself for the next election. As a result, the president's proposals make up a smaller percentage of the congressional agenda in the second half of a president's term under divided government.

Success of Presidential Proposals

We have determined that presidential initiatives make up a significant portion of the congressional agenda, particularly under conditions of unified government. But what happens to these proposals once they obtain agenda status? We hypothesized that presidential initiatives are more likely to pass than congressional initiatives, especially under unified government.

In Table 6–6 we can see that presidential initiatives are much more likely than congressional initiatives to become law. Forty-two percent of the major presidential legislative initiatives that make it onto the congressional agenda become law, while only 25 percent of congressional initiatives achieve that status.

We also see that the average success rates for the forty-four years of our study mask a substantial variation over time. We have hypothesized that the president is more likely to succeed under unified government. When we separate the success rates of presidential and congressional initiatives of Congresses during divided and unified government, we find that the success rate for presidential initiatives rises to 53 percent under unified government. Because only 20 percent of congressional initiatives became law under unified government, presidential initiatives enjoy a thirty-three-percentage-point advantage over congressional initiatives. Under divided government, however, the success rate for presidential initiatives falls to 28 percent. The success rate for congressional initiatives actually rises to 26 percent, so there is no real difference between the success of presidential and congressional initiatives under divided government.

The surprising difference between the success rates for congressional initiatives under unified and divided governments can be explained by the very large percentage that passed during the eight years of the presidencies of Richard Nixon and Gerald Ford. In fact, fifty (37 percent) of the

Table 6–6

Presidential and Congressional Initiatives that Became Law

Years	Presidential Initiatives			Congressional Initiatives			Difference
	Initiatives	Became Law	Percent	Initiatives	Became Law	Percent	
1953–54	9	5	56%	14	4	29%	+27
1955–56	6	2	33	16	3	19	+14
1957–58	11	7	64	17	3	18	+46
1959–60	4	0	0	17	3	18	−18
1961–62	24	13	54	11	0	0	+54
1963–64	21	9	43	19	3	16	+27
1965–66	30	17	57	22	5	23	+34
1967–68	19	13	68	15	2	13	+55
1969–70	16	4	25	23	10	44	−19
1971–72	17	4	24	37	11	30	−6
1973–74	17	5	29	39	17	44	−15
1975–76	15	2	13	40	12	30	−17
1977–78	19	7	37	21	4	19	+18
1979–80	17	9	53	18	1	6	+47
1981–82	11	3	27	25	5	20	+7
1983–84	10	0	0	25	2	8	−8
1985–86	5	1	20	27	7	26	−6
1987–88	2	1	50	35	9	26	+24
1989–90	8	3	38	31	5	16	+22
1991–92	4	3	75	31	3	8	+67
1993–94	15	9	60	22	9	41	+19
1995–96	0	0	0	40	16	40	− 40
Total	280	117	42%	545	134	25%	+17 t=4.86*
Unified	154	82	53%	142	28	20%	+33 t=6.35*
Divided	126	35	28%	403	106	26%	+2 t=.43

*significant at .01 probability level

congressional initiatives that passed during the forty-four years of our study did so in these eight years.[10] During that same period, only fifteen major presidential initiatives became law. The two Republican presidents, especially in the unusual context of the years 1973 through 1976, ended up supporting many Democratic congressional initiatives, including a large number of environmental protection and social welfare measures.

---

10. The opposition party is energized to take initiatives under divided government, and it does. There are twelve more congressional initiatives on major legislation per Congress in the House when the majority is of the party in opposition to the president than under unified government, and nine more per Congress in the Senate.

Without the Nixon-Ford years, the success rates for congressional initiatives in divided and unified government are nearly identical, 21 percent and 20 percent, respectively. Major congressional legislative initiatives, then, almost always face substantial obstacles to becoming law.

What explains the disparity between the ultimate success rates of presidential and congressional initiatives? We can begin to explore this question by asking what occurs within each house. The data in Tables 6–7 and 6–8 show that congressional initiatives *within* each chamber pass at high rates, especially in divided government. Moreover, congressional initiatives are *just as likely* as presidential initiatives to pass each chamber. The results are similar in each house. Under unified government, about two-thirds of

Table 6–7

Presidential and Congressional Initiatives that Passed the House

Years	*Presidential Initiatives*			*Congressional Initiatives*			
	Initiatives	*Became Law*	*Percent*	*Initiatives*	*Became Law*	*Percent*	*Difference*
1953–54	9	6	67%	9	5	56%	+11
1955–56	5	3	60	11	5	46	+14
1957–58	11	8	73	14	6	43	+30
1959–60	4	2	50	15	9	60	−10
1961–62	23	14	61	6	2	33	+28
1963–64	20	10	50	12	6	50	0
1965–66	25	21	84	20	10	50	+34
1967–68	18	15	83	9	4	44	+39
1969–70	14	9	64	21	16	76	−12
1971–72	17	8	47	33	20	61	−14
1973–74	17	7	41	36	26	72	−31
1975–76	14	5	36	40	26	65	−29
1977–78	18	10	56	20	12	60	−4
1979–80	17	13	76	13	5	39	+37
1981–82	8	5	63	18	10	56	+7
1983–84	6	1	17	19	15	79	−62
1985–86	3	3	100	24	19	79	+21
1987–88	2	1	50	33	21	64	−14
1989–90	8	7	88	26	20	77	+11
1991–92	4	3	75	28	19	68	+7
1993–94	14	10	71	21	14	67	+4
1995–96	0	0	0	40	27	68	−68
Total	257	161	63%	468	297	63%	0 t=0
Unified	144	99	69%	110	58	53%	+16 t=2.67*
Divided	113	62	55%	358	239	67%	−12 t=2.4*

*significant at .01 probability level

Table 6–8
Presidential and Congressional Initiatives that Passed the Senate

	Presidential Initiatives			Congressional Initiatives			
Years	Initiatives	Became Law	Percent	Initiatives	Became Law	Percent	Difference
1953–54	9	5	56%	13	8	62%	–6
1955–56	6	3	50	14	5	36	+14
1957–58	9	8	89	16	10	63	+26
1959–60	4	1	25	15	11	73	– 48
1961–62	23	16	70	8	3	38	+32
1963–64	18	15	83	16	6	38	+45
1965–66	29	21	72	18	8	44	+28
1967–68	18	14	78	12	6	50	+28
1969–70	16	6	38	22	15	68	–30
1971–72	14	6	43	30	25	83	– 40
1973–74	15	9	60	36	32	89	–29
1975–76	14	5	36	34	26	77	– 41
1977–78	15	8	53	19	13	68	–15
1979–80	15	11	73	15	5	33	+40
1981–82	10	3	30	24	13	54	–24
1983–84	10	3	30	22	8	36	–6
1985–86	5	2	40	24	17	71	–31
1987–88	1	1	100	29	18	62	+38
1989–90	8	4	50	29	17	59	+15
1991–92	3	3	100	26	13	50	+50
1993–94	14	10	71	16	11	69	+2
1995–96	0	0	0	32	20	63	–63
Total	256	154	60%	470	290	62%	–2 t=.54
Unified	166	108	65%	187	98	52%	+13 t=2.55*
Divided	90	46	51%	283	192	68%	–17 t=2.83*

*significant at .01 probability level

presidential initiatives pass, while just over half pass under divided government. The results are the mirror image of the record for congressional initiatives, with two-thirds passing under divided government and just over half passing under unified government.

Thus, the party with the congressional majority succeeds most of the time in passing legislation in each chamber. Congressional initiatives are not disadvantaged in passing individual chambers. Congressional initiatives, unlike presidential initiatives, do not often become law, however. How can we explain the fact that presidential and congressional initiatives pass each chamber of Congress at similar rates, but presidential initiatives are much more likely to become law?

One possibility is that congressional bills that pass one chamber do not pass in the other while presidential initiatives pass both. The data in Table 6–9 show the differences between presidential and congressional initiatives. Eighty-two percent of presidential initiatives that pass the House also pass the Senate, compared to 76 percent of congressional initiatives. Similarly, 86 percent of presidential initiatives that pass the Senate also pass the House, compared to 78 percent of congressional initiatives.

Thus, the president has a modest advantage in obtaining passage of his initiatives in both houses of Congress. The most important reason for this advantage is the president's ability to exercise his role as party leader to achieve agenda status for his initiatives in *both* houses (only 17 percent of presidential initiatives do not attain agenda status in both houses, whereas 28 percent of congressional initiatives fail to make the agenda of the second chamber). This presidential advantage is most likely to occur during unified government, when his party's congressional leadership, which controls the agendas, typically supports presidential initiatives. At the same time, congressional initiatives under unified government are likely to come from the opposition party, which will experience more difficulty in obtaining agenda space. As we have noted, if legislation is not on the agenda, it cannot pass.

Nevertheless, the differences in the rates at which presidential and congressional initiatives pass both houses of Congress are not large enough to explain the entire seventeen-percentage-point difference between the ultimate success of presidential and congressional initiatives. We must turn to other elements of presidential-congressional relations for the rest of the explanation.

Under unified government, the president's initiatives enjoy a high level of success because of the support of his party, which has a majority in each house. Congressional initiatives under unified government pass at a low

Table 6–9
Initiatives Passing Both Houses of Congress

	Presidential Initiatives	*Congressional Initiatives*
Passed the House and also the Senate	82%	76%
Divided Government	71	76
Unified Government	89	76
Passed the Senate and also the House	86%	78%
Divided Government	82	79
Unified Government	88	73

rate, however, because the majority defers to the White House in proposing initiatives and the minority, which *does* propose potentially significant legislation, lacks the votes to pass them. Over the forty-four years of our study, only forty-four congressional initiatives passed both houses during unified government. The president successfully vetoed four of these. For example, during the 96th Congress, President Carter pocket vetoed the 1981 State, Justice, and Commerce appropriations bill because it contained a provision that would have prevented the Justice Department from bringing lawsuits that could lead to court-ordered school busing for desegregation. The appropriations bill was eventually passed without the antibusing provision because of Carter's veto. Thus, there is a substantial gap between the success of presidential and congressional initiatives in becoming law.

Under divided government, presidential initiatives do less well than under unified government because of the opposition of the majority party. Congressional initiatives, which come from the majority party under divided government, pass at a higher rate than under unified government. However, the opposition of the president is an important impediment to congressional initiatives becoming law, especially under divided government. During the period under study, the president successfully vetoed 54 of the 181 of the congressional initiatives that passed both houses of Congress under divided government—*30 percent of the total.* For example, during 1991 and 1992, President George Bush vetoed a number of bills involving issues such as tax increases, China's most-favored-nation trade status, urban aid, family and medical leave, campaign finance, and voter registration. Similarly, in the 104th Congress, President Clinton vetoed several Republican initiatives, including bills regarding product liability and late-term abortions. (A number of bills may have also failed to pass the second house because the threat of a presidential veto discouraged the investment of time, energy, and political capital necessary to obtain passage.)

Under divided government, then, presidential initiatives typically cannot obtain congressional support in both houses, and the president vetoes a large percentage of congressional initiatives. Neither the president nor Congress can pass its initiatives, and neither side enjoys an advantage in seeing its proposals become law.

Conclusion

Can the president influence Congress's legislative agenda? The answer is straightforward: the president is very successful in obtaining agenda space for his potentially significant legislative proposals. This stage of the legislative process rarely poses an insurmountable barrier to his ultimate success in establishing new public policies. At the same time, the president does not dominate the congressional agenda, even under unified government, when the majorities in Congress are most likely to defer to the White House's lead. Congress is quite capable of taking its own initiatives and frequently does, especially during divided government.

Setting the congressional agenda is the prerequisite for obtaining passage of any legislation. Once on the agenda, 42 percent of presidential initiatives become law, a rate two-thirds greater than that for congressional initiatives. The White House is more likely than congressional initiators to obtain agenda status and approval in both houses of Congress. In addition, presidential initiatives do not face the considerable hurdle of the presidential veto.

The president's advantage over Congress in the success of initiatives is restricted to unified government, however. His initiatives do not enjoy special advantages in the face of the opposition of a congressional majority. As Edwards (1989) and Bond and Fleisher (1990) have argued, the key to success for presidential proposals is the size and support of his political party in each house. There is no special magic associated with the presidential initiatives. Congress displays no exceptional deference toward the president, and the president demonstrates no unusual persuasiveness with Congress.

The lack of special advantage for the president's initiatives magnifies the importance of presidential agenda setting. Once on the agenda, the president's proposals have a reasonable chance of passing. Although it remains important to understand the president's congressional support on floor votes, we have found that we must understand the agenda-setting process if we are to truly explain the president's success in Congress.

CHAPTER 7

Hostile Partners: The President, Congress, and Lawmaking in the Partisan 1990s

Barbara Sinclair

Barbara Sinclair's chapter, "Hostile Partners: The President, Congress, and Lawmaking in the Partisan 1990s," looks at interactions between Congress and the president at several points in the lawmaking process. Much of the quantitative analysis of presidential-congressional relations has focused on roll call votes and vetoes. What is not taken into account is what happens earlier in the legislative process. In the U.S. Congress the legislative process is decentralized, involving the participation of numerous actors in different institutional settings, such as the various committees and subcommittees in both the House and Senate, floor action in each chamber, and conference committees. The Constitution requires not only that there be agreement across both chambers of the bicameral legislature, but that there be a working partnership between Congress and the president. Over the past several decades, we have witnessed significant changes in the way this complex process works. As a result, simple textbook descriptions are less likely to apply to policy making in Congress. In a previous book, Sinclair (1997) described how the changes in the legislative process produced what she characterized as "unorthodox lawmaking." In this chapter, she continues to explore how and why the legislative process has changed, focusing on shifts in the working partnership between the president and Congress, especially the effects of increased partisan conflict.

Sinclair argues that the growth in partisanship has made legislating more difficult, and she presents evidence that more partisan conflict is showing up at several different stages of the process. Her analysis also demonstrates that party control of government matters. Consistent with Edwards and Barrett's chapter, Sinclair finds that the president has an advantage in setting the congressional agenda, at least under unified government. But, since the end of World War II, divided government has been more common than unified government. Until the Republicans captured control of Congress in 1994, divided government meant that Democratic majorities in Congress had to respond to the agendas of Republican presidents. In the 1970s and 1980s Democratic senators and representatives began proposing a congressional agenda. Over time, the behavior of congressional leaders changed, and they have now become more prominent agenda setters. In terms of the production of major legislation, Sinclair's findings show that under unified government, committees and conferences are more likely to report legislation the president supports; under divided government there is more disagreement. Although more interbranch cooperation takes place under unified government, the Senate filibuster gives the minority a powerful tool to block the majority from adopting its preferred legislation. Under divided government, the majority also must contend with the threat and actual use of the presidential veto to block its legislative agenda. Sinclair notes that in the intensely partisan environment in the 1980s and 1990s, relations between the president and Congress became more hostile. This environment prompted presidents and congressional leaders to adopt more aggressive strategies to attain their policy goals.

When a Republican House of Representatives impeaches a Democratic president on an almost strictly party line vote, few observers would contest that partisanship has come to play a more central and perhaps even fundamentally different role in American politics. Certainly the bitterly divided, stridently partisan House that Americans saw on their television screens in December 1998 bore little resemblance to the collegial body of fluid alignments depicted in the congressional scholarship of the 1950s, 1960s, and 1970s. How typical is such partisanship in Congress? How has it affected the policy process and policy outputs? Specifically, what has been the impact on the president's role in and capacity to influence the legislative process?

Legislating in the American System: Structure and Preference

A systematic answer to these questions requires a brief explication of what enacting legislation at the national level entails, structurally and politically, and an analysis of how party and partisanship may facilitate or hinder the process.

The structure of the American national government makes legislating difficult (Brady and Volen 1997; Jones 1994). To enact legislation, a majority of both houses of Congress must approve it. Increasingly, approval in the Senate requires a supermajority of sixty votes (Binder and Smith 1997; Sinclair 1997). Once it has passed both houses in identical form, the president must approve the legislation. If he exercises his veto, a two-thirds majority in both chambers is required to override the veto and enact the bill into law.

The degree of difficulty of enacting legislation in any given case depends on the preferences of the relevant actors—members of Congress and the president. If all are agreed, the seemingly cumbersome process presents few obstacles, and legislation may fly through the process in days or even hours. However, the constitutionally specified fact that these actors are elected by different sets of voters and often at different times makes such agreement on a broad range of issues unlikely, whether within each chamber or between the chambers or between the branches. Those electoral arrangements also have worked against the development of a strong, centralized party system that, through control over nominations and election campaigns, would tie together the electoral fate of members of the same party, whether they are members of the House or the Senate or the president. Although the president is considered his party's leader, members of Congress are seldom likely to feel they owe their election directly to the president or that the president's success is the single most important determinant of their future reelection. The party system does not provide the president with great leverage vis-à-vis his fellow partisans in Congress (Bond and Fleisher 1990; Edwards 1989).

Nevertheless, even in our loose party system, members of a party do tend to have similar electoral interests, and these tend to translate into shared legislative preferences. The extent of shared legislative preferences has varied over time but, when substantial, has provided the basis for the cooperation within and across the chambers and branches that facilitates legislating (Rohde 1991; Sinclair 1995). The extent to which the two parties differ in their legislative preferences has also varied over time. The U.S. constitutional system makes it possible for one party to control the presidency and the other to command majorities in one or both houses of Congress, and, in fact, that situation frequently has been the case during the last half century. Cohesive and distinct parties whose members share legislative preferences within the party and disagree with the other party should make cooperation between the congressional majorities of one party and the president of another more difficult.

The president and members of Congress are, by assumption, goal-directed actors. Therefore, one would expect that when the environment in which they pursue their goals changes, their strategies would change as well. A change in the cohesiveness and distinctiveness of the parties would represent a major change in context. I will argue that during the period under consideration here, other environmental changes also occurred that called for—and elicited—new strategies.

In this chapter, I examine the structure of coalitions at several stages in the legislative process and how those coalitions have changed over time. Are coalitions more likely to be partisan in the 1990s, indicating greater disagreement between the parties in legislative preferences? What is the extent of presidential-congressional agreement and disagreement and how is it related to whether control is divided or unified and to partisanship? What are the roles of the president and of congressional leaders in setting the congressional agenda in the 1990s? What strategies are the major actors using to advance their legislative preferences and hinder those of their opponents? And, finally, what is the impact on outcomes, especially on the president's success in the legislative process?

To answer these questions, I look at the legislative process on major legislation in three Congresses of the 1990s and compare it with the legislative process in three selected Congresses from earlier decades. Specifically, I examine the 91st (1969–1970), 97th (1981–1982), 101st (1989–1990), and the 103d, 104th, and 105th Congresses (1993–1998). These include the first Congresses of Presidents Nixon, Reagan, Bush, and Clinton—the first Congress of a presidential term is generally thought to be a president's most productive—as well as the Republican Congresses of the 1990s. By reflecting a range in time and in the values of political variables, the data make possible a number of worthwhile comparisons. Major legislation is defined here as those measures that Congressional Quarterly lists as such, augmented by those measures on which there were key votes, again according to Congressional Quarterly.

The Changing Structure of Congressional Coalitions

If congressional rhetoric and highly aggregated voting scores are taken as indicators, partisanship is much higher in the Congresses of the 1990s than at any time during the last half century. Between 1990 and 1998 (the data do not include 1999) a majority of Democrats voted against a majority of Republicans on 59 percent of roll call votes in the House and on 57 percent in the Senate. During the 1970s, in contrast, Republican and Democratic majorities opposed each other on 37 percent of the recorded votes in the House and 42 percent in the Senate (CQWR, January 9,

1999, 93). To what extent does the higher partisanship permeate the legislative process? Have legislative battles become typically partisan? Is this the case in the Senate as well as in the House and in committees as well as on the floor?

The committee process on each major measure was examined in each house and categorized in one of three ways: as partisan, as reflecting another sort of split (for example, along constituency or ideological lines), or as reflecting either consensus or a bipartisan compromise.[1] As Table 7–1 shows, the committee process has become more partisan over time. This change is true of the Senate as well as the House, although the Senate lags the House in the extent of partisanship. The 91st Congress conforms to the picture the literature paints of committee processes during the era of committee government: committees in both chambers seldom split along partisan lines and often either worked out a bipartisan compromise or acted by consensus (Fenno 1973). Even in President Reagan's first Congress, partisan committee splits were still unusual, although committee conflict had clearly increased; other splits—most often ideological—had become much more frequent, while bipartisan deals and consensus decision making had decreased precipitously. In the late 1980s and the 1990s, partisan committee decision making rose steeply, especially in the House.

The increase in committee partisanship extended to the floor stage (see Table 7–2). The floor process on major measures was much more likely to be partisan in the 1990s than before, but as was the case with commit-

Table 7–1
Increasing Committee Partisanship in the House and Senate

Congress (Years)	House Committee Process			Senate Committee Process		
	Partisan	Other Split	Consensus	Partisan	Other Split	Consensus
91st (1969–1970)	10%	48%	42%	4%	47%	49%
97th (1981–1982)	22	61	17	13	68	19
101st (1989–1990)	29	46	25	20	60	20
103d (1993–1994)	41	54	6	12	76	12
104th (1995–1996)	55	36	9	34	49	17
105th (1997–1998)	42	28	31	25	28	47

1. The coding is based on CQ's account and on committee votes where available. For legislation reported from several committees, the action of the lead committee, if such existed, was coded. If there were several committees with more or less equal responsibility, those committees all had to meet the criteria for committee partisanship.

Table 7–2
Increasing Floor Partisanship in the House and Senate

Congress (Years)	Median Percentage of Party Roll Calls per Bill		Median Absolute Party Difference on Passage Vote	
	House	Senate	House	Senate
91st (1969–1970)	0%	0%	5%	4%
97th (1981–1982)	50	26	26	16
101st (1989–1990)	40	26	32	8
103d (1993–1994)	60	44	61	27
104th (1995–1996)	61	44	62	47
105th (1997–1998)	57	45	55	15

tee partisanship, this change occurred over time. Two indicators are used. First, the percentage of roll calls that were party votes was calculated for each major measure.[2] Then the median percentage for each chamber in each Congress was calculated. This provides an indicator of how frequently issues that were decided by a roll call vote were decided along partisan lines. The second is the median absolute party difference on passage votes (that is, the absolute value of the percentage of Democrats voting yes minus the percentage of Republicans voting yes). This calculation provides an indicator of how differently the members of the parties voted on final passage. Both lead to the same conclusions: floor partisanship on major measures has been increasing in both chambers and is much higher in the 1990s than in earlier decades.[3] (The second measure, but not the first, shows some receding of the very high partisanship in the Senate in the 105th Congress. Amendments continued to be frequently decided by party votes, but passage votes less often pitted most Democrats against most Republicans.)

What has elevated partisanship meant for the president in the legislative process? How has the president fared in the legislative process over this period of time? To answer these questions I examined agreement and disagreement between the president and Congress on each major measure at the committee and floor stage in each house and on the final bill. Based on the Congressional Quarterly account, I coded the president as supporting, having a mixed response, or opposing the bill as it emerged from

2. Only measures that reached the floor and on which there were roll calls are included.

3. Including voice votes (coded as zero party difference) would strengthen the over time trend as the number of such votes declines monotonically over these Congresses.

the House/Senate committee, as it passed the House/Senate, and as it emerged from whatever House/Senate reconciliation process was used.

Table 7–3 illustrates a complex but intelligible pattern. In the House committee and on the House floor, agreement between the president and Congress has declined over time—with the notable exception of the 103d Congress, the only Congress in the series in which the president and the House majority were of the same party. In the highly partisan 1990s, a president seems to benefit from partisanship when his party controls the House but suffers more when the opposition party does. There are two cases of single-party control of the presidency and the Senate (in the 97th, the first Reagan Congress, Republicans controlled the Senate but not the House), and, in both cases, that condition significantly boosted the level of presidential-congressional agreement. Otherwise, patterns are broadly similar to those in the House—a decline in the level of agreement, especially since the early part of the period under study. The pattern for presidential support of the final bill suggests that the president benefits from his party controlling one chamber and even more from his party controlling both chambers. It also shows that, when control is divided, the president is increasingly likely over time to be confronted with legislation he opposes at this stage. Thus, during the 104th Congress, President Clinton opposed almost half of the measures that emerged from House-Senate agreements.

An examination of the relationship between the character of the committee process and whether the president supports the resulting bill demonstrates no relationship when the president and the chamber are of the same party. That is, the president tends to support the bills reported by committees controlled by his co-partisans, whether or not the bills were drafted through a partisan process. In contrast, when control is divided, partisan committee processes are more likely than other processes to produce bills that the president opposes. (The only exception to this generalization is the 91st Senate for which the relationship is not significant; however, the small number of partisan committee bills makes the question moot.)

Setting the Agenda and Shaping the Debate

During the twentieth century, especially with the presidency of Franklin Roosevelt, Americans came to expect their presidents to propose a legislative agenda (Light 1991). Although the Constitution does not give the president the power to compel Congress to consider—much less pass— his legislative program, presidents are advantageously situated to act as

Table 7-3

Presidential/Congressional Agreement on Legislation

Congress (Years)	House Committee Bill		House Floor Bill		Senate Committee Bill		Senate Floor Bill		Conference Bill	
	Agree	Disagree	Agree	Disagree	Agree	Disagree	Agree	Disagree	Agree	Disagree
91st (1969–1970)	57	16	61	16	44	35	42	33	53	18
97th (1981–1982)	39	44	57	26	62	11	**80**	**5**	68	18
101st (1989–1990)	24	55	21	61	26	41	31	39	30	27
103d (1993–1994)	**94**	**0**	**94**	**0**	**89**	**4**	**83**	**0**	**83**	**0**
104th (1995–1996)	18	78	22	71	27	61	38	49	33	48
105th (1997–1998)	18	52	12	71	24	41	26	37	42	29

Note: Bold indicates unified government.

agenda setters. The president and vice president are the only government officials elected nationwide. As the single head of government, and lacking a single competitor from Congress, the president is by far the most visible elected official in the United States. The spread of radio and television significantly enhanced this presidential advantage; the president can focus the public's attention on a particular problem or issue more effectively than any other political actor. His media access also gives the president an edge in shaping debate on issues to enhance his position.

Frequent divided control of Congress and the presidency in the post–World War II era led to a growing dissatisfaction among congressional majority party members with a situation in which an opposition party president set the congressional agenda. Democrats, who were the majority during most of this period, began to pressure their elected party leaders to challenge the president with a Democratic Party agenda, and, as the congressional parties became more ideologically homogeneous in the 1980s, congressional party leaders became more aggressive in attempting to do so (see Sinclair 1995, 1997).

Majority party congressional leaders have become much more prominent agenda setters over time. Table 7–4 shows that, throughout the period under consideration, presidents have been highly prominent agenda setters in their first Congress and less so later in their terms.[4] Thus, during Nixon's,

Table 7–4
The President and Congressional Majority Party Leaders as Agenda Setters

Congress (Years)	Congressional Agenda of Major Measures (N)	Percent Presidential Agenda Items	Percent Majority Party Leaders' Agenda Items
91st (1969–1970)	53	47%	2%
94th (1975–1976)	48	23	17
97th (1981–1982)	53	45	8
100th (1987–1988)	46	20	28
101st (1989–1990)	57	18	11
103d (1993–1994)	55	45	NA
104th (1995–1996)	56	4	41
105th (1997–1998)	42	31	36

4. The president's agenda is defined as those items mentioned in the State of the Union address or its equivalent and in special messages of some prominence. Majority party leadership agenda setting, if it occurs, is announced in the Speaker's speech upon being elected to the office, the party's reply to the president's State of the Union address, the leadership's reply to special presidential addresses, or in major news conferences.

Reagan's, and Clinton's first two years in office, about half of the congressional agenda of major legislation consisted of presidential agenda items. (The exception is Bush, but his term might better be seen as a third Reagan term.) Majority party congressional leaders played an ever greater agenda-setting role during this period: as party polarization increased in the late 1980s and 1990s, so did party leaders' agenda setting. Furthermore, during the latter years the congressional majority party's agenda became even more clearly a direct challenge to the president's agenda. The Republican agenda in the 104th Congress is the best-known example; it consisted of the Contract with America and budget balancing legislation. But the Democrats' agenda in the 100th Congress also consisted mostly of items the president opposed, as did the Republicans' agenda in the 105th Congress.

Early attempts at congressional majority party agenda setting can be traced back at least to the 94th Congress, when the huge Democratic House majority elected in the wake of the Watergate scandal pressured its reluctant leader, Speaker Carl Albert, to develop within the party an anti-recession and energy policy agenda and attempt to enact it (but see Bader 1996 for evidence on earlier efforts). Disagreements within the party frustrated the effort, and the Democrats ended up with little accomplished, as Albert had feared (Sinclair 1995).

In the 1980s, however, increased ideological homogeneity within the Democratic Party, as well as the threat that President Reagan posed to the party, gave renewed impetus to that thrust. Reagan was a conservative, confrontational president who threatened all the Democrats' goals. An adept media performer, Reagan showed Democrats the danger of ceding the public forum to the president. Not only did he use television to build support for his own agenda, but also he used it to paint a highly negative portrait of the Democratic Party as addicted to wasteful federal spending and out of touch with the American people. Fearing electoral as well as policy consequences and unable to counter Reagan as individuals, congressional Democrats demanded that their leaders become more active participants in national debates.

During the 1980s and 1990s, the congressional parties became more adept at media relations and more engaged in public discourse (Blatz and Brownstein 1996; Koopman 1996). Press secretaries became central players in leadership offices, and the parties developed mechanisms aimed at getting their message out most effectively. For example, the House Democrats in the late 1980s set up a message group of party leaders and other media-savvy members who met daily when the House was in session to craft a message of the day. When Republicans took control of the House, the party leaders instituted a daily conference call among the top leadership press aides and the press secretaries of each of the committees to coordinate messages. Today, party committees and organizations—for example, the Senate policy committees, the House Democratic Caucus, and the House Republican Conference—produce and disseminate reams of information aimed at trying to get the membership to "all sing from the same hymn book" and at influencing party images in the media.

The impetus for change was not one-sided, however. Major alterations in the news media and in their political role spurred and shaped these developments as well. During the second half of the twentieth century, the mass media, especially television, played an increasingly important role in American politics. The Vietnam War and the Watergate scandal began a trend toward a more negative and confrontational press. By the late 1980s media coverage of politics had become poisonously cynical. Accelerating competition in the media business and among reporters and the advent of twenty-four-hour TV news also affected the character of news coverage. The media in the 1990s displayed a voracious appetite for conflict and for stories that were simple, negative, and sensational (Patterson 1993). Current media styles advantage political actors whose messages fit those criteria and amplify the intensity and bitterness of partisan conflict.

Strategies for a High-Intensity Partisan Environment

When the strategic environment changes, adept political actors change their strategies in response. Increased partisan polarization means that, when control is divided, the policy distance between the president and the congressional majority is great. As the data presented earlier make clear, presidents and congressional majorities of the opposition party now seldom agree on legislation. With a more intrusive, confrontational, and consequential news media, political actors naturally concern themselves with how they and their positions and policy proposals are portrayed as well as how their adversaries fare. The president continues to have an advantage but faces greater competition in setting the agenda and attempting to shape debate.

These changes in political context have led both presidents and congressional party leaders to make greater—and more aggressive—use of the procedure-based and structure-based strategies available to them, to employ media-based strategies more routinely, and often to combine the two.

The character of the media environment and the ideological distance between the parties encourages political actors to "go public" in an attempt to frame the issue in terms favorable to their stance and thereby improve their bargaining position (Kernell 1997). Bargaining between partisan opponents behind closed doors still takes place but most often in a context shaped by the actors' media strategies and sometimes by "grass roots" (or "astroturf") campaigns that the actors have orchestrated as well. The appeal of "going public" is not that the strategy is so easy to carry out successfully—it is not. The reasons for choosing this strategy, however, are compelling: the payoff for success can be huge; feasible alternatives for increasing one's bargaining resources are often lacking; the cost in good will is limited because party polarization has largely extinguished good will and trust between the parties; and actors know their opponents are likely to "go public" and are unwilling to risk yielding the public forum to them.

The one unequivocal legislative power the Constitution gives the president is the veto. As partisanship has increased over the period under study, presidents have made greater use of that power as a bargaining tool. When the opposition party controls Congress, presidents use the veto threat more often (see Table 7–5). Thus, Nixon threatened to veto 14 percent of major measures subject to veto during his first Congress; Bush threatened to veto more than half in the 101st; and Clinton issued veto threats against 60 percent of such major measures in the 104th Congress and 69 percent in the 105th.[5] The number of actual vetoes on these major measures did not, however, increase in any consistent way.

Often the purpose of a veto threat is not to kill the legislation, but to extract concessions from an opposition majority that has major policy differences with the president but lacks the strength to override his vetoes. When the opposition party controls at least one house of Congress, partisan

Table 7–5
Percentage of Major Measures Subject to Veto Threats and Filibusters and Number of Actual Vetoes

Congress (Years)	Veto Threats	Filibuster Problem	Actual Vetoes
91st (1969–1970)	14%	12%	5
97th (1981–1982)	23	22	4
101st (1989–1990)	52	28	9
103d (1993–1994)	**4**	**47**	**0**
104th (1995–1996)	60	49	10
105th (1997–1998)	69	50	5

Note: Bold indicates unified government.

5. Coding is based on Congressional Quarterly's account of the bill's legislative history.

committee processes stimulate veto threats. Over all, 38 percent of the measures on which neither the House nor the Senate committee process was partisan faced a veto threat; presidents threatened to veto 57 percent of the measures on which either the House or the Senate committee process was partisan; and, when committee processes in both chambers were partisan, fully 70 percent of the measures faced veto threats.

The Senate's permissive rules give minorities considerable opportunities to obstruct and sometimes foil the plans of majorities. To cut off a filibuster and bring legislation to a final vote over opposition requires a supermajority (sixty votes since 1975; two-thirds of those present and voting before that). During the 1970s senators became more willing to use their prerogatives expansively (see Binder and Smith 1997; Sinclair 1989). As Table 7–5 shows, the likelihood of a major measure encountering some sort of filibuster problem—either the threat of a veto or an actual veto—has increased enormously over the Congresses under study.

The 1990s, especially the 103d and 104th Congresses, have seen the emergence of a filibuster-centered partisan strategy. In the past, filibusters were often partisan in the sense that the obstructionists came predominantly from one party. In some cases, the obstructionists were directed by the party leadership. But in the 103d Congress filibuster-based obstructionism emerged as a systematic partisan strategy.

The 103d Congress marked the return of unified control of both houses of Congress for the first time since the late 1970s. The new Democratic president had a big, ambitious agenda, but he had been elected with only 43 percent of the vote and in an era of popular distrust of politicians and government. Those circumstances, combined with the increased ideological polarization of the congressional parties, made it possible and profitable for Senate Republicans under Majority Leader Robert Dole to pursue a systematic filibuster strategy. In the 103d Congress, almost half of all major legislation encountered some filibuster-related problem identifiable from the public record, and most of these were partisan. In the 104th, Democrats, now in the minority, returned the favor; about half the major legislation encountered extended debate–related problems and, again, most were partisan. Half of the major measures ran into filibuster problems in the 105th Congress.

During the earlier part of the period under study, bills that emerged from a partisan committee process in either or both houses were no more likely to encounter a filibuster problem than those that did not. For the 101st, 103d, 104th, and 105th Congresses, in contrast, partisanship at the committee stage increased the likelihood of a filibuster problem later on; when the committee process was partisan in either or both chambers, 58 percent of measures subject to filibuster encountered such problems;

when the committee process was not partisan in either chamber, only 39 percent faced filibuster problems.

Maintaining a filibuster requires a degree of public indifference. Few senators want to be seen blocking a measure with intense popular support. Consequently, efforts to frame the debate and influence public opinion often become a part of the strategy. Those who want to overcome a filibuster problem have the harder task because they need to arouse at least the attentive public. A successful public relations effort by President Clinton and his allies was instrumental to the enactment of the Brady bill, which imposed a seven-day waiting period for buying a gun. The Republican filibuster of the Brady bill collapsed when a number of Republican moderates began to fear the political price of their participation. In contrast, Clinton's effort to build public support for his economic stimulus bill was a failure. Republicans won that PR battle by persuading the public that the measure consisted mostly of wasteful pork-barrel spending.

The Senate's permissive rules combined with an adept PR strategy can be, and now often are, strategically employed to try to wrest agenda control away from the congressional majority, as Democrats' successful effort in 1996 to raise the minimum wage illustrates. In the wake of their astonishing electoral victory in 1994, congressional Republicans totally dominated agenda setting (McSweeney and Owens 1998). In his State of the Union address on January 24, 1996, Clinton advocated raising the minimum wage. Although the proposal was popular with the American public, it was expected to go nowhere because it was anathema to the conservative Republicans who led and made up the bulk of the Republican majorities in the House and Senate.

Because amendments to most Senate bills need not be germane, the Democrats' strategy was to offer the minimum wage increase as an amendment to every piece of legislation the majority leader brought to the floor. Lacking the votes to kill the minimum wage or impose cloture on legislation he did want to pass, Dole was forced to pull bill after bill off the floor, prompting news stories of Senate gridlock. House and Senate Democrats, the White House, and organized labor all worked to keep the issue in the news and to put pressure on moderate Republicans. Public approval of a minimum wage increase went up to 85 percent. With an election approaching, Senate and House Republicans capitulated. The Democrats, less than two years after being demoralized and discredited by the 1994 election debacle, managed through skill and good luck to thrust the issue to the center of the agenda and force the most conservative Congress since the pre–New Deal era to pass an increase in the minimum wage.

The power that Senate rules give the minority can aid a president when his party does not control the Senate, if his party's senators are willing to work with him. When the president's party is in the majority, it is his partisan opposition that is advantaged by those rules. In the 103d Congress, Republicans forced a number of issues—most notably, gays in the military—onto the congressional agenda that Clinton and the Democratic congressional majority would have preferred to avoid.

The House majority party leadership has long had more control over the floor than its Senate counterpart. Since the 1970s, House party leaders have gained additional powers and resources and, as the parties have become more internally homogeneous, the leaders have also been allowed and often encouraged by their members to use their powers more aggressively (Sinclair 1995, 1997). House party leaders of the 1990s were more likely to intervene in committee or directly thereafter to ensure that the legislation that reached the floor conformed to the preferences of a party majority or even to bypass the committee altogether to that end (Aldrich and Rohde 1997). They were more likely to use restrictive special rules to advantage the majority party's position during floor consideration (Sinclair 1998). Well-organized whip-led efforts to mobilize votes for party objectives became routine.

For the president, the House majority party leadership is a more valuable ally and a more formidable opponent than its Senate counterpart. With the increase in partisan polarization, a president whose party controls the House can expect considerable help from the leadership; when the opposition party controls the House, presidents can expect the leaders to use their powers and resources against them. Thus, the Democratic leadership in the 103d Congress largely adopted President Clinton's agenda as their own and used their powers and resources aggressively to speed its components through the House. The leadership employed quite restrictive rules with great frequency, but closed and modified closed rules were still more likely to be used to protect the president's agenda items than other measures (on 67 percent of the president's agenda versus 57 percent of other items). In the 101st Congress, House Democrats used such restrictive rules more frequently on legislation on which the committee process was partisan, but they actually used them less on legislation President Bush either opposed or had mixed sentiments about than on legislation he supported (41 percent versus 67 percent). By the 104th Congress, in contrast, House Republican leaders used closed or modified closed rules on 33 percent of the legislation that Clinton supported as reported from the committee, on 50 percent when his reaction was mixed, and on 63 percent of legislation that Clinton opposed as reported from the committee.

In the 1980s, when normal processes were, for one reason or another, incapable of producing legislation and the costs of failing to reach an agreement were very high, the president and Congress began to resort to summits (Gilmour 1990; Sinclair 1995)—relatively formal negotiations between congressional leaders and high-ranking administration officials representing the president directly. The deficit and the budget process, especially as revised in the mid-1980s by the Gramm-Rudman automatic spending cut provisions, often provided the sense of emergency and the statutory deadline that made inaction politically costly. But partisan polarization underlay the resort to summits. As the parties became more ideologically homogeneous and more distant from each other and as congressional leadership strengthened, presidents were less able to bypass the opposition majority party leadership and make deals directly with committee chairmen or dissenting members of the opposition party on issues of this magnitude. With the further intensification of partisan hostility in the 1990s, summits often were preceded and accompanied by fierce public relations campaigns to frame the issues and influence public opinion. Success in the PR battle translated into a stronger hand at the bargaining table and often into policy victories. Thus, the political and policy outcomes of the budget summits of 1990, 1995, and 1997 were strongly shaped by the PR campaign that accompanied them. President Bush lost the public opinion fight in 1990 and consequently did not prevail on the final policy outcomes. In contrast, President Clinton won the PR battles in 1995 and 1997, which made it possible for him to come out on top in political and policy terms as well (Drew 1996).

The budget process has become the mechanism of choice for those attempting to effect comprehensive policy change (Sinclair 1997). Packaging myriad legislative changes into one bill reduces the number of legislative fights that have to be won—an important consideration in a system with a strong status quo bias. Leaders can ask members to cast a handful of tough votes, not dozens. Crucially important as well, the special rules that pertain to the budget process protect the legislation from a Senate filibuster. Unified government and the procedural advantages that the budget process confer made it possible for Clinton and congressional Democrats to enact their massive economic policy/budget legislation in 1993, almost completely by party line votes. The Democrats paid dearly for that policy success, however, because the Republicans' PR strategy of depicting the legislation as containing tax increases on the middle class contributed to the Democrats' defeat in the 1994 elections.

Partisanship and Presidential Policy Success

As the media environment changed and the parties polarized, the president and congressional party leaders altered their strategies. How have

150 BARBARA SINCLAIR

these changes affected presidential success in Congress? Given that a level of agreement between the president and Congress is required to enact legislation, how has the combination of divided control and heightened partisanship affected presidential success? Table 7–6 shows presidential success on the legislative agenda.

Whether we examine presidential success on the broad congressional agenda of major legislation or on presidential agenda items only, we find no clear and consistent trend over time.[6] Excluding consideration of the 104th and 105th Congresses for the moment, the likelihood that the president's position prevailed on balance is strongly related to whether the president's party controlled at least one house of Congress. Reagan in the 97th, when Republicans controlled the Senate, and Clinton in the 103d are most successful.[7] Nixon in the 91st is considerably more successful on all major legislation and a great deal more successful on his agenda than Bush is in

Table 7–6
Presidential Success on the Legislative Agenda

| Congress (Years) | Total Agenda | | | President's Agenda | | | Percentage of Pres.'s Wins that Are Enactments |
	Won	Lost	(N)*	Won	Lost	(N)	
91st (1969–1970)	53%	27%	49	52%	36%	25	85%
97th (1981–1982)	68	17	47	70	17	23	75
101st (1989–1990)	41	29	51	20	50	10	43
103d (1993–1994)	**67**	**25**	**52**	**68**	**32**	**25**	**91**
104th (1995–1996)	65	19	54	50	50	2	37
105th (1997–1998)	60	20	40	54	31	31	50

Note: Bold indicates unified government.
*Total items on which the president took a position.

6. Based on the Congressional Quarterly account, a judgment was made as to whether the president had on balance won or lost on final disposition. Because most major legislation involves some compromise after committee consideration— most frequently in conference—the classification of winning on balance is considerably less demanding than the classification of winning on the floor and just requires that the president achieved a favorable compromise. Where a measure involved a clear-cut conflict between two sides and the result appeared to be an even compromise, the measure is placed into a middle, no clear winner, category.

7. I argue elsewhere (Sinclair 1985) that the perception that the 1980 elections had conferred a mandate on Reagan contributed significantly to his legislative success.

the 101st. Both presidents faced Congresses controlled by the opposition party, but the Democratic Party Bush confronted was more ideologically homogeneous and more strongly led than the one Nixon faced.

Clinton's high success rate in the 104th Congress, when he confronted an aggressive, ideologically conservative new Republican majority, prompts a further examination of these data. The measure used gauges whether the president won or lost the legislative battle on balance: the president can win by the enactment of legislation in a form he, on balance, favors; he can also win when legislation that he opposes is not enacted. In the 91st, 97th, and 103d Congresses, most presidential wins were of the former type: legislation the president supported was enacted. In the 103d, the only period of fully unified government in our dataset, 91 percent of Clinton's victories were enactments. In the 101st, 104th , and 105th Congresses, when the president won, it was much more likely to be when legislation died. Although Clinton sports a quite impressive win rate of 65 percent on the major legislation of the 104th Congress, more than 60 percent of those victories came when legislation that Clinton opposed failed enactment; in the 105th, 50 percent of Clinton's victories took the form of defeated legislation. The contrast between the 91st Congress, on the one hand, and the 101st and 104th Congresses, on the other, suggests that the higher partisanship of the 1990s, combined with divided control, reduces a president's chances for positive achievements. Although Nixon won just slightly more than half the time (considerably lower than either Reagan in the 97th or Clinton in the 103d), most of those victories were positive—bills that he supported, quite a few of them his agenda items, were enacted into law.

As these results would lead us to expect, the relationship between partisanship and presidential success on a bill-by-bill basis is quite contingent.[8] Overall, there is no relationship. On legislation that failed enactment, presidential success and partisanship at the committee stage tend to be positively if weakly related, suggesting that high partisanship helps the president kill legislation he does not like. However, on legislation that is enacted, there is no relationship overall; only in the 104th is partisanship at the committee stage strongly and significantly related to presidential failure.

The filibuster, I argued earlier, has become a partisan weapon. How has its increased use affected presidents' legislative success? A filibuster problem depresses presidential success, but the relationship is fairly weak.

---

8. The analyses reported in this and the following paragraphs is preliminary.

When the relationship is examined on a Congress-by-Congress basis, considerable variation is evident. In the 91st Congress, Nixon was hurt by filibuster problems, but they occurred so rarely that the practical impact was negligible. In the 97th, Reagan's success was unrelated to whether the legislation encountered filibuster problems, which were more frequent but still not pervasive. Bush and Clinton in the 101st and 103d Congresses, respectively, were hurt by filibuster problems. In the 103d, in fact, Clinton clearly lost on one-third of all measures that encountered a filibuster problem, and about half of all measures did. In the 104th and 105th, however, there is no relationship.

Finally, how do veto threats affect the president's likelihood of legislative success? Because presidents threaten to veto legislation with which they have serious problems, one might expect the outcome on such legislation to be worse for the president than legislation that is more to his liking. This is, in fact, the case for Nixon in the 91st Congress, although the relationship is weak.[9] The president may, however, threaten a veto in order to strengthen his bargaining position. Is there evidence that a veto threat has that effect? When the bills in the other divided-control Congresses are considered, the president does slightly better when he issues a veto threat than when he does not.[10] And often the president's threat results in changes to the legislation, not in its demise. Thus, threatening a veto seems to strengthen the president's hand and results in an outcome more to his liking, explaining why presidents in the 1990s used veto threats often.

Conclusion

What then is the impact of increased partisanship on the president's role in the legislative process and his impact on the process? The question has no simple answer because the legislative process is complex and myriad factors influence the course of any given legislative battle. Moreover, the increase in partisan polarization was not the only important change in the political context during the period under study. The example of the 103d Congress suggests that when the president and the congressional majority are of the same party, greater partisanship can lead to greater presidential success as long as the legislation in question is neither subject to a

---

9. Measures the president cannot veto are excluded from this analysis.

10. The relationship is not statistically significant.

filibuster nor provokes one—a major caveat. When control of the presidency and the Congress is divided, higher partisanship tends toward gridlock. To be sure, when the major actors have a strong incentive to enact legislation despite their ideological differences, summits and other special procedures can aid them in reaching agreement. Presidents facing opposition party–controlled Congresses have become adept at veto bargaining and seem to gain positive legislative influence by using veto threats aggressively. However, the distance between the parties in what they perceive as good public policy means that one or both parties must make major concessions to reach agreement, and this provides a huge incentive for both to use whatever strategies are available to them to try to change the strategic balance to their advantage. Impeachment can be seen as the most drastic such strategy to date. The media environment encourages "going public," so increasingly contentious PR campaigns are now almost always a core element of presidents' and the congressional parties' strategies.

The Constitution requires a partnership between the president and Congress just to get the most essential legislative business of the country done. In the 1990s, when control of the branches was divided between the parties, Congress and the president were at best hostile partners, who neither trusted each other nor perceived themselves to have much of a common interest.

CHAPTER 8

Partisanship and the President's Quest for Votes on the Floor of Congress

Richard Fleisher and Jon R. Bond

In "Partisanship and the President's Quest for Votes on the Floor of Congress," Richard Fleisher and Jon Bond examine changes in the levels of support that presidents have received from their partisans and members of the opposition during the partisan period that began in the mid-1980s. This chapter updates their previous analysis in *The President in the Legislative Arena* (Bond and Fleisher 1990). That analysis was based on the view that congressional behavior toward the president can be understood in terms of predispositions resulting from the interaction of members' party and ideology. Because of ideological diversity in congressional parties, it was useful (until the mid-1980s anyway) to view Congress not in terms of two parties, but as four party factions. Each party had a mainstream faction—liberals in the Democratic Party and conservatives in the Republican Party—and a smaller cross-pressured faction—conservative Democrats and liberal Republicans. Presidents typically are chosen from the mainstream faction of their party, so they tend to get the most consistent support from their party base and the least from the base of the opposition party. The support from the two cross-pressured factions falls somewhere between the two party mainstreams. As several essays in this volume demonstrate, parties in Congress have become less ideologically diverse, and the differences between the parties have grown. With the decline of ideological diversity, the cross-pressured factions in both parties have almost ceased to exist. How is presidential support in Congress likely to be affected by the disappearance of the middle?

Not surprisingly, Fleisher and Bond find that patterns of support changed, with the president receiving more support from his own partisans and less from the opposition party. These changes, however, are not symmetrical: the opposition party is more cohesive in opposition than the president's party is in support. But the analysis of these voting patterns also indicates that there continue to be considerable rates of defection by

154

members of both parties. These high defection rates signal that coalition building on the floor of Congress remains uncertain. Neither the president nor the congressional party leadership can routinely count on the votes of members of their party, even those whose ideological predispositions suggest that they should support the party position. Even party and committee leaders continue to defect from the preferred party position on a substantial percentage of presidential votes. Finally, increased partisanship has not resulted in greater certainty of outcomes. Other things being equal, the probability of a presidential win on the floor is lower in the partisan period than previously. And this increased difficulty in winning characterizes majority as well as minority presidents.

———

What the president ultimately needs from Congress is votes. It is certainly the case that many significant instances of presidential-congressional interaction—struggles to define the party position on issues, set the agenda, get a committee hearing, schedule a bill for floor consideration, and so on—occur long before a floor vote. Still, there is little of significance that does not eventually come to the floor of the House or Senate, giving members of Congress the opportunity (or perhaps the duty) to go on the public record with a yea or nay. Nearly two decades ago, political scientist Anthony King (1983, 247) summarized the president's dependence on congressional votes with a prophetic list:

> All you [the president] really need from Congress is votes, but you need those votes very badly. Moreover, under the American system, you need votes all the time and all kinds of votes: votes for and against bills, votes for and against amendments, votes to appropriate funds, votes not to appropriate funds, votes to increase the budget, votes to cut the budget, votes to enable you to reorganize the executive branch, votes to strengthen you (or not to weaken you) in your dealings with administrative agencies, votes to sustain your vetoes, votes to override legislative vetoes, votes in the Senate to ratify the treaties you have negotiated and to confirm the nominations you have made, votes (every century of so) in opposition to efforts to impeach you. You need votes to enable you to build up a record, to win reelection, to win—who knows?—a place in history.

Presidents must take votes where they can get them. Unlike executives in parliamentary systems, the U.S. president cannot count on members of his party to support his policy preferences. But the other side of the coin is that the opposition party frequently fails to oppose. Ideological diversity within each of the parties, as well as members' need to satisfy parochial reelection constituencies, introduces considerable uncertainty into the president's quest for support. When angling for votes, therefore, the president must fish on both sides of the stream. Given the ideological diversity in the parties, presidents at various times have found the pickings plentiful on the other side of the aisle.

Since the mid-1980s, however, politics in the U.S. Congress has become more partisan. One might suppose that as members increasingly vote on the basis of party, uncertainty for the president would be reduced. More partisan predictability, however, is a mixed blessing in the American system of fragmented power, which frequently produces divided government. Majority party presidents may profit from greater partisan predictability and win more votes on the floor, but minority presidents cannot win without votes from the opposition and are likely to suffer more losses if floor voting is more predictably partisan (Bond and Fleisher 1990, 113–16; Fleisher and Bond 1996b).

Yet features of the American system of "separated institutions *sharing* power" (Neustadt 1960, 33) lead us to question whether more partisan voting has significantly reduced uncertainty for any president. The rise of party voting in recent Congresses resulted in part from a decline in the ideological heterogeneity of congressional Republicans and Democrats. Even though congressional parties have become more ideologically united, considerable diversity still remains. Furthermore, party leaders in Congress lack the tools available to leaders in a disciplined party system. In this context, party government is "conditional" (Rohde 1991; Sinclair 1995), and defections from party positions are still common. Moreover, the multiple decision points in Congress where a determined minority can slow down or stymie the majority make it unlikely that even cohesive parties will be able to enact policies without compromise (Brady and Volden 1998; Krehbiel 1998). Although compromise is still required, cohesive parties make it more difficult to achieve.

The most recent case of escalated partisanship—impeachment of the president by the lame-duck 105th House—was characterized by considerable uncertainty at the floor stage of the deliberations. The vote on the first article of impeachment was as partisan as it gets in the U.S. Congress; with only five defections in each party, 98 percent of Republicans voted against 98 percent of Democrats. The vote on the second article was also highly partisan—88 percent of Republicans against 98 percent of Democrats. The near perfect party unity on impeachment, however, belies the uncertainty surrounding these historic votes. Article I passed, but Article II failed because additional Republicans defected while Democrats held firm. Both the president and Republican leaders were scrambling to the very end trying to determine how many partisans on both sides of the aisle would defect from their parties' positions.[1]

In this chapter, we argue that the uncertainty on the impeachment issue was common even in the face of heightened partisanship. We present evidence that increased party cohesion has contributed to greater uncertainty in the president's quest for votes, rather than reducing it. We begin with an overview of our predispositions model of presidential success on the floor of Congress. We discuss how the decline of ideological diversity in congressional parties since the mid-1980s increased the level of partisanship. Next, we look at changes in the roll call voting behavior of congressional Democrats and Republicans on presidential votes, observing that defections—and therefore uncertainty—remain common in recent Congresses characterized by elevated partisanship. We then look at patterns of party and committee leaders support for the president's positions. We find that although party and committee leaders (particularly opposition leaders) have become more partisan, their behavior falls far short of the highly predictable behavior expected of administration and opposition leaders in legislatures with disciplined parties. Finally, we present an analysis of the effects of leaders' positions on levels of presidential support within both parties and on whether the president wins or loses on the floor. This analysis reveals that with more cohesive and opposing parties, majority as well as minority presidents continue to face considerable uncertainty on the floor.

A Predispositions Model of Presidential-Congressional Relations

In an earlier work, we adopted (with slight modification) James MacGregor Burns's (1963) thesis that Congress had four rather than two parties: liberal Democrats, conservative Democrats, liberal Republicans, and conservative Republicans (Bond and Fleisher 1990).[2] Undisciplined, ideologically

---

1. The House voted on two additional articles. Article III passed with 95 percent of Republicans voting against 98 percent of Democrats; Article IV failed with "only" 64 percent of Republicans voting against 98 percent of Democrats. The unity of Democrats was remarkable across these four votes, as well as other procedural votes related to impeachment. Republican unity was only slightly less consistent: the low of 64 percent Republican cohesion on Article IV is still high enough to define this vote as "partisan" using a typical definition.

2. Burns argued that the four parties in Congress were (1) presidential Democrats, (2) presidential Republicans, (3) congressional Democrats, and (4) congressional Republicans. In his view, liberal Republicans were the presidential wing of

diverse parties in Congress result in large part from the American electoral system. The president is the nominal head of his party, but his co-partisans in Congress have little say about his selection or the policy positions he takes. The reverse is also true: the president has little control over who wears his party's label in Congress or the policies they support. To get nominated, elected, and reelected, members of Congress must satisfy local political preferences. Supporting positions of the national party and the president that conflict with local interests can be costly; the costs of opposing the national party and the president are minimal. Recall, for example, the fate of Rep. Marjorie Margolies-Mezvinsky, D-Pa. When President Clinton's 1993 reconciliation bill came to a vote, she initially followed the sentiment of her Republican-leaning district and voted against the party position. But yielding to intense pressure from the White House and Democratic leaders, she changed her vote just before floor voting closed to save the president's (and the party's) policy. This vote to support party leaders instead of her constituency probably led to her defeat in the 1994 election (Hager 1996, 1654). Examples such as this are rare because, when faced with such intense conflict, members typically take the safer route and side with constituency over party. This electoral system produces ideological diversity within each party and low levels of party cohesion and discipline.

The Effect of Four Party Politics

Our theory of presidential-congressional relations is that congressional behavior toward the president can be understood in terms of predispositions resulting from the four party politics framework. We begin with the observation that on any controversial issue, members of Congress are predisposed to take one side or the other. Although each member's political predispositions vary along a number of dimensions, party and ideology have been shown to be among the most important (Kingdon 1981). When the president takes a position, the coalition that forms reflects choices made by members with different partisan and ideological predispositions.

(*continued*) the party (Burns 1963, 199). In our framework, liberal Republicans are the cross-pressured faction that is less predisposed to support a Republican president than are conservative Republicans. Burns's view seems justified for the period he studied: Eisenhower was the last Republican president in his study. We found that Eisenhower took some positions that appealed to the small number of liberal Republicans in Congress. Republican presidents after Eisenhower took more conservative positions that appealed to the conservative Republican mainstream and created greater cross-pressures for liberal Republicans (Bond and Fleisher 1990).

When members cast a roll call vote on a controversial issue, they must decide whether to vote yea, vote nay, or be strategically absent.[3] In making these decisions, members are motivated by (1) their own partisan and ideological predispositions; (2) constituency interests; and (3) other actors both in and out of government, including party leaders, committee leaders, staff, state delegations, interest groups, and bureaucrats, as well as the president's position and his activities to get their vote. Note that the president is only one of several competing cues, and he is seldom the dominant actor in members' calculus. The literature on congressional behavior clearly establishes that party, ideology, and constituency are the dominant forces (Jackson 1974; Kingdon 1981; Matthews and Stimson 1975).

On most issues, members do not experience conflict between their own predispositions and constituency interests either because they share constituency values or the constituency is indifferent. Some members—those we have characterized as cross-pressured—do, however, experience frequent conflict between party and ideology. Because partisan and ideological values are reinforcing for some members and conflicting for others, the effects of predispositions vary across members.

The effects of predispositions show up clearly on presidential issues. With few exceptions, presidents are selected from the ideological mainstream of their party; the policies they propose and the positions they take are usually compatible with the preferences of the mainstream faction of their party in Congress. Hence, in analyzing presidential-congressional relations, it is useful to orient the four party factions—(1) the president's party base, (2) cross-pressured members of the president's party, (3) cross-pressured members of the opposition party, and (4) the opposition party base—in terms of how the interaction of party and ideology affects their predisposition to support or oppose the president's preferences. The president's party base is the mainstream faction of his party; these members have the greatest predisposition to support his positions because they share with the president both a party affiliation and an ideological outlook. Cross-pressured members—conservative Democrats and liberal Republicans—have ideological orientations outside their party mainstream; these members are often cross-pressured on presidential roll calls because party

---

3. Strategic nonvoting is not common in the U.S. Congress. Most members feel that it is their duty to vote on roll calls. The proportion voting on roll calls typically exceeds 90 percent, and, when members must miss a vote, they often express a public position by pairing with another member or announcing a position in the *Congressional Record*. There is evidence, however, that a small number of cross-pressured members of the president's party do occasionally miss votes to avoid voting against the president (Covington 1988).

pushes them in one direction while ideology pulls in the other. The opposition party base is the other party's mainstream faction; these members have the least predisposition to support the president because they share neither a party affiliation nor an ideological orientation with the president.

A presidential position occupies a point along a partisan-ideological spectrum. Members' partisan and ideological predispositions determine how close they are to the president's position. The coalition that forms reflects choices made by members with different partisan and ideological predispositions that vary not only in content (Democrat versus Republican, liberal versus conservative) but also in strength (mainstream predispositions versus cross-pressured predispositions). Because presidential positions are typically closest to the preferences of their party mainstream, support from the president's party base is the highest and most consistent; support from the opposition base is the lowest and least consistent; and support from cross-pressured members of both parties is in between (Bond and Fleisher 1990).

We need to keep in mind, however, that predispositions create a tendency, not an imperative. Because members of Congress have different, often conflicting, institutional and political perspectives, even members who are predisposed to support or oppose the president may fail to do so. Members of Congress are individual politicians who interpret each vote in light of the current political context. Although each member's interpretation is influenced by partisan and ideological predispositions, even members with the same predispositions may come to different conclusions. In the end, members of Congress are political entrepreneurs free to follow their own predispositions if doing so serves their interest or to defect if they decide another choice is more beneficial.

Within this context of uncertainty the president searches for votes. Although members' party and ideology create a predisposition, members' decisions are not made in isolation. Rather, congressional decision making takes place in an institutional context defined by rules and norms peculiar to each chamber. In addition, two of the most important elements of the institutional structure of Congress are the party caucuses, which are directed by elected party leaders, and the committee system, in which each committee is ruled to a great extent by its leaders—the chair and ranking minority member.

Institutional Structure: Party and Committee Leaders

Congressional leaders occupy a pivotal position between the White House and rank-and-file members of Congress. The leaders are the primary channels of communication between Congress and the president, and they have the power to manipulate resources that can directly affect members' careers and the fate of legislation.

Each chamber has two sets of leaders: party leaders elected by a majority of each party caucus and committee chairs and ranking minority members chosen in part on the basis of committee seniority. The two types of leaders—elected and seniority—perform different institutional roles. Although reforms have reduced reliance on seniority in selecting committee leaders and obliged them to be more responsive to the preferences of the caucus, committee leaders' role remains different from that of party leaders.

Party Leaders. Members of Congress expect their party leaders to perform several important functions, including (1) organizing and running the chamber in a way that allows individual members to meet their goals; (2) being articulate communicators and defenders of the party's positions; and (3) building coalitions on legislation of importance to party members (Herrnson 1998; Sinclair, 1983, 1995). These expectations hold for both majority and minority party leaders, although minority leaders' influence over running the chamber is limited.

In their efforts to promote the programs of the national party, the president's party leaders typically assume the role of administration lieutenants in Congress. Party leaders from the president's party, however, do not always support the administration. Leaders in Congress are constrained by institutional interest and loyalty. They may be the administration's lieutenants, but they are leading an undisciplined army that makes its own demands on them. Tensions arise between the congressional party leadership and the White House because at times party leaders in Congress need to meet demands that are inconsistent with presidential needs. Moreover, institutional loyalty often leads congressional leaders to view themselves as the president's peers, not his servants. In a recent orientation speech given to senators, Robert Byrd, D-W.Va (a former majority leader) said, "Remember, you don't serve under any president. You serve with a president. They can't fire you. They can't do anything to you. It's you who raises an army for him to command. Remember this: you're the boss" (Achenbach 1999, A1). Such independence from the president, however, is the exception rather than the rule.

Opposition party leaders may choose from a number of roles. They may decide to be a constructive opposition that proposes alternative programs and seeks to win concessions from the president. Or they may decide to be obstructionist and attempt to defeat the president's policy preferences without proposing any alternatives. Which role the opposition plays is influenced by whether it is the majority or minority party.

Whether government is unified or divided, the majority party shares with the president the responsibility for governing and must participate in building majority coalitions in Congress. Traditionally, a majority opposition was likely to be limited either to proposing and passing its own programs over the president's objection or reaching a compromise with the president if there were not enough votes to override a veto. In recent Congresses, increased acrimony between Republicans and Democrats has made compromise more difficult.

A minority opposition party has more leeway to choose from the full range of roles. The choice depends on variables such as the closeness of the party division in the chamber and how aggressive and partisan the president is (Dodd and Oppenheimer 1997; Jones 1970). In recent Congresses, opposition parties have more frequently adopted the obstructionist role.

Thus, party leaders are likely to exercise considerable influence over presidential-congressional relations. As noted above, however, party leaders' support for or opposition to the president is constrained by institutional forces in Congress. Standing committees are among the most important congressional institutions.

Committee Leaders. In the period of four party politics before the reforms of the 1970s, seniority automatically elevated members to positions as committee leaders. These members often came from the cross-pressured faction of their party, and the seniority rule insulated them from pressure to support the positions of party majorities. As a result, compared to party leaders, committee leaders from the president's party were less likely to support his preferences, and opposition committee leaders were more likely to support him (Bond and Fleisher 1990, 132).

Reforms adopted by Democrats in the 1970s and by Republicans in the 1990s reduced the influence of seniority and obliged committee leaders to be more responsive to the wishes of their caucuses. Furthermore, the virtual disappearance of cross-pressured members means that committee leaders are likely to have policy preferences similar to the mainstream of their party. These changes should reduce the frequency of conflict between party and committee leaders.

Yet differences in the behavior of party leaders and committee leaders are likely to persist for at least two reasons. First, reforms in the 1970s and 1990s weakened, but did not eliminate, the seniority system. Seniority may continue to provide committee leaders some limited insulation from pressure from the party. Second, and more important, party and committee leaders still have different institutional roles. Party leaders are expected to be visible, articulate spokespersons for party positions across the entire range of issues. This institutional party role encourages the president's party leader to support his positions and the opposition party leader to oppose them. Although the institutional interest of Congress or the leaders' own policy preferences may cause them to defect from their party role on some issues, they are likely to support the party position on a large majority of votes. Committee leaders, in contrast, have a more complex institutional role. Like party leaders, committee leaders have an allegiance to their party and to the institution of Congress and personal preferences that sometimes conflict with the party position. But committee leaders also develop loyalty to their committee and its work. Although committee leaders now must be responsive to the wishes of the party caucus, their participation in the details of policies under the committee's jurisdiction and their loyalty to the committee's work causes conflicts with partisan expectations on some issues. These conflicts may draw committee leaders away from their party's position more often than is the case for party leaders.

Leader Influence in Congress. Leaders' actions prior to the floor vote often determine whether a bill passes or fails. Leaders also wield influence on the floor, but determining how much is problematic. We can observe whether leaders and the rank and file vote together on roll calls, but we cannot observe the causal process that leads to the agreement. Agreement may result from several causal processes, including (1) leaders' using their powers to persuade (or sometime pressure) members to vote with the party; (2) members' using leaders' positions as voting cues; (3) leaders and members voting together because they share the same values; and (4) leaders' anticipating and responding to the preferences of the members. Furthermore, because all four causal processes operate simultaneously, with each one accounting for some of the agreement on any given vote, it is not possible to determine the mix of causes.

Regardless of how the process produces agreement, analyzing the extent to which leaders and followers vote together contributes to understanding presidential success in Congress. If members vote with leaders because of bargaining or cue taking, then support from leaders would produce some additional votes for the president's position. But even if agreement results from shared values or from leaders' being influenced by the rank and file, the analysis of leader-follower agreement is useful. If there is an association between the votes of leaders and followers in Congress, then knowing whether party and committee leaders support the president's position forecasts likely levels of support from factions in Congress. In short, leaders may be viewed as barometers that can be used to test the climate in Congress.

The Decline of Four Party Politics in Congress

We have seen that four party politics in Congress results from (1) ideo-logical diversity in the parties; (2) members' willingness to cast votes in response to something other than their partisan-ideological predisposi-tion; and (3) leaders' lack of formal authority to control nominations and discipline members. Beginning in the 1980s, party cohesion in Congress began to rise, leading to what David Rohde (1991) calls conditional party government.[4] According to this theory, leaders can be strong if members are cohesive. Because partisan behavior has a number of dimensions, and the House and Senate are different institutions with different rules and norms, pinpointing a precise line of demarcation between less and more partisan periods is difficult. Evidence from previous research (Fleisher and Bond 1996a, 1996b; Rohde 1991; Sinclair 1995), however, suggests that the beginning of President Reagan's second term (1985) is a reasonable point. Reagan's second term and the time following may be characterized as a partisan era.

The newfound party unity in Congress resulted from changes within the institution and in the electorate. First, congressional reforms in the 1970s gave the party mainstreams tools to foster party unity. Both Repub-licans and Democrats adopted reforms between 1971 and 1973 that made committee leaders subject to election by secret ballot. The defeat of sev-eral senior House committee chairs in the 1970s and 1980s demonstrated that the Democratic Caucus would use its power to hold unresponsive committee chairs accountable. These reforms weakened the seniority sys-tem and obliged committee chairs to be more responsive to the wishes of the caucus (Rohde 1991). After Republicans captured control of Congress in the 1994 elections, they adopted reforms giving party leaders more con-trol of the policy-making apparatus.

Second, ideological shifts in both the Democratic and Republican par-ties reduced the ideological diversity in congressional parties. Electoral forces in the states and districts reduced the differences between the con-stituencies of southern and northern Democrats. Changes in electoral pol-itics in the South brought on by implementation of the 1965 Voting Rights Act contributed to the development of a viable Republican Party in the region. Redistricting efforts aimed at ensuring the election of black candidates had the effect of making more seats available for conservative Republicans in 1992 and 1994 (Hill 1995).

---

4. Others view party leadership in similar terms (see Aldrich 1995; Dodd and Oppenheimer 1997; and Sinclair 1995).

In addition, changes within the Republican Party reduced the number of liberal Republicans elected to Congress. Beginning with the Goldwater revolution at the 1964 Republican convention, and reinforced by Reagan's electoral success in 1980, the party machinery was taken over by hard-line conservatives.[5] Moreover, activists who support the party with money, volunteer activities, and votes became more conservative, making it more difficult for liberal candidates to get a share of campaign resources and win Republican primaries. The result was the election of greater numbers of avid conservatives. Led by Newt Gingrich of Georgia, the right wing of the party won control of the top leadership offices in the House. In addition, Trent Lott, R-Miss., a Gingrich ally before moving to the Senate, became Senate majority leader in 1996. Thus, congressional Republicans, pushed by conservative presidents and strident congressional leaders, shifted to the right and became less willing to compromise on the Republican agenda.

In the heyday of four party politics, the conflict of party and ideology created a substantial number of cross-pressured members; these numbers were reduced by the electoral and institutional changes discussed above. Table 8–1 shows the number of members in the four party factions in each Congress from the 1950s to the 1990s. Cross-pressured members are defined as those who have ideological preferences closer to the mean of the other party (Bond and Fleisher 1990, Fleisher and Bond 1996b).[6] This definition of cross-pressured members sets a rather stringent benchmark. Yet note that from the 1950s to the mid-1980s there were substantial numbers of cross-pressured members: between one-fifth and one-third of Democrats and Republicans in both chambers had ideology scores closer to the mean of the other party than to their own (Bond and Fleisher 1990, 89). By 1994 liberal Republicans had all but disappeared from both chambers, and conservative Democrats also had become an endangered species. With the disappearance of cross-pressured members, four party politics in Congress was reduced to two. The actual size of the majority party's base

---

5. Republican and Democratic activists who attended state party conventions in 1988 were more polarized on issues than were convention delegates in 1980 (Stone, Rapoport, and Abramowitz 1990). And data reported by Harold Stanley and Richard Niemi (1998, 69) suggest that delegates to the national party conventions became more polarized ideologically in the 1980s and 1990s. Although activists are more ideologically extreme than rank-and-file voters, Republican convention delegates shifted farther to the right in the 1980s than Democratic delegates shifted to the left.

6. See the appendix for a description of how the factions were identified.

Table 8–1

Number of Members in the Party Factions

	House				Senate			
	Democrats		Republicans		Democrats		Republicans	
Congress (Years)	Base	Cross-pressured	Cross-pressured	Base	Base	Cross-pressured	Cross-pressured	Base
83d 1953–54	170	43	19	201	35	13	12	36
84th 1955–56	157	74	74	129	36	12	3	44
85th 1957–58	196	37	22	178	34	15	13	34
86th 1959–60	248	33	12	141	45	21	11	23
87th 1961–62	188	74	31	143	42	22	11	25
88th 1963–64	166	90	32	146	45	22	8	25
89th 1965–66	203	91	19	121	51	16	4	29
90th 1967–68	180	65	16	173	44	20	9	27
91st 1969–70	162	81	31	160	41	17	11	31
92d 1971–72	179	75	34	146	38	18	12	32
93d 1973–74	180	62	35	157	43	15	14	28
94th 1975–76	224	68	22	120	47	15	13	25
95th 1977–78	223	66	21	124	44	18	12	26
96th 1979–80	230	45	16	143	51	8	7	34
97th 1981–82	191	51	24	168	34	13	10	43
98th 1983–84	242	25	17	150	37	9	11	43
99th 1985–86	224	29	18	164	41	6	11	42
100th 1987–88	236	22	20	158	49	5	8	38
101st 1989–90	223	37	15	163	50	5	6	39
102d 1991–92	248	20	8	159	54	3	6	37
103d 1993–94	222	36	1	176	53	3	4	40
104th 1995–96	191	11	4	229	46	0	2	52

Source: 83d–98th Congresses are from Jon R. Bond and Richard Fleisher, *The President in the Legislative Arena* (Chicago: University of Chicago Press, 1990), 87; 99th–104th Congresses updated by the authors.

in the House has exceeded an absolute majority (218) in every Congress since the 98th. In the Senate, the majority base has been greater than fifty-one since the 102d Congress (although it never exceeded the sixty votes necessary to break a filibuster). In the earlier period, it was rare for the majority party's base to exceed a majority.

Political commentators continue to speak of "moderate" Republicans in the contemporary Congress, and we can identify some Republicans who are less conservative than their colleagues. But unlike the liberal wing of the party in the past, the so-called moderates today have ideological preferences closer to their own party mean than to the Democrats'. And the "conservative" Democrats are not as conservative—or as numerous—as they once were.

The disappearance of the cross-pressured members in both parties may have contributed to the acrimonious partisanship and the difficulty in reaching compromises we have witnessed in recent Congresses. When one-fifth to one-third of each party's caucus had policy preferences closer to the other party, leaders and the majority in each caucus had to accommodate these members' preferences on at least some issues. When compromises within the party caucuses did not go far enough, cross-pressured members defected from the party, often forming winning coalitions based on ideology (Brady and Bullock 1980; Frymer 1994; Manley 1970; Shelley 1983). These members—Democrats with Republican ideologies and Republicans with Democratic ideologies—have all but disappeared. Some switched parties. Others were defeated or retired. Cross-pressured members who left Congress were replaced by a member of the same party with preferences in the party mainstream, or the seat was won by someone in the other party's mainstream. Those who remain are too few to influence caucus decisions. The disappearance of the cross-pressured members means that neither party needs to move much in the other party's direction to achieve majority support within the caucus.

With the disappearance of cross-pressured members, the average ideology in the party caucuses shifted in opposite directions and the variance declined. Table 8–2 reports the mean and standard deviation in "liberalism" scores for selected Congresses from the 1960s to the 1990s to demonstrate this process.[7] We see that the Democratic average grew more

Table 8–2
Average Liberalism Scores by Party

	House				Senate			
	Democrats		Republicans		Democrats		Republicans	
Years	Mean	Std. Dev.	Mean	Std. Dev.	Mean	Std. Dev.	Mean	Std. Dev.
1965–66	50.0	31.5	15.8	15.4	64.3	26.3	26.2	20.5
1975–76	64.7	26.1	25.7	19.0	72.7	26.4	38.9	33.0
1985–86	74.4	20.2	22.1	16.6	74.4	18.4	30.4	23.9
1995–96	79.4	12.5	12.5	11.4	88.3	9.9	13.8	15.4

Source: Calculated by the authors.

---

7. To construct a measure of general ideology we started with the list votes selected by the Americans for Constitutional Action or the American Conservative Union (conservative groups) and Americans for Democratic Action (a liberal group) and purged from the lists votes on which the president took a position. We recalculated ideology scores ranging from 0 (most conservative) to 100 (most liberal) for all members in each Congress, 1953–1996. Although such indexes have been criticized (Jackson and Kingdon 1992), there is evidence that they are reliable and generally valid proxies of members' ideology (Herrera, Epperlein, and Smith 1995; Hill, Hanna, and Shafqat 1997; Smith, Herrera, and Herrera 1990).

liberal over time and the Republican average became more conservative. The standard deviation around each party's mean ideology declined over time, indicating that fewer members had ideologies far from the party mainstream. These ideological shifts in the parties resulted in greater ideological polarization—the distance between the two party means in the 1950s and 1960s is about half what it is in the 1990s. And note that parties in the Senate have become as ideologically homogeneous and polarized as parties in the House.

But there is still a range of ideological preferences in each party—Democrats to the right and Republicans to the left of their party medians. These members are just not as far right or left as the cross-pressured members who have left. Because the party caucuses no longer must move as far toward the other party's preferences, some party positions may be too far left for the less liberal Democrats and too far right for the less conservative Republicans. Consequently, there are still defections, but fewer than when there were large numbers of cross-pressured members.

Less need to compromise within the caucus results in less compromise with the other party. And the greater ideological polarization between the parties makes finding the middle ground more difficult. Partisanship is stronger in the House because House rules permit a cohesive majority to rule. In the Senate, where the rules protect the power of individuals, compromise is more common, even though partisanship and ideological polarization have increased there as well.

As a result of the declining ideological heterogeneity, cohesion in the party caucuses increased, and congressional leaders could act with greater authority (Rohde 1991; Sinclair 1995). As roll call voting became more predictably partisan, the uncertainty that traditionally characterizes the president's quest for votes should have been reduced. From the president's perspective, this change means that there are fewer uncertain votes on his side of the aisle, but less opportunity to pick up votes on the other side. In short, congressional parties should begin to look more like their parliamentary counterparts, with more consistent presidential support from the president's partisans and more consistent opposition from the opposing party.

Presidential Support and Opposition in a Partisan Era

A look at presidential support from the parties over time reveals that defections on presidential votes have remained common in the partisan era since Reagan's second term. Table 8–3 presents descriptive statistics on levels

Table 8–3
House Support for the President's Position

Admin.	President's Party			Opposition Party		
	Mean	*Median*	*Std. Dev.*	*Mean*	*Median*	*Std. Dev.*
Eisenhower	66	69	28	39	42	28
Eisenhower	61	62	27	44	51	28
Kennedy	78	83	17	27	19	24
Johnson	74	78	19	27	20	23
Nixon	66	71	25	44	46	24
Nixon	63	69	26	33	27	23
Ford	62	67	27	32	25	25
Carter	63	68	22	30	23	24
Reagan	65	68	27	30	26	24
Reagan	62	69	30	21	14	23
99th	66	75	27	24	16	23
100th	58	65	33	20	11	23
Bush	69	77	27	24	17	23
101st	66	76	27	25	16	25
102d	72	78	26	24	17	21
Clinton	75	82	23	26	16	28
103d	75	84	24	36	31	29
104th	74	81	23	18	9	24

Note: Entries are the percentage of party members voting in agreement with the president's position on roll call votes.

of support for the president's position on conflictual roll calls in the House from the 83d Congress (1953–1954) to the 104th Congress (1995–1996).[8] Several points emerge from these results. First, although other studies show a rise in overall party voting beginning in the mid-1980s (Fleisher and Bond 1996a; Ornstein, Mann, and Malbin 1998, 210; Rohde 1991), average levels of presidential support from the president's partisans do not increase until the 1990s. During Reagan's two terms in the White House, when the rise in party voting first appeared, support from the president's party was no higher than during the administrations immediately preceding his. Not until the second Bush Congress and the two Clinton Congresses do we see signs of

---

8. A conflictual roll call is defined as one on which less than 80 percent of members in the chamber vote in agreement with the president's position. We excluded consensual votes in Congress to limit the analysis to important issues on which there was some controversy. The issues that passed by near unanimous margins with the president's support were, with rare exceptions, minor and routine issues. Votes that the president lost with more than 80 percent voting against him remain in the analysis. These relatively unusual cases—the president standing alone against a united Congress—represent important institutional conflict and belong in the analysis.

increased support for the president from members of his own party. Even in these cases, however, support for the president barely reaches the levels seen during the Kennedy-Johnson years.

A second observation that emerges from the figures in Table 8–3 is that in most Congresses the mean level of support is less than the median, indicating that the distribution is skewed. The distribution is skewed because there are a number of votes on which large numbers of the president's partisans vote against his position. Because the median is unaffected by these cases with large numbers of defections, it is a better measure of central tendency. Yet even the median reveals evidence of frequent party defection. During the second Reagan and Bush Congresses, one of four Republicans voted against the president's position on more than half of the votes. Although Clinton received higher levels of support from Democrats, on half of the votes at least one in five Democrats opposed him. In concrete terms, if the president's party controls two hundred seats, a median score of eighty means that on 50 percent of the votes, at least forty members of the president's party voted against his position.

Finally, with the decline in the ideological heterogeneity of the parties, we might expect greater stability; that is, variability in levels of support across presidential roll calls should decline. The standard deviation measures the degree of variability across the votes. We find that the standard deviation in support for the president's position from his own partisans has remained relatively stable over the entire period. The lowest level of variability occurred during the Kennedy and Johnson administrations. Standard deviations during the Reagan and Bush administrations increased slightly compared to previous years. The slight decline in the 103d and 104th Congresses is a return to levels typical of the pre-Reagan years. Although the ideological heterogeneity of the parties decreased in the 1990s, variability in support of the president's positions on the floor remains relatively high.

Thus, heightened partisanship increased support for the president from his partisans in the House, but the increase occurred later than we might have expected given the trends in other indicators of partisanship on floor votes. And even with elevated partisanship, defections within the president's party remain sufficiently common to warrant a conclusion that the president and other party leaders face considerable uncertainty as they attempt to attract majority support for the administration's preferred position on the House floor. The decline in ideological heterogeneity in the parties marked by the virtual disappearance of cross-pressured members did not result in more certain support for the president's preferences.

To highlight the degree of uncertainty remaining in the recent period of heightened partisanship, let us look at the percentage of presidential partisans who supported the president less than 75 percent of the time.[9] For the 101st to 104th Congresses, the numbers were 78 percent, 54 percent, 46 percent, and 36 percent, respectively. Although there is a sharp decline in the number of partisans who fail to cross the 75 percent support threshold, defections remain common on presidential votes. During Bush's term, between one-half and three-fourths of House Republicans had support scores lower than 75 percent; for Clinton, between one-third and one-half of Democrats had support scores lower than 75 percent. Furthermore, only a handful of presidential partisans provided dependable support for the president, support that approached levels expected in parliaments with disciplined parties. In the 101st to 104th Congresses, the percentage of partisans supporting the president's position more than 90 percent of the time was 1 percent, 0, 2 percent, and 3 percent, respectively. Even in this highly partisan era, only a tiny handful of House members provide loyal, dependable support for the president. Attracting support from the president's partisans remains uncertain.

Because historically presidents also have derived votes from members of the opposition party, especially those who were cross-pressured, we turn next to the trends in House opposition party support for the president. These results are also presented in Table 8–3.

In some respects, the behavior of the opposition party reflects the weaknesses of American parties. If the president's partisans fail to act as loyal supporters, the opposition party frequently fails to act as an opposition. Eisenhower and Nixon typically received support from more than 40 percent of opposition party members in the House; Nixon, Ford, and Carter typically received about 30 percent, and Kennedy and Johnson received only slightly less. During the second Reagan term and continuing under Bush, Democrats in the House began to act more like an opposition party. The median level of support from Democrats in the 99th through 102d Congresses was 17 percent or less. Thus, on most votes, fewer than one in six Democrats supported the positions of Presidents Reagan and Bush. In the 103d Congress, on most votes Clinton received about 30 percent of Republican votes. This level of support is unusual for this period, and may have resulted from Clinton taking relatively conservative positions on foreign policy and defense votes (Fleisher et al. 2000). In the Republican-controlled 104th

9. These figures are similar to Congressional Quarterly's individual members' Presidential Support Scores, except we calculate support only on conflictual roll calls—those on which less than 80 percent of members voted in agreement with the president's position.

Congress, Republican support for Clinton's positions dropped to a record low 9 percent or less on most votes.

Note that elevated partisan opposition occurred earlier than elevated partisan support. The Democrats' more cohesive opposition started at the beginning of Reagan's second term (in the 99th Congress), but we do not see a rise in support from the president's partisans until Bush's second Congress (102d). And note that the opposition was more cohesive in opposition than the president's party is in support—on most votes only about one-sixth defected from the opposition, while between one-fifth and one-third defected from the president's party. These findings indicate that Reagan, Bush, and Clinton were finding fewer fish across the stream without a comparable increase in the prospects of successful fishing on their own side. The standard deviation remains fairly high into the partisan period, indicating that opposition party support varies considerably from one vote to the next. Parties in the House became more partisan, but uncertainty remains.

Patterns of support from Senate partisans are presented in Table 8–4. As in the House, the distributions are somewhat skewed, making the median a better indicator of central tendency. While the rise in overall party voting in the Senate lagged the House by a number of years (Fleisher

Table 8–4
Senate Support for the President's Position

Admin.	President's Party			Opposition Party		
	Mean	Median	Std. Dev.	Mean	Median	Std. Dev.
Eisenhower	75	83	23	37	37	25
Eisenhower	73	77	21	37	37	25
Kennedy	71	77	21	34	30	25
Johnson	64	68	20	47	47	27
Nixon	68	72	20	37	37	23
Nixon	59	65	27	25	20	22
Ford	63	70	23	31	30	23
Carter	68	72	21	39	38	20
Reagan	75	83	24	33	31	22
Reagan	76	82	19	29	26	22
99th	81	86	16	28	26	19
100th	69	74	20	30	25	26
Bush	78	82	17	31	25	26
101st	76	78	18	34	30	27
102d	81	85	16	27	21	24
Clinton	83	91	22	24	14	27
103d	83	93	23	29	18	29
104th	82	89	22	20	9	25

Note: Entries are the percentage of party members voting in agreement with the president's position on roll call votes.

and Bond 1996a; Ornstein, Mann, and Malbin 1998, 210), presidential support from the president's partisans in the Senate increased earlier, during the first Reagan term. Before Reagan, on most votes presidents received support from between two-thirds to three-fourths of the senators in their party. During Reagan's first term, median support from Republicans increased to 83 percent. This level of party support was matched only during Eisenhower's first term. The elevated level of Republican support continued through Reagan's second term and into Bush's. When Clinton was elected, partisan support on most votes in the Senate increased again, rising to about 90 percent. The standard deviation declined somewhat during the Reagan and Bush years, but then returned to more typical levels under Clinton. Compared to the House, therefore, presidential support in the Senate has become more partisan and the increase occurred earlier. Senators may be more individualistic than House members, but when issues got to the Senate floor, Reagan and Bush typically lost only two in ten Republicans, and Clinton lost only one in ten Democrats.

The behavior of opposition party senators did not become more partisan until Reagan's second term. In earlier Congresses, the president typically received votes from more than 30 percent of opposition party senators. During Reagan's second term and continuing through Bush's presidency, support from Senate Democrats declined to about 25 percent. Under Clinton there was a precipitous decline in opposition party support. On most votes in the 103d Senate, Clinton received votes from only 18 percent of Republicans, and in the 104th median Republican support dropped to 9 percent. These scores indicate the most partisan behavior of any Senate party for the period we studied. Once again, we see no downward trend in the standard deviation, indicating no change in the variability of support from one vote to the next.

Congressional leaders are pivotal actors in interactions between the president and Congress. Indeed, the leaders' actions are likely to have more influence on how members of Congress respond to presidential preferences than anything the president can do personally. Therefore, we analyzed the influence of congressional leaders on presidential-congressional relations. We explore the support that presidents receive from party and committee leaders in Congress and the impact that leaders' support has on party support for the president's positions.

Congressional Leaders in a Partisan Era

In this section we look at presidential support from four leaders in each chamber—the majority and minority floor leaders, and the chair and ranking committee members of the committee that considered the bill in question.[10] We were interested in whether elected leaders are more supportive than committee leaders chosen on the basis of seniority and whether the differences discovered changed after reforms weakening the seniority system.

Leader Support

Table 8–5 reports the percentage of roll call votes on which party and committee leaders supported the president's position. Support from the president's party leader is very high throughout the entire period of study. Most presidents receive the support of their party leader more than 80 percent of the time; support from the president's party leader was never less than 75 percent in the House, and it fell below 75 percent only three times in the Senate (Nixon II, Ford, and Carter). This generally high level

Table 8–5

Party and Committee Leader Support for the President

| | House | | | | Senate | | | |
| | President's | | Opposition | | President's | | Opposition | |
Admin.	Party Leader	Comm. Leader	Party Leader	Comm. Leader	Party Leader	Comm. Leader	Party Leader	Comm. Leader
Eisenhower	87	74	52	54	87	87	44	48
Eisenhower	76	66	60	47	91	77	42	52
Kennedy	93	87	35	39	87	63	32	38
Johnson	92	87	35	43	77	57	56	55
Nixon	92	83	61	59	78	67	26	53
Nixon	88	79	29	45	56	61	11	39
Ford	87	83	31	52	66	74	27	49
Carter	77	74	33	46	72	66	49	56
Reagan	81	71	39	47	88	71	33	44
Reagan	77	57	18	22	89	68	31	41
99th	83	59	18	20	96	70	28	40
100th	72	55	18	24	79	64	36	43
Bush	87	68	17	30	92	69	32	39
101st	83	62	18	30	88	68	36	38
102d	90	73	15	30	96	64	28	41
Clinton	82	83	27	28	90	81	18	25
103d	87	85	41	43	90	88	23	27
104th	78	81	16	17	90	75	12	24

Note: Entries are the percentage of votes on which the leader supported the president's position.

---

10. We are not able to analyze the Speaker of the House because he rarely votes.

of support creates a ceiling effect, so there is not much room for it to increase further when Congress becomes more partisan. In the Senate since Reagan, however, support from the president's party leader has increased to near 90 percent or more.

Opposition party leaders have become more partisan in recent Congresses. In the House, we see a sharp decline in support from the opposition party leader in Reagan's second term. Presidents before Reagan typically got the support of the opposition party leader on more than 30 percent of conflictual roll calls. Since 1985 the opposition party leader has supported the president less than 20 percent of the time (with the exception of Clinton in the 103d Congress).[11] Opposition committee leaders in the House were also less supportive after 1985. In the Senate, we do not see a large decline in opposition party or committee leaders' support until Clinton's presidency.

Differences in the behavior of party leaders and committee leaders discovered previously (Bond and Fleisher 1990, 132) continue to appear during much of the recent partisan period: the president's party leader is more supportive than the president's committee leader; the opposition party leader is less supportive than the opposition committee leader. The behavior of party and committee leaders may reflect their different institutional roles. Thus, even after the general rise in partisanship, committee leaders continued to be somewhat less partisan on presidential issues than party leaders. Until Bill Clinton, that is. During his first term, the difference in support from party and committee leaders disappeared.

The analysis of each leader separately, however, overstates the level of certainty in leaders' presidential support. The party and committee leader each defect from their party's position on a meaningful number of votes, and these defections are often on different votes. Therefore, we need to look at how often both leaders in each party are unified on the party position—in other words, how often both the president's party and committee leaders support his position and how often both the opposition party and committee leaders oppose. Table 8–6 reports the results.

Looking at the frequency of unified cues from party and committee leaders, we see that considerable uncertainty continues to prevail in the partisan era. In the less partisan period from Eisenhower through Reagan's first term, both the president's party and committee leaders supported his positions about three-fourths of the time in the House and

---

11. As noted above, the unusually high opposition support for Clinton in the 103d Congress is likely due to his relatively conservative positions on foreign and defense issues.

Table 8-6

Unity of Party and Committee Leader Position

Admin.	President's Party in Support of the President		Opposition Party in Opposition to the President	
	House	Senate	House	Senate
Eisenhower	72	82	38	39
Eisenhower	58	73	28	38
Kennedy	87	63	48	56
Johnson	86	50	49	35
Nixon	78	59	32	35
Nixon	75	47	51	57
Ford	80	61	47	38
Carter	65	55	45	31
Reagan	65	69	48	44
Reagan	52	64	71	47
99th	53	70	73	49
100th	51	53	71	45
Bush	65	64	67	53
101st	60	61	68	52
102d	71	69	71	54
Clinton	72	75	66	69
103d	80	82	48	65
104th	66	70	77	71

Note: Entries are the percentage of roll call votes on which both leaders from the president's party supported his position and the percentage of votes on which both opposition leaders opposed it.

about two-thirds of the time in the Senate. We do not see an increase in unified support from the leaders of the president's party in the more partisan period. Indeed, in the House during Reagan's second term, these leaders provided unified support for the president's position barely half the time. In the Senate, unified support from these leaders is similar in both periods, although there is a slight rise during Clinton's first term.

Opposition party and committee leaders exhibit more consistent partisan opposition in the recent period, but considerable uncertainty prevails in their behavior. In the pre-partisan era, opposition party and committee leaders in the House unified in opposition less than half the time. In the partisan era, these House leaders unified in opposition to the president's position about two-thirds of the time. There is an increase in the Senate as well, but there the pattern differs from the House. In the less partisan period, opposition party leaders and committee leaders opposed the president an average of about 38 percent of the time, slightly less than House leaders during this time. They become slightly more partisan during the two Reagan terms, but still unified against the president on fewer than half the votes. Under Bush, Democratic party and committee leaders opposed the president slightly more than half the time. Then under Clinton, Republican leaders in the Senate unified against the president's position about two-thirds of the time, the same level as House opposition leaders.

Thus, increased partisan voting in Congress has not resulted in more consistent support from leaders in the president's party. Although opposition leaders are somewhat more likely to unify in opposition to the president in recent Congresses, their behavior falls far short of consistent party opposition. Consequently, the president's quest for votes is still characterized by uncertainty. And keep in mind that this analysis focuses on the behavior of only two leaders. The party whips are also important party leaders, and subcommittee chairs and ranking members have become important committee leaders, particularly in the House. Adding the behavior of these leaders to the analysis would certainly reveal even lower levels of consistent partisan behavior on presidential votes in Congress. We turn now to the issue of whether the behavior of congressional leaders has different effects in the more partisan era.

Effects of Leaders on the Support from the Parties

The first place to look for evidence of party and committee leaders' influence is on the behavior of rank-and-file members. As noted earlier, we cannot observe actual leader influence or even their activities to encourage members to support the party. We can, however, analyze patterns of leader-member agreement. The relationships reveal which leaders are likely to be the most relevant predictors of member behavior on presidential roll calls (Bond and Fleisher 1990, 140).

Table 8–7 reports the results of a regression analysis of presidential support from members of each party on party and committee leader support. Because leaders' influence is affected by majority or minority status, the models are constructed to produce separate estimates for majority and minority presidents. We are interested in the effect of elevated partisanship, so the models also estimate separate relationships in the less partisan (1953–1984) and more partisan (1985–1996) periods.

In general, members of Congress tend to respond positively to their own leaders and negatively to the other party's leaders; the positive response to their own leaders is stronger than the negative response to opposition leaders; and the associations are stronger for party leaders than for committee leaders. These overall patterns hold for both majority and minority presidents, both the House and Senate, and in the less and more partisan periods. In the more partisan period, however, these relationships

Table 8–7

Relationships Between Leader Support and Support from Party Members

	House		Senate	
	Pres. Party	*Opp. Party*	*Pres. Party*	*Opp. Party*
Majority Presidents				
President's Party Leader				
Pre-Partisan Period	26.8 (2.6)***	−6.3 (2.2)**	29.7 (1.2)***	−0.9 (1.3)
Partisan Period	34.6 (5.6)***	−13.5 (4.7)**	34.7 (5.0)***	−8.4 (5.4)
President's Committee Leader				
Pre-Partisan Period	16.3 (2.2)***	−4.3 (1.9)*	13.6 (1.1)***	0.1 (1.2)
Partisan Period	20.5 (5.4)***	11.4 (4.6)**	15.1 (5.0)***	−3.1 (5.4)
Opposition Party Leader				
Pre-Partisan Period	− 3.3 (1.7)*	26.4 (1.5)***	−3.1 (1.1)**	26.3 (1.2)***
Partisan Period	− 16.2 (4.6)***	35.8 (3.8)***	−8.4 (4.9)*	43.9 (5.3)***
Opposition Committee Leader				
Pre-Partisan Period	− 0.8 (2.4)	12.0 (1.4)***	−1.4 (1.1)	12.6 (1.2)***
Partisan Period	0.8 (4.5)	13.5 (3.8)***	−4.9 (4.3)	11.3 (4.6)**
Minority Presidents				
President's Party Leader				
Pre-Partisan Period	33.8 (2.1)***	0.5 (1.7)	24.5 (1.5)***	−0.7 1.7)
Partisan Period	37.7 (1.9)***	3.6 (1.6)*	35.8 (2.6)***	−11.7 (2.9)***
President's Committee Leader				
Pre-Partisan Period	12.7 (1.8)***	−2.5 (1.5)*	15.9 (1.5)***	−2.4 (1.7)
Partisan Period	16.2 (1.6)***	−0.6 (1.3)	9.1 (1.9)***	1.3 (2.0)
Opposition Party Leader				
Pre-Partisan Period	5.6 (1.7)**	31.7 (1.5)***	1.7 (1.4)	23.4 (1.5)***
Partisan Period	9.5 (2.2)***	33.0 (1.9)***	3.9 (2.1)*	23.4 (2.3)***
Opposition Committee Leader				
Pre-Partisan Period	− 0.6 (1.8)	12.0 (1.5)***	0.1 (1.4)	17.9 (1.5)***
Partisan Period	− 2.4 (2.0)	18.5 (1.7)***	−1.9 (2.0)	21.7 (2.1)***
Partisan Period (Yes =1)	− 2.0 (1.8)	8.4 (2.0)***	3.4 (2.8)	3.4 (3.0)
Majority Control (Yes=1)	6.2 (2.8)*	4.9 (2.3)*	0.5 (0.0)***	0.0 (0.0)
Constant	30.1 (1.8)***	18.1 (1.6)***	37.7 (0.9)***	20.8 (1.0)***
R–Squared	.45	.61	.46	.47
N	2,202	2,202	2,570	2,570

Note: Entries are Ordinary Least Squares regression coefficients. Standard errors in parentheses.
* −p<.05; ** −p<.01; *** −p<.001

tend to be stronger; that is, members' positive response to their own leaders and the negative response to opposition leaders are stronger in the period since 1985.

Uncertainty remains high in the more partisan period. Even if the president gets his party and committee leaders' support, defections are still common. And, as we see in Tables 8–4 and 8–5, the president does not automatically get the support of his leaders. There is, nonetheless, an association between leader support and the level of support from rank-and-file partisans, and the association is stronger in the recent period. The cost of not getting leader support, therefore, is quite high, and higher in the recent period. For example, when a majority party president failed to get the support of the majority leader in the recent period, he received about 35 percent fewer votes from his partisans in both chambers.

Our previous analysis revealed that the president faces trade-offs in his quest for votes from members with different partisan and ideological predispositions (Bond and Fleisher 1990, 118–20). Those trade-offs are still present. Getting the support of a leader increases support from members of that party, but reduces support from members of the other party. Because the relationships are stronger in the partisan period, the trade-offs are also greater.

Effects of Leaders on Winning and Losing

Although the relationships between leaders' support for the president's position and support from rank-and-file party members is interesting, the more important issue is whether the president's preferences win or lose on the floor. Table 8–8 reports a logit analysis of the effects of leaders' support on whether the president wins or loses (win = 1, lose = 0). Logit analysis is a technique, similar to ordinary regression analysis, that allows us to estimate the effect of one or more independent variables on a dependent variable that has a limited number of categories. In our analysis, the number of possible outcomes on the dependent variable is two: the president either wins or loses the vote. Unlike in regression analysis, the magnitude of the coefficients produced by logit analysis cannot be interpreted directly but must be converted to probabilities. We constructed the models to estimate separate relationships for majority and minority presidents in the less partisan and more partisan periods. To have a more complete model, we also included controls for honeymoons (the first nine months of a newly elected president's term) and public approval of the president's job performance at the time of the vote. The logit analysis reveals that support from party leaders and from committee chairs significantly affects the probability that the president's position will win on the floor. The proportional reduction in error (PRE) is 47 percent in the House model and 35 percent in the Senate. In addition, the president is more likely to win during the honeymoon period and if his party controls the chamber. To see the substantive effects of leader support, we also reported the predicted change in probability of victory if the president gets support from a particular leader (Greene 1993, 638-41).[12]

12. This technique estimates the change in probability from .5, when the variable changes from zero, to 1 (that is, if the president gets the leader's support). Since the logit curve is steepest at .5 probability, these estimates indicate the maximum effect each variable can have in the model.

Table 8–8
Logit Analysis of Leader Support and Presidential Success

	House		Senate	
	Logit Coeff.	Δ p	*Logit Coeff.*	Δ p
Majority Presidents				
President's Party Leader				
Pre-Partisan Period	1.85 (.33)***	.36	2.46 (.18)***	.42
Partisan Period	2.44 (.70)***	.42	2.78 (.83)***	.44
President's Committee Leader				
Pre-Partisan Period	1.39 (.28)***	.30	1.44 (.18)***	.31
Partisan Period	1.86 (.69)**	.37	1.12 (.72)	
Opposition Party Leader				
Pre-Partisan Period	1.26 (.29)***	.28	1.42 (.21)***	.31
Partisan Period	−.07 (.80)		2.75 (1.05)**	.44
Opposition Committee Leader				
Pre-Partisan Period	.46 (.25)*	.11	.37 (.19)*	.09
Partisan Period	1.19 (.82)		−.62 (.69)	
Minority Presidents				
President's Party Leader				
Pre-Partisan Period	1.42 (.30)***	.31	1.00 (.23)***	.23
Partisan Period	1.82 (.33)***	.36	1.53 (.44)**	.32
President's Committee Leader				
Pre-Partisan Period	.23 (.25)		.33 (.23)	
Partisan Period	.19 (.22)		.49 (.26)*	.12
Opposition Party Leader				
Pre-Partisan Period	2.20 (.23)***	.40	1.84 (.22)***	.36
Partisan Period	1.62 (.28)***	.32	1.95 (.36)***	.38
Opposition Committee Leader				
Pre-Partisan Period	1.32 (.22)***	.29	1.45 (.19)***	.31
Partisan Period	1.46 (.23)***	.31	1.61 (.27)***	.33
Partisan Period (Yes =1)	−.39 (.43)		−.41 (.49)	
Majority Control (Yes =1)	.73 (.43)*	.17	.04 (.01)***	.01
Honeymoon (Yes =1)	.68 (.21)***	.17	.61 (.18)***	.15
Presidential Approval	.00 (.01)		.00 (.00)	
Constant	−2.86(.41)***		−2.24(.28)***	
N	2,190		2,546	
% modal category/% correctly predicted/PRE	53%/ 80%/ 57.4		65%/ 80%/ 42.8	

Note: Entries are logit coefficients. Standard errors in parentheses.
*–p< .05; **–p < .01; ***–p < .001

The results of this analysis reveal that the rise in partisanship since the mid-1980s has not reduced uncertainty for the president. Instead, under similar circumstances, the probability of victory is lower in the partisan period. While we might have expected minority presidents to have more difficulty winning in a more partisan environment (Fleisher and Bond 1996b), this analysis shows that the decline in probability characterizes majority presidents as well. First, let us look at the constant terms. In the less partisan period, majority control increased the chances of victory .17

in the House. In the Senate the coefficient is statistically significant, but the change in probability is trivial. Majority control is less of an advantage in the Senate because traditions nurture individualism, and Senate rules bestow great power on the minority to frustrate majority rule. Howard Baker, R-Tenn., a former Senate majority leader, once likened his job to "herding cats." He explained, "It is trying to make 99 independent souls act in concert under rules that encourage polite anarchy and embolden people who find majority rule a dubious proposition at best" (quoted in Merida 1999, C1). The coefficient for the partisan period variable indicates the change in the intercept. Since this coefficient is negative (though it is not significant), it suggests that the benefits of majority control are less (or at least no greater) than in the less partisan period. Overall, elevated partisanship has not increased the probability of victory for majority presidents, and may even have decreased it.

For majority presidents, the benefit of attracting support from his own party leaders is higher in the partisan period, but not by much. Keep in mind that the only majority presidents in the partisan period are Reagan in the 99th Senate and Clinton in the 103d House and Senate. In the partisan 103d House, the probability of victory with majority leader support was only .06 higher than in the pre-partisan period, and .07 higher with the support from the chair of the committee of jurisdiction. But appealing to opposition leaders no longer helps. Although taking positions that gained support of the House minority leaders increased the president's probability of victory in the pre-partisan period, getting opposition leader support in the partisan period has no significant effect. In the Senate, the effect of majority leader support is only .02 higher in the partisan period, and the effect of committee chair support is no longer significant. Getting support from the Senate minority leader, however, increases the chances of a floor victory more in the partisan period (the probability is .13 higher). This finding may reflect the difficulty of winning on the Senate floor with a simple majority. Needing sixty votes to break a filibuster requires even majority presidents and the Senate majority leader to accommodate the views of minority senators. Support from the minority leader may indicate that such an accommodation has been reached.

For minority presidents in the partisan period (Reagan, Bush, and Clinton in the 104th Congress), uncertainty is greater. In the House, there is little difference in the effect of gaining support of the president's own party and committee leaders in the two periods. Getting the House majority leader's support increases the probability of victory, but the effect is less in the partisan period. Getting the committee chair's support is about the same in both periods. In the Senate, minority presidents who got the support of their own party and committee leaders were more likely to win in the partisan period, but getting the support of the majority party and committee leaders has about the same effect in both periods.

Conclusion

We began this chapter with the observation that party leaders in the 105th Congress faced considerable uncertainty as they tried to anticipate members' votes on articles of impeachment against President Clinton. Although all of the impeachment votes turned out to be highly partisan, leaders had difficulty predicting how many of their co-partisans would defect from the party's preferred position. Our view is that the uncertainty on the impeachment votes was not unusual. By analyzing a large number of votes, we found that the president's quest for support in Congress remains uncertain even in this era of elevated partisanship. The continued uncertainty results because defections from members' partisan and ideological predispositions are still quite common. The American system is indeed one of *separate* institutions sharing power. This institutional separation means that even highly partisan members of Congress can and do act in ways independent of the president and party because frequently their political and institutional interests conflict with their partisan and ideological predispositions.

Although defection from partisan predispositions is common in both parties, we found that the degree of partisanship on presidential votes is not symmetrical—it occurred first and with greater intensity in the party in opposition than among the president's co-partisans. One result of the asymmetry in the increase in partisanship in the two parties is that presidents often find it more difficult to attract support from the opposition party without a corresponding increase in the certainty of support from their own partisans. Consequently, increased partisanship has made the president's job of governing more difficult rather than less.

Greater party cohesion resulted in part from the disappearance of the cross-pressured faction in each party. The disappearance of the middle made it easier for party caucuses to agree on policy proposals, but made it more difficult to reach compromises across the aisle. Yet the fact remains that individual members still defect and support the other party's position when they believe that doing so is in their interest. These defections continue to occur with considerable frequency. American politics during the past fifteen years, therefore, has produced the sharp, partisan, and ideological divisions found in responsible party systems, but not the certainty associated with political control of the policy-making process.

Defections are common not only among the rank and file, but also among party leaders. The behavior of party and committee leaders on presidential votes has also become more partisan in recent Congresses—leaders of the president's party are more likely to support his positions, and leaders of the opposition party are more likely to oppose. But leader support of the president's positions remains far from certain, with one or more leaders defecting from the president's position on between one-fourth to one-third of votes. Regression analysis indicates that while leaders continue to affect the votes of the rank and file in expected ways, support from the leadership does not automatically translate into universal support from the "back benchers." The loss of support of the leadership is associated with significant decline in support from the members. Our analysis of presidential wins and losses on conflictual roll calls indicates that even with more cohesive and opposing parties, majority as well as minority presidents continue to face considerable uncertainty on the floor.

Appendix

Research Design

The basic unit of analysis is the roll call vote in Congress. A victory is a vote on which the president's position prevails on the floor of the House or Senate, given the decision rule on that vote. If the president's position requires a supermajority to win, it is coded as a presidential victory only if the required supermajority votes in agreement with the president.

The data base is all conflictual roll calls in the House and Senate on which the president expressed a position (n = 2,886 House votes, 3,325 Senate votes). A conflictual roll call is defined as a vote on which there is less than 80 percent agreement with the president's position. We eliminate nonconflictual presidential victories to filter out minor and routine issues on which there is little disagreement. A spot check of these near unanimous presidential victories reveals that, with rare exceptions, these are votes dealing with minor or routine issues. Votes on which 80 percent or more vote *against* the president's position remain in the data set. Although there are only a small number of votes on which the presidents stands alone against a virtually unanimous Congress, we decided to retain these cases in the analysis because they represent institutional conflict and therefore are neither trivial nor routine.

This research design allows us to analyze variation in presidential wins and losses, as well as variation in levels of presidential support from the four party factions across roll call votes. Presidential positions on roll calls are identified by Congressional Quarterly (*Congressional Quarterly Almanac* 1953–1997).

Identification of Party Factions

As noted above, for most of the last half century, both parties in Congress contained a mainstream and cross-pressured faction. Students of presidential-congressional relations are aware of the ideological diversity of American parties. Because there is a geographical cast to these party factions, a common method of dealing with this diversity is to divide members along regional lines: many conservative Democrats are from the South; many liberal Republicans are from the Northeast. A common measure of ideology is the conservative coalition—votes on which a majority of southern Democrats and Republicans vote against a majority of nonsouthern Democrats are defined as "conservative coalition votes" (Congressional Quarterly 1953–1997). The "conservative" side of an issue (yea or nay) is the one supported by a majority of southern Democrats and Republicans. Some studies divide Republicans into a northeastern ("liberal") wing and all other Republicans.

As a measure of ideology, however, region is an indirect and imprecise indicator. Furthermore, for a number of reasons, southern Democrats have become more like their nonsouthern colleagues (Rohde 1991; Fleisher 1993), and conservative Democrats are no longer exclusively from the South (Bond and Fleisher 1995). In the House in recent years, for example, about one-third of southern Democrats were African American or Hispanic. These southern Democrats have voting records on the liberal side of the distribution. And even white Democrats from the South have more liberal voting records in recent Congresses. Because southern Democrats are no longer uniformly conservative, the traditional definition of the conservative coalition is suspect as a measure of the conservative position on a vote. The regional split in the Republican Party has not been as distinct as in the Democratic Party, and, as a group, northeastern Republicans are no longer much more liberal than their colleagues from other regions. We have the ability to measure the ideological orientation of members of Congress more precisely in order to identify cross-pressured members regardless of the region from which they come.

Indexes calculated by the Americans for Constitutional Action or the American Conservative Union (conservative groups) and Americans for Democratic Action (a liberal group) are frequently used indicators of general ideology. Using these indexes to analyze presidential-congressional relations, however, is problematic because some votes used in the indexes are also presidential roll calls used to measure members' support for the administration's position. To minimize this circularity, we purged votes on which the president expressed a position from the lists of ideological votes selected by ACA/ACU and ADA and recalculated liberalism scores for all members of Congress from 1953 to 1994.

We use the lists of votes selected by two ideological groups to identify a subset of roll calls that evoke a strong liberal/conservative division on the floor and to determine *a priori* what the "liberal" position is. A liberal position is defined as a vote in agreement with the ADA position or against the ACA/ACU position.[13] We use the list of votes selected by both groups and calculate scores for each Congress (two years) in order to have enough votes for a stable measure. Although each group typically selects between ten and twenty votes per year in each chamber, eliminating votes on which the president takes a position reduces the number of usable ideological votes. Using votes selected by two groups and calculating scores for a Congress increases the chances that there are enough votes remaining on which to calculate stable ideology scores for members of Congress (we adopted a standard of a minimum of ten votes).[14]

We use the mean liberalism score for each party to define the party mainstreams for each chamber. Cross-pressured members are defined as those who have liberalism scores closer to the mean of the opposition party than to the mean of their party.[15] Levels of support from each party faction were coded as variables on each presidential roll call. We also coded the positions of party and committee leaders on each vote. Thus, we can observe differences in presidential support from each party faction and from congressional leaders across the sample of roll calls.

---

13. ADA votes are used for the entire time series. ACA votes are available from 1958 to 1984. After 1984 ACU votes are used.

14. Only in the 87th House and Senate and the 88th House were there less than ten votes on the ACA and ADA lists on which the president did not express a position. In these cases, we had no choice but to supplement the list with conservative coalition votes on which the president did not take a position. In the 1950s and early 1960s, the coalition of a majority of Republicans and a majority of southern Democrats consistently expressed the conservative position on issues.

15. Some might have preferred using the party medians. We found that the means and medians are close and the mid-points between them similar (Bond and Fleisher 1990, 85). During the period from 1985 to 1994, for example, only ten cases out of more than two thousand would have been classified differently had we used the median.

CHAPTER 9

Polarized Politics: Does It Matter?

Richard Fleisher and Jon R. Bond

Every two years the electoral process puts into positions of power individuals representing different constituencies, having different ideas about what form policy should take, and acting out different personal ambitions. Conflict among these actors empowered by the "rules of the game" is a constant feature of American politics. At various times in the nation's history, the struggle between such individuals to influence the content of government policy has manifested itself in heightened partisanship, as has been the case for much of the past two decades.

The chapters in this book systematically address how polarized politics has affected interaction between the president and Congress in the formation of public policy. The authors explore a diverse set of activities: elections, the setting of the policy agenda, and the journey of legislation through the complexities of a decentralized, bicameral process characterized by multiple decision points. The contestants involved in this process not only battle one another in the formal processes of government, but also extend the battle to words waged in print, over the airways, and in cyberspace.

While each of the chapters explores presidential-congressional interactions from the author's own perspective, there are some common themes. In this concluding chapter we consider some of these as we address the questions raised in Chapter 1.

Party Control of Governing Institutions: Does It Matter?

The first and most basic question is whether party matters in American politics. If party does not matter, then it should make no difference whether partisan control of Congress and the presidency is the same or different. A related question is what are the effects of divided party control of government. The tendency of the American electoral process to produce divided government is not new; in fact, it was common in the nineteenth century. For much of the first half of the twentieth century, however, the same party controlled the presidency and both houses of the Congress. In the post–World War II period, divided party government again became the norm.

Given the frequency of divided government, it should not be surprising that political scientists began to ask whether party control of the federal government's political institutions matters. The literature on national-level policy making often observes that unified party control of the national government does not result in quick, efficient enactment of the ruling party's program as one might expect. The president in consultation with the majority party leadership in Congress cannot simply announce a platform and expect it to be routinely adopted. Reforms adopted early in the twentieth century, as well as those that came just after World War II, weakened party leadership in Congress and strengthened the power of committees and committee chairs. Party leaders in the United States lack the tools to compel the rank and file to support party positions. As governing agents, U.S. political parties are noted for their weakness, and students of American politics observed a further weakening during the 1960s and 1970s (Brady, Cooper, and Hurley 1979; Hurley and Wilson 1989).

Yet some commentators argue that the difficulty in adopting policies—especially those intended to solve the nation's social and economic problems—became more acute in recent decades. The culprit responsible for this difficulty is the increased frequency of divided government (Cutler 1988; Ginsberg and Shefter 1990; Sundquist 1988). If party leaders cannot control the policy-making machinery when party control is unified, they become even less able to do so when the institutions are controlled by different parties. The negative effects of divided government are exacerbated by yet another change in U.S. politics: the rise of partisanship in Congress and the presidency. As a result, *gridlock* and *stalemate* have become common terms in the political lexicon.

Other commentators caution against blaming these ills exclusively on divided government. According to Morris Fiorina (1996, 106–7), the limited amount of systematic research "fails to support the stronger claims of the critics of divided government." A number of scholars argue that the idea of divided party control producing policy gridlock is a gross oversimplification. David Mayhew (1991) was among the first to challenge the conventional wisdom about divided government. He presents evidence showing that the system produces approximately the same amount of important legislation under divided party control as it does under unified government. Subsequent research identified a number of problems with Mayhew's analysis. Studies that correct these problems show that divided government does indeed hold back legislation (Edwards, Barrett, and Peake 1997; Kelly 1993a). Other scholars argue that the difficulty in enacting legislation is not a function of which party controls the institutions of government; rather it results from the need to fashion majority coalitions among members representing diverse constituency preferences (Brady and Volden 1998). Furthermore, the rules of the process require that those trying to enact new legislation build supermajorities to overcome the opposition of other actors in the process (Brady and Volden 1998; Krehbiel 1998). These features of the American system retard the passage of legislation even under unified party control.

Still, it is clear from this research that the U.S. government can and does legislate whether party control is unified or divided. Terms such as *gridlock* and *stalemate,* suggesting a lack of movement toward solving the nation's problems, do not accurately describe the operation of the American political system. Looking back at the budget battles of the 1990s, we see that even with partisan conflict between President Clinton and Republicans in Congress at a maximum and the mutual trust and respect necessary to promote compromise at a minimum, the system eventually produced a budget. But saying that gridlock is not an apt metaphor does not suggest that divided government presents no problems; those who argue that party control of the government matters little may be equally wrong in their conclusion. The evidence presented in this book clearly shows that party does matter in American national government.

If party matters, how does it matter? In their chapter, John Aldrich and David Rohde (2000a) offer theory and evidence of how party matters in the House. They argue that the power of majority and minority parties is not the same, but asymmetric. The majority party's advantage derives in large part from the ability to structure the choices available to members. The majority party controls access to the floor, the rules of debate and amendment, and the timing of votes. The minority party has much less ability to control these resources. In addition, when party leaders need to attract votes from recalcitrant members, the majority party's inducements are more valuable than those available to the minority. As a result, the majority party wins more policy battles than the minority. Because of the majority party's asymmetric influence, the minority party is motivated to become the majority and is constantly trying to make this happen. If party control does not matter as some argue (Krehbiel 1998), then why would the minority try so hard to become the majority?

Aldrich and Rohde refer to their theory as *conditional party government*. Because the U.S. electoral system produces weak, undisciplined parties, the majority party's ability to use its greater influence for policy advantage is not automatic. Instead, majority party power is "conditional." The condition necessary for party government is homogeneous preferences within the majority party—that is, relative consensus on certain important policy proposals on the party agenda (Aldrich 1995; Aldrich and Rohde 2000a; Rohde 1991). If that condition is met, the majority party caucus will give leaders additional powers to enact the agenda (or at least those items on which there is agreement) and will expect the leaders to use those powers. Beginning in the mid-1980s, the condition was met. The voting records of Democrats and Republicans in Congress diverged, while the intraparty differences in voting decreased (Fleisher and Bond 1996a, 2000; Jacobson 2000; Ornstein, Mann, and Malbin 1998; Rohde 1991). As a result, today the two parties are more homogeneous internally and farther apart from each other than was the case for much of the twentieth century.

The condition of greater homogeneity within the parties and the greater polarization between them is due in part to changes in the electoral system (Fleisher 1993; Fleisher and Bond 1996a, 2000; Jacobson 2000; Rohde 1991). These changes are significant even for those who believe that behavior in the legislative process is fundamentally a reflection of each member's preferences. When partisan constituencies in different parts of the country had diverse policy preferences, parties in Congress reflected that diversity. Each party contained a sizable cross-pressured minority—conservative Democrats and liberal Republicans—with policy preferences that reflected their constituencies but differed from the mainstream of their party. Indeed, these cross-pressured members had policy preferences closer to the mean of the other party than to their own (Bond and Fleisher 1990). When the changes in the electoral system produced more homogeneous partisan constituencies, the cross-pressured partisans in Congress all but disappeared (see Table 8–1, page 166). Compare the bar graphs in Figure 2–1 (page 12) to see how congressional parties became more internally homogeneous over time.

The disappearance of cross-pressured members changed the bargaining process in Congress. As the conditional party government theory suggests, a more ideologically homogeneous majority party caucus was willing to give party leaders more power to increase the likelihood that agreed-upon policies were enacted (Rohde 1991). But compromise on divisive issues became more difficult. The few cross-pressured members that remain in each party are less able to influence caucus decisions. With less need to compromise to accommodate diverse interests within each party, there is also less incentive for the majority party to compromise with the minority party. Partisanship is stronger in the House, because House rules permit a cohesive majority to rule. In the Senate, where the rules protect the power of individuals, compromise is more common even though partisanship has increased there as well (Fleisher and Bond 1996a, 2000).

The greater polarization of the parties has increased the leaders' propensity to use their resources and powers to enact legislation containing more of the majority party's preferences and fewer of the minority party's. In an earlier study, we found that the president's positions are more likely to prevail on roll call votes if his party controls the chamber (Bond and Fleisher 1990). Research reported in the present volume finds that this relationship characterizes interactions between the president and Congress at stages prior to the roll call vote. George Edwards and Andrew Barrett (2000) and Barbara Sinclair (2000) show that under the conditions of unified party control and increased partisanship, presidents are more likely to be in agreement with congressional decisions, including the agenda and what is adopted in committee and on the floor.

Party control affects the words spoken by actors in the policy process as well as deeds to enact party policies. Tim Groeling and Samuel Kernell (2000) observe that words have strategic value because they send signals to other actors in the policy process as well as to supporters in the outside world. Under divided government, they find that talk changes as "party members can find common advantage in attacking the opposition" rather than criticizing members of their own party. A political party is like a family. As with most families, there are diverse preferences and frequent conflicts. Yet, if the family is threatened by an outsider, the members come together. As Richard Neustadt (1960, 187) observes, "Bargaining 'within the family' has a rather different quality than bargaining with members of the rival clan."

Although the rise of conditional party government has increased the majority party's power to influence policy, especially under unified government, enacting policy under the American system is still a difficult task for at least two reasons. First, even with greater homogeneity within the parties, the votes of party members cannot be taken for granted. On any given issue, there is always considerable uncertainty whether any particular member will vote with fellow partisans (Fleisher and Bond 2000). And as Groeling and Kernell (2000) point out, members of the same political party frequently criticize their fellow partisans. Second, government power in the American system remains fragmented among different institutions. The Constitution divides power not only among the different branches of government, but also between the House and Senate. Congress is actually two separate legislative institutions with different rules and traditions. Senate rules—the filibuster in particular—allow the minority to block legislation preferred by the majority (Binder 1997; Binder and Smith 1997; Brady and Volden 1998; Krehbiel 1998). Historically, the filibuster was a tool individual members could use to block legislation they personally opposed. Once an unusual occurrence, the use of the filibuster has become more common in recent decades. In the 1950s there was an average of about one filibuster per Congress; in the 1990s the average was more than thirty. The filibuster has been used in the Senate for more than 150 years, but "nearly half of all identifiable filibusters . . . have occurred since 1980" (Democratic Study Group 1994, 1). And there is evidence that rules afforded to individual members are now used as part of a coordinated partisan strategy. Sarah Binder and Steven Smith (1997, 148) note that Republicans using the filibuster during the 103d Congress "seemed to be targeting the majority party's reputation as much as its legislation."

The battle by each party to gain control of policy making has changed the legislative process in other ways. During the late nineteenth and early twentieth centuries, both the House of Representatives and the Senate adopted formal rules and developed informal norms to make debate and discussion by the members more civil (Polsby 1968). Members were expected to act toward one another with civility. As Eric Uslaner (1993) documents, the past several decades have seen a decline of comity in Congress as members violated both the rules and norms of civil behavior more often. To be sure, the lack of civility was not all directed at the opposition party. Members in both chambers have become less civil even toward members and presidents of their own political party. But the tensions produced by increased partisanship and higher stakes associated with majority party control have made the legislative process less collegial. Kathleen Hall Jamieson and Erika Falk (2000) look at two indicators of breaches of civility: when words spoken on the House floor were ruled out of order and when members requested that the words spoken by another member "be taken down" by the Speaker. Analysis indicates that between 1952 and 1978 such actions were rare. After 1978 both indicators show an increase, reaching a peak in 1995. If *gridlock* does not accurately describe policy making in the U.S. government, another traffic metaphor, *road rage,* might be used to characterize the highly charged partisan environment of the recent period. Political elites show little hesitation at venting their frustration at figures from the opposition party, even over trivial differences in policy. The old norm of political discourse that encourages one "to disagree without being disagreeable" seems to have been replaced by members who are "disagreeable even when they don't disagree."

Evaluating Democratic Institutions in a Partisan Era

A second theme is democratic responsiveness and accountability. When American political parties were at their weakest and the policy-making system was more decentralized, critics cried out against a system that was perceived to sacrifice certain values thought to be crucial to democracy. Some observed that this system produced responsiveness to constituent desires but minimized collective responsibility for the performance of the policy-making system (Fiorina 1977; Jacobson 1997). Others noted that a decentralized system tilted the process in favor of the organized and the affluent at the expense of the less organized and less affluent (Baumgartner and Leech 1998; Schattschneider 1960; Schlozman and Tierney 1986). Leading political scientists writing in the 1940s and 1950s produced a manifesto urging the strengthening of the political parties to improve American democracy.

Yet the emergence of stronger, more coherent, and more polarized political parties has not stemmed dissatisfaction with the state of American politics. Indicators abound. Everett Ladd and Karlyn Bowman (1998) document the dissatisfaction of citizens with the performance of government. John Hibbing and Elizabeth Thiess-Morse (1995) attribute the dissatisfaction to the public's general dislike of the "messiness" of democratic politics in a presidential system.

Although this dissatisfaction likely has a number of sources, we believe it is safe to attribute some of it to the rise in partisan behavior. The data presented by Hibbing and Thiess-Morse indicate that the public does not like the need for compromise and bargaining, preferring a more efficient system. The combined effects of divided government and heightened partisanship make more visible exactly those aspects of a democratic political process that citizens find distasteful. The need for bargaining and compromise and the greater difficulty in working out bargains acceptable to both parties exacerbates the public's dissatisfaction with politics. As Gary Jacobson (2000) notes, the 1998 National Election Studies survey found that 84 percent of the public expressed the view that Congress was "too involved in partisan politics."

Dissatisfaction with the highly charged partisan atmosphere is not limited to ordinary citizens. A number of elites directly involved in the policy-making process have expressed a similar dissatisfaction. Some members of Congress who voluntarily retired said that intense partisanship contributed to their decision not to run again. In 1997 members from both political parties met in Hershey, Pennsylvania, to discuss ways to reduce the incivility of congressional partisanship. Just two years later, another retreat to Hershey continued the effort.

The rise of intense partisan conflict in both words and deeds set against the backdrop of public dissatisfaction with the condition of the political system offers an opportunity to assess the consequences of this state of affairs. Has the development of a partisan political system affected the health of American democracy?

To answer this question, we need to be clear about what we mean by democracy. One way of defining democracy is in terms of the concepts of representation, responsiveness, and accountability. Although these are central concepts in many theories of democracy, their definitions remain quite ambiguous. One prominent scholar suggests that Congress is a representative body where "we expect members to bring into the legislative process the views, needs, and desires of their constituents, and we expect Congress as an institution to provide the forum where the interests and demands of all segments of society are expressed" (Sinclair 1997, 231). Others view representation as reflecting a congruence between the behavior of the individual legislator and the policy preferences of citizens (Clausen 1973; Jacobson 1997; Miller and Stokes 1963). Policy congruence can come about because policy makers hold views that are similar to the views of the constituents that elected them. Another way to achieve policy congruence is to create some incentive for policy-making elites to take the views of citizens into account when making policy decisions (Luttbeg 1974). The competitive election, in which elites must secure the support of citizens to gain a position in the policy process, is typically viewed as the primary means by which elites are made responsive to the preferences of those who elect them. Accountability means having to answer to citizens for past behavior. When making choices between competing elites, voters can consider the future behavior of the various candidates or they can hold them accountable by judging their past performance.

Does the current system encourage or discourage policy representation, responsiveness, and accountability? There is little evidence to support a claim that members of Congress have become less responsive to constituent preferences. The classic tradeoff between voting constituency or voting party noted by some scholars (for example, Turner 1951; Turner and Schneier 1970) is most likely to occur when members of a particular party represent a local constituency with policy preferences different from the party mainstreams. It is cross-pressured members that frequently confront this tradeoff. The increase in partisan behavior does not mean that members have sacrificed constituents' preferences to vote with party leaders. Quite the contrary. The theory of conditional party government assumes that members act as representatives of local constituent interests (Aldrich and Rohde 2000; Rohde 1991). Increased partisanship comes about not because members are shunning constituency for the sake of party but because the constituencies represented by members of a political party have become more similar. There are fewer cross-pressured members who must confront the trade-off between party and constituency (Fleisher and Bond 2000; Jacobson 2000). The increase in party voting, therefore, is not at odds with responsiveness to constituents. Members still speak passionately for the interests they believe put them in office and whose support is crucial to remain there. If anything, some have expressed the concern that the process has become too open, and government officials are too accessible to the public (Mayer and Canon 1999). Those who take the time to look will find that much more of the policy-making behavior of members is carried out in the open than was the case several decades ago. And many citizens do not like what they see.

If members have not diminished their attention to constituency, why are constituents unhappy with Congress? First, we need to keep in mind that it has long been the case that the institution of Congress receives lower marks than individual members (Fenno 1975; Hibbing and Thiess-Morse 1995; Parker and Davidson 1979). Second, we should take a closer look at the type of constituents being spoken for by members of Congress. As Richard Fleisher and Jon Bond (1996a) and Jacobson (2000) point out, the polarization of the parties in Congress is reflected in a polarization of the electorate—the core electoral constituencies within each party have become more polarized. This polarization is particularly characteristic of active citizens who contribute money and work on election campaigns. But not all voters have polarized. Many citizens hold moderate policy views and base their electoral choices on retrospective performance-based evaluations. These centrist voters have been left behind by the parties, which have become more extreme.

What about accountability? One of the hallmarks of a political system based on strong parties is that citizens can hold the governing party responsible for its policy-making behavior and the consequences of the policies adopted. When the government is divided, however, strong parties make attributing responsibility for its performance extremely difficult. Both sides engage in a "blame game" in which they try to convince voters to hold the other party accountable for the failures of government. Just as diverse parties operating in a decentralized policy-making process make it difficult for voters to assign blame and credit, more homogeneous, cohesive parties accompanied by divided party control have the same effect (Fiorina 1996).

However, voters do not have to hold policy makers accountable to promote responsiveness. Sometimes just the fear that they might is enough. As we noted above, the gridlock metaphor, which implies an absence of movement, is too strong to accurately describe government responsiveness. Polarized parties in separate institutions *do* come together to pass needed legislation. Two conditions promote such agreement. One is consensus. Much of the legislation that makes its way past the roadblocks in the fragmented American system does so because there is a general consensus in the nation about the need for it. This observation implies that many of the policies stalled by so-called gridlock are those on which there is not yet a sufficient consensus on the need for government action—or at least for *this* action. The other condition that fosters agreement between warring parties and branches of government is fear—fear that voters will hold them accountable for failure. Fear of voters' retribution seems to have contributed to the compromise between Clinton and congressional Republicans on the 1998 budget. Some level of responsiveness and accountability is achieved through a process of anticipated reactions.

Presidential-Congressional Relations: Will Polarized Politics Continue?

We end with some consideration and speculation about the future and longevity of polarized politics. The polarized politics we have observed since the 1980s is unlikely to last forever. We have witnessed earlier periods when political parties displayed high levels of internal cohesion and external differences, only to see polarized politics give way to calmer competition. From observing these past cycles, we can speculate about what might cause the party system to once again turn away from partisan politics, but we have no way of predicting when this might happen.

By specifying the conditions necessary for polarized parties, the theory of conditional party government identifies a set of conditions that could ameliorate the conflict. The theory starts with the assumption that individual members of Congress seek to adopt policies that are at least partially shaped by the desires of the constituents they represent. Changes in voters' policy preferences could register either in a change in the voting behavior of elected officials or the election of a new representative whose policy preferences are closer to constituent preferences than the previous incumbent's.

In this vein, Rohde (1991) discussed how the shift in electoral politics in the South changed the type of Democrats elected from the region and helped reinvigorate the Republican Party there. After the 1965 Voting Rights Act was implemented, southern blacks began voting in greater numbers and overwhelmingly backed Democratic candidates. Consequently, the electoral constituencies of southern Democrats moved to the left. The election of more liberal southern Democrats also depended on a sufficient number of white voters joining with blacks to back these candidates (Fleisher 1993). One result was that electoral politics in the South changed from a one-party system into a competitive two party system. Voters, activists, candidates, and a few Democratic members of Congress who held the most conservative policy preferences found a home in the Republican Party. The movement out of the Democratic Party of those holding the most conservative policy views moved the party to the left.

Redistricting in the 1990s also played a role. Drawing districts to increase the number of African Americans and Latinos elected to Congress worked, and record numbers of African Americans and Latinos won House seats in the 1990s. But a side effect of packing large blocs of these reliably Democratic voters into "majority minority" districts was the defeat of several moderate white Democrats by conservative Republicans (Hill 1995). In the 106th Congress, Republicans hold 71 of 125 (57 percent) southern House seats. Of the 54 remaining southern Democrats, 21 (39 percent) are black or Latino. Republicans also hold 14 of 22 (64 percent) of southern Senate seats. As the South elected fewer cross-pressured Democrats, the most intense regional split within the Democratic Party disappeared, resulting in a more homogenous Democratic caucus in Congress.

A similar but less dramatic shift occurred in the Republican Party, with fewer cross-pressured Republicans being elected from the Northeast. Historically, northeastern Republicans were less conservative than Republicans elected elsewhere. But while the South was experiencing its realignment, a less pronounced electoral transformation was taking place in the frost belt. Party activists, Republican contributors, and core Republican voters shifted to the right, making it increasingly difficult for moderate Republicans to win their party's nomination. For example, in 1980 Jacob Javits of New York, a liberal Republican with four terms in the Senate, lost a primary election to Alfonse D'Amato. Whereas Javits was more likely to vote with the Democrats than with his own party, D'Amato compiled a mainstream Republican voting record. Even current northeastern Republicans frequently described as "moderates" are more conservative than the cross-pressured Republicans elected from the region during the earlier period.

If significant electoral changes were partly responsible for the disappearance of the cross-pressured members of both parties, then we might look for future electoral changes to cause other constituency-based splits within the parties. The literature on party realignment suggests that it is impossible to predict when significant electoral change will occur.[1] But it does give us some idea about the process that produces electoral change. Just as the Voting Rights Act helped increase the electoral participation of African Americans in the South and set in motion changes that contributed to the polarization of the parties, we might expect the political behavior of other ethnic groups in American society to produce similar changes. During the last quarter of the twentieth century, America became home to "the new ethnics," Latinos, Asians, and immigrants from the Caribbean islands and the former countries of the Soviet bloc. Several of the most populous states—California, Florida, Illinois, New York, and Texas—have large concentrations of the new ethnics.

Among these groups, Latinos have the greatest potential for influencing electoral politics in the near future. Hispanic Americans are one of the fastest growing groups in the population, but until recently they have been among the least likely to vote (Abramson, Aldrich, and Rohde 1999; Stanley and Niemi 1998). Should Latinos begin to vote in greater numbers, their impact on the electoral strategy of candidates in both parties will undoubtedly grow. In addition, politicians in both parties believe they can make Hispanics a core part of their constituency profile. As a result, neither party is willing to cede the large majority of the growing Hispanic vote to candidates of the other party. In Texas, for example, population forecasts indicate that Anglos will be a minority of the state's population sometime early in the twenty-first century. When this happens, any party that writes off the Latino vote, also writes off the state.

Finding ways to appeal to such voters may be more problematic for the Republicans, whose message—especially that delivered by the more ideologically extreme elements within the GOP—has not been perceived as supportive of Hispanic interests. A number of Republican strategists have

---

1. Early proponents of a theory of electoral realignment based much of their thinking on time: a major overhaul of the electoral system should occur about every forty years. Some realignment theorists, therefore, expected a realignment during the late 1960s or early 1970s. When it failed to materialize, many students of electoral politics were confused and frustrated. The result was some serious debate concerning whether realignment was a useful concept, whether we had entered a new "dealigned" period in U.S. politics, and what are the mechanisms of electoral change. The literature on realignment is too voluminous to cite, but we suggest that interested readers explore Burnham (1970); Carmines and Stimson (1989); Lawrence (1996); and the various essays in Shafer (1991).

urged their party to adopt policy positions more in line with positions held by Hispanics or face dire electoral consequences. Some Republican candidates have heard the message and have begun looking for ways to bring larger numbers of Hispanic voters into the Republican fold. Such appeals, however, may create tensions within the party. For example, while campaigning for the Republican presidential nomination in 1999, George W. Bush attempted to put together a message and an image that would appeal to a larger percentage of the new ethnic voters (Berke 1999a). At a campaign stop in California in June, Bush stated his opposition to California state propositions denying services to illegal immigrants. In addition, he refused to endorse a state proposition that outlawed affirmative action. Such positions were intended to define the meaning of Bush's campaign slogan, "compassionate conservatism." A number of Republican elites rallied behind this more moderate ideological message as a way to attract the new ethnics voters to the party while holding onto traditional Republican voters. But Bush's theme of compassionate conservatism did not sit well with some GOP conservatives who believe that the Texas governor is soft on issues that are important to the party's right wing (Berke 1999b). If Bush should prove successful and other Republicans follow this strategy, it might create significant tensions within the party and produce less cohesion.

If the political emergence of the new ethnics does not produce a restructuring of the electoral constituencies, changes in the class composition of the parties might produce constituency-based cleavages in them. Jeffrey Stonecash and Nicole Lindstrom's (1999) research into electoral change focuses on the effect of income distribution on the coalitions within each party. Their work shows that by the early 1990s, the outcomes of House elections were more closely tied to the class composition of the district than was the case in the 1960s. Yet in the 1994 and 1996 elections, Republicans managed to win in a larger percentage of low-income, rural districts, especially those located outside of the North. In commenting on the possible impact of these shifts, Stonecash and Lindstrom (1999, 82–83) note, "A Republican coalition of low income, rural small town districts and affluent urban districts could easily split over issues of government assistance." Rural, low-income whites who voted for Republican congressional candidates have little interest in cutting the capital gains tax or in producing a favorable investment climate for Wall Street bankers. Similarly, Democratic candidates seeking to regain seats in poorer rural districts will have points of departure with their colleagues representing urban districts.

The ability of a legislative party to vote in a cohesive manner is also affected by the issues on which members have to cast roll call votes. Some votes are likely to exacerbate tensions within the party either because members personally disagree on the issue or because it affects their constituents differently. During the 1970s, energy, the environment, and defense divided congressional Democrats. When economic issues replaced those items on the agenda in the 1980s, Democrats found it easier to achieve party consensus. Even during the recent period of elevated polarization, we saw issues come onto the agenda that divide the party. For example, Democrats have splintered on trade issues such as the North American Free Trade Association, as well as on health care reform. We also see signs of more moderate Republicans breaking ranks to oppose their party leaders on abortion, gun control, and campaign finance reform. The debate on gun control in the 106th Congress produced splits with a geographical dimension, albeit not quite like the North/South split in the Democratic Party. Rather, suburban voters seem to be moving to a pivotal position in electoral politics—at least on this issue. Representatives from rural districts strongly opposed new gun control regulations; those from urban districts strongly supported them; and suburban representatives split (Carney 1999).

Another change that might affect polarization is the budget surplus. Since the Reagan administration, huge budget deficits structured much of the policy debate. The parties have different policy priorities, but the deficits precluded creating any expensive new programs to satisfy either party's goals. The constraints of scarcity did, however, contribute to achieving consensus within each party over which programs to protect. With the end of the budget deficit, the parties are struggling to adjust from the politics of scarcity to the politics of surplus. The parties may find that achieving consensus over what to protect during a time of scarcity is much easier than deciding how to spend a windfall.

Should the focus of the agenda change and bring nonbudget issues to the forefront, party polarization may decline. The shift from budget deficits to surpluses did not reduce partisan fighting over fiscal policy. Furthermore, to the extent that presidents and party leaders have some control of the agenda, they will use their influence to focus attention on those issues that most strongly advantage their political party. However, political actors do not have complete control of the policy agenda, and we can anticipate that problems will arise on which partisans will find it difficult to agree. At the beginning of the twentieth century, the reform agenda pushed by the progressives in the GOP split the party and ultimately contributed to the adoption of reforms that greatly weakened the congressional party leadership (Binder 1997; Cooper and Brady 1981). New issues appeared during the late 1930s that fractured Franklin Roosevelt's

New Deal coalition (Patterson 1967). The emergence of civil rights as a major focus of government attention created a wedge between northern and southern Democrats (Carmines and Stimson 1989).

If the development of a new set of problems that produce significant disagreement within the political parties is to be the basis upon which party polarization recedes, it is difficult to predict what that new policy agenda might be. Perhaps the most significant change in contemporary society is the information explosion. A few policy pioneers are seeking to develop telecommunication policies so that the information age will serve the public interest. So far, these changes have not produced new social movements or issues that are reshuffling the parties. Nor are there obvious new social problems in sight that will reshuffle the partisan deck. But our ability to forecast such turns is not very good. Often we find that we have changed course only after we have spent some time heading in the new direction. We suspect that will be the case when there is a significant change in party polarization.

REFERENCES

"A Real Record." 1993. *Roll Call,* December 6. Editorial. Lexis–Nexis.

Abramowitz, Alan I., and Kyle L. Saunders. 1998. "Ideological Realignment in the U.S. Electorate," *Journal of Politics* 60 (August): 634–52.

Abramson, Paul R., John H. Aldrich, and David W. Rohde. 1999. *Change and Continuity in the 1996 and 1998 Elections.* Washington, D.C.: CQ Press.

Achenbach, Joel. 1999. "The Proud Compromisers." *Washington Post,* January 9: A1.

Adams, Greg D. 1997. "Abortion: Evidence of an Issue Evolution." *American Journal of Political Science* 41 (July): 718–73.

Aldrich, John H. 1995. *Why Parties? The Origin and Transformation of Party Politics in America.* Chicago: University of Chicago Press.

Aldrich, John H., and David W. Rohde. 1996. "A Tale of Two Speakers: A Comparison of Policy Making in the 100th and 104th Congresses." Presented at the annual meeting of the American Political Science Association, San Francisco.

Aldrich, John H., and David W. Rohde. 1997. "Balance of Power: Republican Party Leadership and the Committee System in the 104th House." Presented at the annual meeting of the Midwest Political Science Association, Chicago.

Aldrich, John H., and David W. Rohde. 1997–1998. "The Transition to Republican Rule in the House: Implications for Theories of Congressional Politics." *Political Science Quarterly* 112 (4): 541–67.

Aldrich, John H., and David W. Rohde. 1998. "Measuring Conditional Party Government." Presented at the annual meeting of the Midwest Political Science Association, Chicago.

Aldrich, John H., and David W. Rohde. 2000a. "The Consequences of Party Organization in the House: The Role of the Majority and Minority Parties in Conditional Party Government." In *Polarized Politics: Congress and the President in a Partisan Era,* ed. Jon R. Bond and Richard Fleisher. Washington, D.C.: CQ Press.

Aldrich, John H., and David W. Rohde. 2000b. "The Republican Revolution and the House Appropriations Committee." *Journal of Politics* (forthcoming.)

American Political Science Association, Committee on Political Parties. 1950. "Toward a More Responsible Two-Party System." *American Political Science Review* 44 (September): Supplement.

Anderson, James E. 1975. *Public Policy-making.* New York: Praeger.

Bach, Stanley, and Steven S. Smith. 1988. *Managing Uncertainty in the House of Representatives.* Washington, D.C.: Brookings.

Bacon, Donald. 1995. "Violence in Congress." In *Encyclopedia of the United States Congress,* ed. Donald C. Bacon, Roger H. Davidson, and Morton Keller. New York: Simon & Schuster.

Bader, John. 1996. *Taking the Initiative: Leadership Agendas in Congress and the "Contract with America."* Washington, D.C.: Georgetown University Press.

Balutis, Alan P. 1976. "Congress, the President, and the Press." *Journalism Quarterly* 53 (Autumn): 509–15.

Balutis, Alan P. 1977. "The Presidency and the Press: The Expanding Presidential Image." *Presidential Studies Quarterly* 7 (Spring): 244-51.

Barone, Michael, and Grant Ujifusa. 1997. *The Almanac of American Politics 1998.* Washington, D.C.: National Journal.

Barr, Stephen. 1995. "House Moves Record Closer to the Truth." *Washington Post,* January 9.

Baumgartner, Frank R., and Bryan D. Jones. 1993. *Agendas and Instability in American Politics.* Chicago: University of Chicago Press.

Baumgartner, Frank R., and Beth L. Leech. 1998. *Basic Interests: The Importance of Groups in Politics and Political Science.* Princeton: Princeton University Press.

Berke, Richard. 1999a. "Bush Moves Toward the Center on Immigration and Quotas." *New York Times,* June 29.

Berke, Richard. 1999b. "G.O.P.'s Right Talks of Bolting Faithless Party." *New York Times,* June 30.

Bianco, William T. 1998. "Reliable Source or Usual Suspects? Cue-Taking, Information Transmission, and Legislative Committees." *Journal of Politics* 59 (August): 913–24.

Binder, Sarah A. 1997. *Minority Rights, Majority Rule: Partisanship and the Development of Congress.* New York: Cambridge University Press.

Binder, Sarah A., Eric D. Lawrence, and Forrest Maltzman. 1999. "Uncovering the Hidden Effect of Party." *Journal of Politics* 61 (May): 815–31

Binder, Sarah A., and Steven S. Smith.1997. *Politics or Principle: Filibustering in the United States Senate.* Washington, D.C.: Brookings.

Black, Earle, and Merle Black. 1987. *Politics and Society in the South.* Cambridge: Harvard University Press.

Blalock, Hubert M. 1960. *Social Statistics.* New York: McGraw-Hill.

Blatz, Dan, and Ronald Brownstein. 1996. *Storming the Gates: Protest Politics and the Republican Revival.* Boston: Little Brown.

Bohrnstedt, George W., and David Knoke. 1988. *Statistics for Social Data Analysis,* 2d ed. Itasca, Ill.: F. E. Peacock Publishers.

Bond, Jon R., and Richard Fleisher. 1990. *The President in the Legislative Arena.* Chicago: University of Chicago Press.

Bond, Jon R., and Richard Fleisher. 1995. "Clinton and Congress: A First-Year Assessment." *American Politics Quarterly* 23 (July): 355–72.

Box-Steffensmeier, Janet M., Gary C. Jacobson, and J. Tobin Grant. 1999.

"Question Wording and the House Vote Choice: Some Experimental Evidence." Ohio State University. Typescript.

Bradley, Jennifer. 1997. "But Republicans Find Trouble on House Floor Wednesday." *Roll Call,* May 15: 1.

Brady, David W., and Charles S. Bullock III. 1980. "Is There a Conservative Coalition in the House?" *Journal of Politics* 42 (May): 549–59.

Brady, David W., Joseph Cooper, and Patricia A. Hurley. 1979. "The Decline of Party in the U.S. House of Representatives, 1887–1968." *Legislative Studies Quarterly* 4 (August): 381–407.

Brady, David W., and Craig Volden 1998. *Revolving Gridlock.* Boulder, Colo.: Westview.

Brody, Richard A. 1991. *Assessing the President: The Media, Elite Opinion, and Public Support.* Stanford: Stanford University Press.

Brown, William Holmes. 1996. *House Practice: A Guide to the Rules, Precedents and Procedures of the House 1974–1994.* Washington, D.C.: U.S. Government Printing Office.

Bryce, James. 1888. *The American Commonwealth.* London: MacMillan & Company.

Burnham, Walter Dean. 1970. *Critical Elections and the Mainsprings of American Politics.* New York: W. W. Norton & Company.

Burns, James MacGregor. 1963. *The Deadlock of Democracy: Four-Party Politics in America.* Englewood Cliffs, N.J.: Prentice-Hall.

Calmes, Jacqueline. 1986. "The 99th Congress: A Mixed Record of Success." *Congressional Quarterly Weekly Report,* October 25, 2647–67.

Cameron, Charles M. 2000. *Veto Bargaining: Presidents and the Politics of Negative Power.* New York: Cambridge University Press.

Campbell, James. 1993. *The Presidential Pulse of Congressional Elections.* Lexington: The University Press of Kentucky.

Cannon, Clarence. 1936. *Cannon's Precedents.* Washington, D.C.: Government Printing Office.

Cannon, Clarence. 1949. *Cannon's Procedure in the House of Representatives.* Washington, D.C.: Government Printing Office.

Cappella, Joseph N., and Kathleen Hall Jamieson. 1997. *Spiral of Cynicism: The Press and the Public Good.* New York: Oxford University Press.

Carmines, Edward G., and Geoffrey C. Layman. 1997. "Issue Evolution in Postwar American Politics: Old Certainties and Fresh Tensions." In *Present Discontents: American Politics in the Very Late Twentieth Century,* ed. Byron E. Shafer. Chatham, N.J.: Chatham House.

Carmines, Edward G., and James A. Simson. 1989. *Issue Evolution: Race and the Transformation of American Politics.* Princeton: Princeton University Press.

Carney, Dan. 1999. "Beyond Guns and Violence: A Battle for House Control." *Weekly Report,* June 19, 1426–32.

Chevalier, Michel. 1839 [1961]. *Society, Manners, and Politics in the United States.* Ed. John William Ward. New York: Doubleday.

Clapp, Charles L. 1963. *The Congressman: His Work As He Sees It.* Washington, D.C.: Brookings.

Clark, Champ. 1920. *My Quarter Century of American Politics* (Vol. 1). New York: Harper.

Clausen, Aage R. 1973. *How Congressmen Decide: A Policy Focus.* New York: St. Martin's.

Cobb, Roger W., and Charles D. Elder. 1983. *Participation in American Politics: The Dynamics of Agenda-Building,* 2d ed. Baltimore: Johns Hopkins University Press.

Cohen, Jeffrey E. 1997. *Presidential Responsiveness and Public Policy-Making.* Ann Arbor: University of Michigan Press.

Collie, Melissa. 1985. "Voting Behavior in Legislatures." In *Handbook of Legislative Research,* ed. Gerhard Lowenberg, Samuel Patterson, and Malcolm E. Jewell. Cambridge: Harvard University Press.

Cong. Rec. 138 H9299, September 24 1992.

Cong. Rec. 141 H13360, November 2, 1995.

Congressional Quarterly Almanac. Annually, 1953–1997. Washington, D.C.: Congressional Quarterly.

Congressional Quarterly, *Weekly Report,* January 9, 1999, 93.

Cooper, Joseph, and David W. Brady. 1981. "Institutional Context and Leadership Style: The House from Cannon to Rayburn." *American Political Science Review* 75 (June): 411–25.

Covington, Cary R. 1988. "Building Presidential Coalitions Among Cross-pressured Members of Congress." *Western Political Quarterly* 41(March): 47–62.

Covington, Cary, R., J. Mark Wrighton, and Rhonda Kinney. 1995. "A 'Presidency Augmented' Model of Presidential Success on House Roll Call Votes." *American Journal of Political Science* 39 (November): 1001–24.

Cox, Gary W., and Mathew D. McCubbins. 1993. *Legislative Leviathan: Party Government in the House.* Berkeley: University of California Press.

Cox, Gary W., and Eric Magar. 1998. "How Much Is Majority Status in the House Worth?" University of California at San Diego. Typescript.

Crook, Sara Brandes, and John R. Hibbing. 1985. "Congressional Reform and Party Discipline: The Effects of Changes in the Seniority System on Party Loyalty in the House of Representatives." *British Journal of Political Science* 15 (April): 207–26.

Cutler, Lloyd N. 1988. "Some Reflections About Divided Government." *Presidential Studies Quarterly* 17 (Summer): 485–92.

Deering, Christopher J., and Steven S. Smith. 1997. *Committees in Congress,* 3d ed. Washington, D.C.: CQ Press.

Democratic Study Group. 1994. "A Look at the Senate Filibuster." *DSG Special Report,* No. 103–28, June 13. Washington, D.C.: Democratic Study Group.

Deschler, Lewis. 1974. *Deschler's Procedures in the House of Representatives.* Washington, D.C.: Government Printing Office.

Deschler, Lewis. 1977. *Deschler's Precedents.* Washington, D.C.: Government Printing Office.

Dion, Douglas, and John Huber. 1996. "Procedural Choice and the House Committee on Rules." *Journal of Politics* 58 (February): 25–53.

Dion, Douglas, and John Huber. 1997. "Sense and Sensibility: The Role of Rules." *American Journal of Political Science* 41 (July): 945–57.

Dodd, Lawrence C., and Bruce I. Oppenheimer. 1997. "Congress and the Emerging Order: Conditional Party Government or Constructive Partisanship?" In *Congress Reconsidered,* 6th ed., ed. Lawrence C. Dodd and Bruce I. Oppenheimer. Washington, D.C.: CQ Press.

Downs, Anthony. 1972. "Up and Down with Ecology: The Issue Attention Cycle." *Public Interest* 28 (Summer): 38–50.

Drew, Elizabeth. 1996. *Showdown: The Struggle Between the Gingrich Congress and the Clinton White House.* New York: Simon and Schuster.

Duncan, Philip D., and Christine C. Lawrence (eds.). 1997. *Politics in America 1998: The 105th Congress.* Washington, D.C.: CQ Press.

Edwards, George C., III. 1989. *At the Margins: Presidential Leadership of Congress.* New Haven: Yale University Press.

Edwards, George C., III, and Andrew Barrett. 2000. "Presidential Agenda Setting." In *Polarized Politics: Congress and the President in a Partisan Era,* ed. Jon R. Bond and Richard Fleisher. Washington, D.C.: CQ Press.

Edwards, George C., III, Andrew Barrett, and Jeffrey Peake. 1997. "The Legislative Impact of Divided Government: What Failed to Pass in Congress?" *American Journal of Political Science* 41 (April): 545–63.

Edwards, George C., III, and B. Dan Wood. 1999. "Who Influences Whom? The President and the Public Agenda." *American Political Science Review* 93 (June): 327–44.

Fenno, Richard F., Jr. 1973. *Congressmen in Committees.* Boston: Little, Brown.

Fenno, Richard F., Jr. 1975. "If, as Ralph Nader Says, Congress is the 'Broken Branch,' How Come We Love Our Congressmen So Much?" In *Congress in Change,* ed. Norman J. Ornstein. New York: Praeger.

Fett, Patrick J. 1992. "Truth in Advertising: The Revelation of Presidential Legislative Priorities." *Western Political Quarterly* 45 (December): 895–920.

Fiorina, Morris P. 1977. *Congress: Keystone of the Washington Establishment.* New Haven: Yale University Press.

Fiorina, Morris P. 1995. "Afterword (But Undoubtedly Not the Last Word)." In *Positive Theories of Legislative Institutions,* ed. Kenneth A. Shepsle and Barry R. Weingast. Ann Arbor: University of Michigan Press.

Fiorina, Morris P. 1996. *Divided Government,* 2d ed. Boston: Allyn and Bacon.

Fleisher, Richard. 1993. "Explaining the Change in Roll-Call Voting Behavior of Southern Democrats." *Journal of Politics* 55 (May): 327–41.

Fleisher, Richard, and Jon R. Bond. 1983. "Assessing Presidential Support in the House: Lessons from Reagan and Carter." *Journal of Politics* 45 (August): 745–58.

Fleisher, Richard, and Jon R. Bond. 1996a. "Why Has Party Conflict among Elites Increased if the Electorate Is Dealigning?" Presented at the annual meeting of the Midwest Political Science Association, Chicago.

Fleisher, Richard, and Jon R. Bond. 1996b. "The President in a More Partisan Legislative Arena." *Political Research Quarterly* 49 (December): 729–48.

Fleisher, Richard, and Jon R. Bond. 2000. "Partisanship and the President's Quest for Votes on the Floor of Congress." In *Polarized Politics: Congress and the President in a Partisan Era,* ed. Jon R. Bond and Richard Fleisher. Washington, D.C.: CQ Press.

Fleisher, Richard, Jon R. Bond, Glen S. Krutz, and Stephen Hanna. 2000. "The Demise of the Two Presidencies." *American Politics Quarterly* 28 (January): 3–25.

Flemming, Roy B., John Bohte, and B. Dan Wood. 1997. "One Voice Among Many: The Supreme Court's Influence on Attentiveness to Issues in the United States, 1947–1990." *American Journal of Political Science* 41 (October): 1224–50.

Flemming, Roy B., B. Dan Wood, and John Bohte. 1995. "Policy Attention in a System of Separated Powers: An Inquiry into the Dynamics of Agenda Setting." Presented at the annual meeting of the Midwest Political Science Association, Chicago.

Friend, Llerena B. 1954. *Sam Houston: The Great Designer.* Austin: University of Texas Press.

Frymer, Paul. 1994. "Ideological Consensus within Divided Party Government." *Political Science Quarterly* 109 (2): 287–311.

Frymer, Paul. 1995. "The 1994 Aftershock: Dealignment or Realignment in the South." In *Midterm: The Elections of 1994 in Context,* ed. Philip A. Klinkner. Boulder, Colo.: Westview.

Gans, Herbert J. 1980. *Deciding What's News: A Study of CBS Evening News, NBC Nightly News, Newsweek and Time.* New York: Vintage Books.

Gilmour, John B. 1990. *Reconcilable Differences?* Berkeley: University of California Press.

Gimpel, James G. 1996. *Fulfilling the Contract: The First 100 Days.* Boston: Allyn and Bacon.

Ginsberg, Benjamin, and Martin Shefter. 1990. *Politics By Other Means: The Declining Importance of Elections in America.* New York: Basic Books.

Greene, William H. 1993. *Econometric Analysis,* 2d ed., Englewood Cliffs, N.J.: Prentice-Hall.

Groeling, Tim, and Samuel Kernell. 1998. "Is Network News Coverage of the President Biased?" *Journal of Politics* 60 (November): 1063–87.

Groeling, Tim, and Samuel Kernell. 2000. "Congress, the President, and Party Competition via Network News." In *Polarized Politics: Congress and the President in a Partisan Era,* ed. Jon R. Bond and Richard Fleisher. Washington, D.C.: CQ Press.

Grove, Lloyd. 1996. "Politics of Politeness: Congressmen Seek a Retreat from Rudeness." *Washington Post,* September 25.

Hager, George. 1996. "Roping Strays." *Congressional Quarterly Weekly Report,* June 15, 1654.

Herrera, Richard, Thomas Epperlein, and Eric R. A. N. Smith. 1995. "The Stability of Congressional Roll-Call Indexes." *Political Research Quarterly* 48 (June): 403–16.

Herrnson, Paul S. 1998. "Directing 535 Leading Men and Leading Ladies: Party Leadership in the Modern Congress." In *Great Theatre: The American Congress in the 1990s,* ed. Herbert F. Weisberg and Samuel C. Patterson. New York: Cambridge University Press.

Hess, Stephen. 1986. *The Ultimate Insiders: U.S. Senators in the National Media.* Washington, D.C.: Brookings.

Hibbing, John R., and Elizabeth Theiss-Morse. 1995. *Congress as Public Enemy: Public Attitudes Toward American Political Institutions.* New York: Cambridge University Press.

Hill, Kevin A. 1995. "Does the Creation of Majority Black Districts Aid Republicans? An Analysis of the 1992 Congressional Elections in Eight Southern States." *Journal of Politics* 57 (May): 384–401.

Hill, Kim Quaile, Stephen Hanna, and Sahar Shafqat. 1997. "Liberal-Conservative Ideology of U.S. Senators: A New Measure." *American Journal of Political Science* 41 (October): 1395–1414.

Hood, M. V., III, Quentin Kidd, and Irwin L. Morris. 1999. "Of Byrd[s] and Bumpers: Using Democratic Senators to Analyze Political Change in the South, 1960–1995." *American Journal of Political Science* 43 (April): 465–87.

Huntington, Samuel P. 1973. "Congressional Response to the Twentieth Century." In *Congress and America's Future,* ed. David P. Truman. Englewood Cliffs, N.J.: Prentice-Hall.

Hurley, Patricia A., and Rick K. Wilson. 1989. "Partisan Voting Patterns in the U.S. Senate, 1877–1986." *Legislative Studies Quarterly* 14 (May): 225–50.

Jackson, John E., and John W. Kingdon. 1992. "Ideology, Interest Group Scores, and Legislative Votes." *American Journal of Political Science* 36 (August): 805–23.

Jackson, John E. 1974. *Constituencies and Leaders in Congress.* Cambridge: Harvard University Press.

Jacobson, Gary C. 1990. *The Electoral Origins of Divided Government: Competition in U.S. House Elections, 1946–1988.* Boulder, Colo.: Westview.

Jacobson, Gary C. 1997. *The Politics of Congressional Elections,* 4th ed. New York: Longman.

Jacobson, Gary C. 2000. "Party Polarization in National Politics: The Electoral Connection." In *Polarized Politics: Congress and the President in a Partisan Era,* ed. Jon R. Bond and Richard Fleisher. Washington, D.C.: CQ Press.

Jacobson, Gary C., and Douglas Rivers. 1993. "Explaining the Overreport of Vote for Incumbents in the National Election Studies." Presented at the Annual Meeting of the Western Political Science Association, Pasadena, Calif.

Jamieson, Kathleen Hall. 1997. *Civility in the House of Representatives: A Background Report.* Philadelphia: Annenberg Public Policy Center.

Jamieson, Kathleen Hall, and Erika Falk. 2000. "Continuity and Change in Civility in the House." In *Polarized Politics: Congress and the President in a Partisan Era,* ed. Jon R. Bond and Richard Fleisher. Washington, D.C.: CQ Press.

Jefferson, Thomas. 1868. *A Manual of Parliamentary Practice.* New York: Clark and Maynard.

Jones, Charles O. 1970. *The Minority Party in Congress.* Boston: Little, Brown.

Jones, Charles O. 1994. *The Presidency in a Separated System.* Washington, D.C.: Brookings.

Kelly, Sean Q. 1993a. "Divided We Govern? A Reassessment." *Polity* 25 (Spring): 475–84.

Kelly, Sean Q. 1993b. "Response: Let's Stick with the Larger Question." *Polity* 25 (Spring): 489–90.

Kernell, Samuel. 1977. "Presidential Popularity and Negative Voting: An Alternative Explanation of the Midterm Congressional Decline of the President's Party." *American Political Science Review* 71 (March): 44–66.

Kernell, Samuel. 1997. *Going Public,* 3d ed. Washington, D.C.: CQ Press.

Kernell, Samuel, and Gary C. Jacobson. 1987. "Congress and the Presidency as News in the Nineteenth Century." *Journal of Politics* 49 (November): 1016–35.

King, Anthony. 1983. "A Mile and a Half is a Long Way." In *Both Ends of the Avenue,* ed. Anthony King. Washington, D.C.: American Enterprise Institute.

Kingdon, John W. 1981. *Congressmen's Voting Decisions,* 2d ed. New York: Harper & Row.

Kingdon, John W. 1995. *Agendas, Alternatives, and Public Policies,* 2d ed. New York: Harper Collins.

Koopman, Douglas L. 1996. *Hostile Takeover: The House Republican Party 1980–1995.* Lanham, Md.: Rowman and Littlefield.

Kramer, Gerald H. 1971. "Short-Term Fluctuations in U.S. Voting Behavior, 1896–1964." *American Political Science Review* 65 (March): 131-43.

Krehbiel, Keith. 1991. *Information and Legislative Organization.* Ann Arbor: University of Michigan Press.

Krehbiel, Keith. 1993. "Where's the Party?" *British Journal of Political Science* 23 (April): 235–66.

Krehbiel, Keith. 1995a. "Cosponsors and Wafflers From A to Z." *American Journal of Political Science* 39 (November): 906–23.

Krehbiel, Keith. 1995b. "Where's the Party Theory?" Stanford University, Typescript.

Krehbiel, Keith. 1997a. "Restrictive Rules Reconsidered." *American Journal of Political Science* 41 (July): 919–44.

Krehbiel, Keith. 1997b. "Rejoinder to 'Sense and Sensibility.'" *American Journal of Political Science* 41 (July): 958–64.

Krehbiel, Keith. 1998. *Pivotal Politics: A Theory of U.S. Lawmaking.* Chicago: University of Chicago Press.

Krutz, Glen S., Richard Fleisher, and Jon R. Bond. 1998. "From Abe Fortas to Zoe Baird: Why Some Nominations Fail in the Senate." *American Political Science Review* 92 (December): 871–81.

Kuklinski, James H., and Lee Sigelman. 1992. "When Objectivity Is Not Objective: Network Television News Coverage of U.S. Senators and the 'Paradox of Objectivity.'" *Journal of Politics* 54 (August): 810–33.

Ladd, Everett C., and Karlyn H. Bowman. 1998. *What's Wrong: A Survey of American Satisfaction and Complaint.* Washington, D.C.: AEI Press.

Lawrence, David G. 1996. *The Collapse of the Democratic Presidential Majority: Realignment, Dealignment and Electoral Change from Franklin Roosevelt to Bill Clinton.* Boulder, Colo.: Westview.

Light, Paul C. 1991. *The President's Agenda: Domestic Policy Choice from Kennedy to Reagan,* rev. ed. Baltimore: Johns Hopkins University Press.

Longley, Lawrence R., and Walter J. Oleszek. 1989. *Bicameral Politics: Conference Committees in Congress.* New Haven: Yale University Press.

Luttbeg, Norman R. 1974. *Public Opinion & Public Policy,* rev. ed. Homewood, Ill.: Dorsey.

Manley, John F. 1970. "The Conservative Coalition in Congress." *American Behavioral Scientist* 17 (November/December): 223–47.

Maraniss, David, and Michael Weisskopf. 1996. *"Tell Newt to Shut Up!"* New York: Touchstone.

Marshall, Bryan W., Brandon C. Prins, and David W. Rohde. 1997. "Theories of Legislative Organization: An Empirical Study of Committee Outliers in the Senate." Presented at the annual meeting of the Midwest Political Science Association, Chicago.

Marshall, Bryan W., Brandon C. Prins, and David W. Rohde. 1998. "Majority Party Leadership, Strategic Choice, and Committee Power: Appropriations in the House, 1995–98." Presented at the annual meeting of the American Political Science Association, Boston.

Matthews, Donald R., and James A. Stimson. 1975. *Yeas and Nays: Normal Decision Making in the U.S. House of Representatives.* New York: John Wiley & Sons.

Mayer, Kenneth R. and David T. Canon. 1999. *The Dysfunctional Congress?: The Individual Roots of an Institutional Dilemma.* Boulder, Colo.: Westview.

Mayhew, David R. 1991. *Divided We Govern.* New Haven: Yale University Press.

Mayhew, David R. 1995. "Clinton, the 103rd Congress, and Unified Party Control: What Are the Lessons?" Yale University. Typescript.

McCarty, Nolan M., Keith T. Poole, and Howard Rosenthal. 1997. *Income Redistribution and the Realignment of American Politics.* Washington, D.C.: AEI Press.

McKelvey, Richard D. 1976. "Intransitivities in Multidimensional Voting Models and Some Implications for Agenda Control." *Journal of Economic Theory* 12 (June): 472–82.

McSweeney, Dean, and John Owens, eds. 1998. *The Republican Takeover on Capitol Hill.* London: MacMillan.

Merida, Kevin. 1999. "Sen. Lott, Trying to Keep Everything in Order." *Washington Post,* January 14: C1.

Michel, Robert. 1993. "Words Taken Down. The History, Evolution and Precedents of an Important House Rule." In Papers, Leadership Box 15. fl. leadership 103rd , October 8. "Dear Colleagues" at the Dirkson Congressional Center, Pekin, Ill.

Miller, Warren E., and the National Election Studies. 1998. American National Election Studies Cumulative Data File, 1952–1996 [Computer File]. 9th ICPSR version. Ann Arbor: University of Michigan, Center for Political Studies [producer], 1998. Ann Arbor, Mich.: Inter-University Consortium for Political and Social Research [distributor].

Miller, Warren E., and Donald E. Stokes. 1963. "Constituency Influence in Congress." *American Political Science Review* 57 (March): 45–56.

Moe, Ronald C., and Steven C. Teel. 1970. "Congress as Policy-Maker: A Necessary Reappraisal." *Political Science Quarterly* 85 (September): 443–70.

Nadeau, Richard, and Harold W. Stanley. 1993. "Class Polarization among Native Southern Whites, 1952–90." *American Journal of Political Science* 37 (August): 900–19.

Nelson, Garrison. 1993. *Committees in the U.S. Congress 1947–1992.* Washington, D.C.: CQ Press.

Neustadt, Richard. 1960. *Presidential Power: The Politics of Leadership.* New York: John Wiley.

Nickels, Ilona. 1995. "Decorum in the House." Washington, D.C.: Congressional Research Service.

O'Neill, Tip. 1987. *Man of the House.* New York: Random House.

Oleszek, Walter J. 1989. *Congressional Procedures and the Policy Process,* 3d ed. Washington D.C.: CQ Press.

Oppenheimer, Bruce I. 1977. "The Rules Committee: New Arm of Leadership in a Decentralized House." In *Congress Reconsidered,* ed. Lawrence C. Dodd and Bruce I. Oppenheimer. New York: Praeger.

Ornstein, Norman J. 1990. "Can Congress be Led?" In *Leading Congress,* ed. John J. Kornacki. Washington, D.C.: CQ Press.

Ornstein, Norman J. 1995. "Ethics and Corruption in Congress." In *The Encyclopedia of the United States Congress* (Vol. 2), ed. Donald C. Bacon, Roger H. Davidson, and Morton Keller. New York: Simon and Schuster.

Ornstein, Norman J., Thomas E. Mann, and Michael J. Malbin. 1998. *Vital Statistics on Congress 1997–1998.* Washington, D.C.: CQ Press.

Paletz, David L., and Robert M. Entman. 1981. *Media Power Politics.* New York: Free Press.

Parker, Glenn R., and Suzanne L. Parker. 1985. *Factions in House Committees.* Knoxville: University of Tennessee Press.

Parker, Glenn R., and Roger H. Davidson. 1979. "Why Do Americans Love Their Congressmen So Much More Than Their Congress?" *Legislative Studies Quarterly* 4 (February): 52–61.

Patterson, James T. 1967. *Congressional Conservatism and the New Deal.* Lexington: University of Kentucky Press.

Patterson, Thomas E. 1993. *Out of Order.* New York: Knopf.

Patterson, Thomas E. 1996. "Bad News, Period." *PS: Political Science and Politics* 29 (March): 17–20.

Penny, Timothy J., and Major Garrett. 1995. *Common Cents*. New York: Avon Books.

Peters, B. Guy, and Brian W. Hogwood. 1985. "In Search of the Issue-Attention Cycle." *Journal of Politics* 47 (February): 239–53.

Peterson, Mark A. 1990. *Legislating Together: The White House and Capitol Hill from Eisenhower to Reagan*. Cambridge: Harvard University Press.

Pianin, Eric, and Kevin Merida. 1998. "How GOP's Enforcer Propelled the Process." *Washington Post*, December 16: A1.

Polsby, Nelson W. 1968. "The Institutionalization of the U.S. House of Representatives." *American Political Science Review* 62 (March): 144–68.

Poole, Keith T., and Howard Rosenthal. 1997. *Congress: A Political-Economic History of Roll Call Voting*. New York: Oxford University Press.

Robinson, Michael J., and Kevin R. Appel. 1979. "Network News Coverage of Congress." *Political Science Quarterly* 94 (Autumn): 407–18.

Rohde, David W. 1991. *Parties and Leaders in the Postreform House*. Chicago: University of Chicago Press.

Rohde, David W. 1994. "Parties and Committees in the House: Member Motivations, Issues, and Institutional Arrangements." *Legislative Studies Quarterly* 19 (August): 341–60.

Rundquist, Barry, and Thomas M. Carsey. 1998. "Party vs. Committee Centered Theories of Legislative Policy Making: Evidence from Defense Spending." Presented at the annual meeting of the Midwest Political Science Association, Chicago.

Sapiro, Virginia, Steven J. Rosenstone, and the National Election Studies. 1999. National Election Studies 1998: Post-Election Study [dataset]. Ann Arbor: University of Michigan, Center for Political Studies [producer and distributor].

Schattschneider, E. E. 1942. *Party Government*. New York: Holt, Rinehart.

Schattschneider, E. E. 1960. *The Semi-Sovereign People*. New York: Holt, Rinehart, and Winston.

Schlozman, Kay Lehman, and John T. Tierney. 1986. *Organized Interests and American Democracy*. New York: Harper & Row.

Seelye, Katharine Q., Stephen Engelberg, and Jeff Gerth. 1995. "Files Show How Gingrich Laid a Grand G.O.P. Plan." *New York Times*, December 3.

Shafer, Byron E. 1991. *The End of Realignment? Interpreting American Electoral Eras*. Madison: The University of Wisconsin Press.

Shelley, Mack C., II. 1983. *The Permanent Majority: The Conservative Coalition in United States Congress*. University: University of Alabama Press.

Shepsle, Kenneth A. 1978. *The Giant Jigsaw Puzzle*. Chicago: University of Chicago Press.

Sigal, Leon V. 1973. *Reporters and Officials: The Organization and Politics of Newsmaking*. Lexington, Mass: D. C. Heath and Company.

Sinclair, Barbara. 1981. "Majority Party Leadership Strategies for Coping with the

New U.S. House." *In Understanding Congressional Leadership,* ed. Frank C. Mackamen. Washington, D.C.: CQ Press.

Sinclair, Barbara. 1983. *Majority Party Leadership in the House.* Baltimore: Johns Hopkins University Press.

Sinclair, Barbara. 1985. "Agenda Control and Policy Success: The Case of Ronald Reagan and the 97th House." *Legislative Studies Quarterly* 20 (August): 291–314.

Sinclair, Barbara. 1989. *Transformation of the United States Senate.* Baltimore: Johns Hopkins University Press.

Sinclair, Barbara. 1992. "The Emergence of Strong Leadership in the 1980s House of Representatives." *Journal of Politics* 54 (August): 658–84.

Sinclair, Barbara. 1995. *Legislators, Leaders, and Lawmaking: The U.S. House of Representatives in the Postreform Era.* Baltimore: Johns Hopkins University Press.

Sinclair, Barbara. 1997. *Unorthodox Lawmaking.* Washington, D.C.: CQ Press.

Sinclair, Barbara. 1998. "Do Parties Matter?" Presented at the annual meeting of the Midwest Political Science Association, Chicago.

Sinclair, Barbara. 2000. "Hostile Partners: The President, Congress, and Lawmaking in the Partisan 1990s." In *Polarized Politics: Congress and the President in a Partisan Era,* ed. Jon R. Bond and Richard Fleisher. Washington, D.C.: CQ Press.

Smith, Eric R. A. N., Richard Herrera, and Cheryl L. Herrera. 1990. "The Measurement Characteristics of Congressional Roll-Call Indexes." *Legislative Studies Quarterly* 15 (May): 283–95.

Smith, Steven S., and Bruce A. Ray. 1983. "The Impact of Congressional Reform: House Democratic Committee Assignments." *Congress and the Presidency* 10 (Autumn): 219–40.

Stanley, Harold W. 1988. "Southern Partisan Changes: Dealignment, Realignment, or Both?" *Journal of Politics* 50 (February): 64–88.

Stanley, Harold W., and Richard G. Niemi. 1998. *Vital Statistics on American Politics, 1997–1998.* Washington, D.C.: CQ Press.

Steger, Wayne. 1997. "Presidential Policy Initiation and the Politics of Agenda Control." *Congress and the Presidency* 24 (Spring): 17–36.

Stimpson, George. 1952. *A Book About American Politics.* New York: Harper and Brothers.

Stone, Walter J., Ronald B. Rapoport, and Alan I. Abramowitz. 1990. "The Reagan Revolution and Party Polarization in the 1980s." In *The Parties Respond: Changes in the American Party System,* ed. L. Sandy Maisel. Boulder, Colo.: Westview.

Stonecash, Jeffrey M., and Nicole R. Lindstrom. 1999. "Emerging Party Cleavages in the House of Representatives, 1962–1996." *American Politics Quarterly* 27 (January): 58–88.

Sundquist, James L. 1981. *The Decline and Resurgence of Congress.* Washington, D.C.: Brookings.

Sundquist, James L. 1988. "Needed: A Political Theory for the New Era of Coalition Government in the United States." *Political Science Quarterly* 103 (4): 613-35.

Taylor, Andrew J. 1998. "Domestic Agenda Setting, 1947–1994." *Legislative Studies Quarterly* 23 (August): 373–97.

Thorson, Greg, and Tasina Nitschke. 1998. "The House Rules Committee: A Test of Three Theories of Legislative Organization." Presented at the annual meeting of the American Political Science Association, Boston.

Tidmarch, Charles M., and John J. Pitney, Jr. 1985. "Covering Congress." *Polity* 17 (Spring): 463–83.

Tufte, Edward R. 1975. "Determinants of the Outcomes of Midterm Congressional Elections." *American Political Science Review* 69 (September): 812–26.

Turner, Julius. 1951. *Party and Constituency: Pressures on Congress.* Baltimore: Johns Hopkins Press.

Turner, Julius, and Edward V. Schneier. 1970. *Party and Constituency: Pressures on Congress,* rev. ed. Baltimore: Johns Hopkins Press.

Uslaner, Eric M. 1993. *The Decline of Comity in Congress.* Ann Arbor: University of Michigan Press.

Walker, Jack L. 1977. "Setting the Agenda in the U.S. Senate: A Theory of Problem Selection." *British Journal of Political Science* 7 (Summer): 433–45.

Watson, Jack. 1985. Interview at United States Military Academy, West Point, New York, October 19.

Wattenberg, Martin P. 1991. "The Building of a Republican Regional Base in the South: The Elephant Crosses the Mason-Dixon Line." *Public Opinion Quarterly* 55 (Autumn): 424–31.

Wildavsky, Aaron. 1986. "On Collaboration." *PS* 19 (Spring): 237–48.

Winneker, Craig. 1995. "Forty Years of Conflict." *Roll Call* , May 15. Lexis-Nexis.

Wood, B. Dan, and Jeffrey S. Peake. 1998. "The Dynamics of Foreign Policy Agenda Setting." *American Political Science Review* 92 (March): 173–84.

Young, James. 1993. "The Washington Community: 1800–1828." In *The American Polity Reader,* 2d ed. Ed. Ann G. Serow, W. Wayne Shannon, and Everett C. Ladd. New York: Norton.

INDEX